The Complete Shade Gardener

The Complete Shade Gardener

George Schenk

TIMBER PRESS

Portland, Oregon

To leaves

Copyright © 1984, 1991 by George Schenk
All rights reserved.
Reprinted by special arrangement with Houghton Mifflin Company.

Reprinted in 2002, with an updated Appendix, by
Timber Press, Inc.
The Haseltine Building
133 S.W. Second Avenue, Suite 450
Portland, Oregon 97204, U.S.A.

ISBN 0-88192-534-9

A CIP record for this book is available from the Library of Congress.

Book design by Dianne Schaefer, Designworks
Printed in the United States of America

People Who Have Helped

The majority of the black-and-white photographs, and all of the color — taken especially for this book — are by Don Normark, who traveled thousands of miles to take the color photographs. Another long-time colleague of mine, garden writer Dick Dunmire, guided him part of the way, to some of the country's finer shade gardens. The two men devoted days to the project, out of sheer friendship.

George Taloumis supplied many vital pictures. My stepfather, Holly Hollingsworth, following my directions mailed from overseas, took one shot for me, goodheart that he is. Photographs not credited were taken by me.

Photographers

E. K. Altmann, *Hinesburg, Vermont*
Dorothy Bonitz, *Wilmington, North Carolina*
Kathryn E. Boydston, *Fernwood, Niles, Michigan*
Hal Bruce, *Winterthur, Delaware*
Elizabeth T. Capen, *Springdale Gardens, Boonton, New Jersey*
Charles O. Cresson, *Swarthmore, Pennsylvania*
Gordon Emerson, *Rock Creek, Ohio*
John English, *Salt Lake City, Utah*
Fred C. Galle, *Callaway Gardens, Pine Mountain, Georgia*
Jim Howard, *Martinez Lake, Arizona*
Ondie N. Huston, *Winnetka, Illinois*
Catherine H. Irwin, *Yuma, Arizona*
Lynn Makela, *Springfield, Virginia*
Marshall Olbrich, *Western Hills Nursery, Occidental, California*
Jim Porter, *Mars, Pennsylvania*
Barry Sugnet, *Salem, Oregon*
Margaret J. Williams, *Sparks, Nevada*

Regional Consultants

I came to know most of the gardeners listed above as customers of my rare-plant nursery in the old days. And I remember them for sending in the most sporting orders for shade plants that I ever received. They were — no doubt they still are — constant gamblers on hundreds of plants new and untried in their respective home climates. Over the years, these customers became my correspondents and friends. I would receive enthusiastic or disparaging reports on the plants with which they won or lost their grower's gamble. When I began writing on shade gardening, I thought at once of these shade gardeners, adventurous and knowledgeable as they are. I got up a questionnaire, with (among many other considerations) the question, What are the best trees, shrubs, and plants for shade in your climate? Their replies have given this book immediacy in all quarters of North America.

Special Consulants and Other Angels

On New Zealand plants, Muriel Fisher has taught me most of what I know. On the growing of Northern Hemisphere ferns, Sue Olsen has provided fresh information I could never have gotten from anybody else. On ivies, the writings of Henri K. E. Schaepman are my authority.

Every one of the shade gardens I've visited in my career of garden viewing has taught me something I've used in this book. I came, I saw, I took away an image or two. Several shade gardeners in particular, if they read my book, will rediscover ideas that could only have come from their work with plants: Sallie Allen, Marvin Black, Roy Davidson, Carl English, Leo Hitchcock, Frances McBride, Betty Miller, Brian and Margaret Mulligan, Herman Ohme, Bob and Evie Putnam, Dennis Thompson, and Mo Yee, this is your book. Of these people, Black, an arborist, and Thompson, a professor of horticultural therapy, have contributed even more. They read the book in galley form, discovered and expunged not a few bloopers, and saved the writer from a writer's Fate Worse Than Death—being found out by his audience.

Finally, I must say that, except for my luck in having worked with a profoundly sympathetic editor, Frances Tenenbaum, this book would never have seen print. There is a huge ingredient of editorial courage and patience in these pages, over which I, after signing the standard one-year contract, labored and dawdled for years. In scores of letters, telegrams, and phone calls, my editor has shaped this book in I don't know how many creative ways. And somehow our battles over the manuscript — for the trail was not entirely lined with violets — have amounted to one of the more rewarding friendships I've ever known.

1990s Update

Since this book came out in 1984, I have carried on with my shade gardening and have gained in experience. Recent findings that I've made appear as an added chapter. My editor's assistant, Linda Clapp, heroically typed the 13,500 words of new text, deciphering my bird-scratch longhand, which covered one hundred pages of yellow foolscap. Publishers usually don't accept manuscript in longhand. This was a special case, a suddenly decided deadline — which at the time found me, a nineteenth-century sort of pen-in-hand writer, located far away from typists.

Have a good read, and then go out and help things grow.

Thank you!
George Schenk

Contents

Introduction

Gardening for pleasure — for the refreshment of the eyes, the body, and the whole being — began with the domestication of shade. The first pleasure gardens were retreats from the Biblical desert, inspired by the natural oasis. To the parched mind and body, the oasis was a place of supernal attraction, a pool of shade, of coolness, and of water. The home garden was conceived as a private fragment of this luxury of nature.

Four thousand years ago, an Egyptian of office and leisure, long life and quiet demise, was entombed with twenty-four miniature dioramas as part of his funerary store. The dioramas represented the best things in the life of the Pharaoh's staunch functionary, Meket-Re: his herd of cattle, prodded past him on parade by his drovers; his kitchen staff baking and brewing; his weavers at their looms. One of the models depicts a shade garden, an area enclosed, for privacy, by high walls, within which a shaded portico faces an oblong reflection pool surrounded by seven fig trees. This cool, private, shady area (much later called the atrium) was one of Meket-Re's favorite places. He even tried to take it with him — in the Egyptian belief that miniaturized possessions would expand to full size and function in the other world.

As things have turned out, we are the heirs who have brought his garden with us into the present. The atrium has passed from Egypt to Greece to Rome to Spain to California to River City and is even now being rebuilt in shapes that Meket-Re could readily inhabit. But more than the shape, it is the mood of his garden that has migrated to all successful shade gardens, from his day to ours — the inherent peace of garden shade. Shade is that other best of places to be, aside from in the sun.

My book will help you plan, plant, prune, and tend your own oasis. The best of it, though, may lie in doing absolutely nothing in shade of your own making.

The oasis, shade gardening's origin. (DON NORMARK)

1

PART I

*The Art, the
Science, and the
Delight of It*

1

The Shade Room

A sunny garden, with its patterns of light and flowers, is a room that stimulates the viewer. A shady garden, with its chiaroscuro of leaves dissolving in shadow, is a room that soothes. But a garden is always a room when it is a place where people live as comfortably as plants — a surround with walls that are either leafy or structural, and with enough green furnishing to make you feel at ease. Even when a garden is several rooms, an alternative home outside the home, the green room is still the garden unit, and it need not be large to contain all the best of gardening.

In the first photograph, you see a shade gardener collecting his dues: rest and recreation in an outdoor den, a small but sufficient shade room of his own making. You see, in fact, me. I'm seated here in a state of grace, which for me is a state of laziness without guilt. I've earned my repose. And now I'm ready to propagate such blessedness as you see.

Let me guide you through an adventure that will inevitably bring you this same bliss — the making of your own shady retreat. I won't expect your shade room to resemble mine very much, if at all, in form and furnishing. That doesn't matter. But I do have something to share that will fit into your garden nicely. It is a dimension special to gardens — because a garden is always, I believe, a room with four dimensions. Height, breadth, and enclosed space are, of course, the basic three. Space-time, I don't know very much about. The fourth dimension of the garden — allow me my little mystery for the moment — is the sum of this chapter.

I started work in a location three or four steps from the side door of my home, in a corner of terrace embraced by the north and east walls of a T-shaped house. This spot was supposed to be the terrace of family ease and

Shade gardener in a royal moment, amidst some favorite leafy subjects. (DON NORMARK)

neighborly get-together, but it was all a visual menace of brick and concrete, in which an exposed downspout lolled like a wino. Nobody had ever made any homey use of the place.

My dead-end terrace begged for plants — tall plants with generous, concealing leaves. Yet, even though adequate ground might easily have been left open for planting, the only soil spared burial beneath concrete was a 3-×-10-foot bed at the base of the north wall. The paving hadn't been designed. As is so often the case, the architect (who certainly didn't owe his clients a garden design) had courteously sketched in a box shape and marked it "terrace." So the contractor's workers had just let it pour. The remaining soil seemed barely sufficient for a few "one-gallon plants" (to use a nursery term derived from container size) — small fry that would require years to achieve growth and leafiness equal to the demands of the site. In fact, the north-wall bed already held just such promissory landscaping that had never paid off: A lone juniper, planted here a good two decades before, had given a remarkable nonperformance, having grown a mere few inches in all these years. (More on this puzzler later.)

I'm not the first gardener in residence here. The first gardeners were the couple who planted the juniper. They had built the house and had lived here as my next-door neighbors for twenty-one years. Both of them are gone now, and I suppose I can speak of them a little more freely and fondly than I might if they were alive. The dismal terrace corner, I hasten to say, would be something of an overmatch for any gardener and was not representative of their cheerful garden. Ralph and Lucille were capable gardeners; they were even inspiring. I learned a book's worth of gardening from them over the years, never admitting to myself that they had a thing to teach me. Acknowledgment has come with retrospection.

In my early days, I was a nature gardener of insufferable purity. I felt duty-bound to ban "unnatural" plants, not only those unnatural in the sense that they had been tinkered with by horticulturists (all garden hybrids, all doubled or enlarged flowers), but also those natural variants that seemed to me botched by nature in off moments of creation (all plants with contorted or fastigiate branches, all variegated, purpled, or jaundiced leaf forms). The wild plants I admitted to my garden were harmoniously forest-green and dryland gray-green, and their flowers were wildflowers, preferably not too big.

One day back then, Lucille returned to her late father's perennial border to salvage floral heirlooms just before a developer's bulldozer erased the family farm — house, flower garden, and all. She brought back root divisions of Chinese poppies and oldtime red peonies and produced from them flowers as big as soup bowls. How I hated having those monstrosities overlooking my nature works. But how I have rejoiced this summer, a quarter-century afterward, in the sure return of that floral opera in orange and red, now that my wildflower garden has gone to greens.

She had an eye decidedly more baroque than mine, my neighbor lady. But we were friends. Casually, quietly, I would observe her weeding, perhaps a bed of marigolds. Four hours or so was her usual stint. There she would be, kneeling before marigolds under an August sun, sequestered beneath a great limpet of a straw hat, saved from the sins of telephone and daytime TV, a marigold woman pure and simple. My neighbor had gardened from her fifth year and she continued until her eightieth (and final) year. Every spring for three-quarters of a century, she planted seeds. Each spring the simple halves of a seed in germination were for her a book of adventure opening up. She was a gardener of growth.

Ralph, on the other hand, was a hard-line gardener, an edger and a sweeper. He was never a planter. Perhaps that is the reason he never thought of himself as a gardener at all. "I'm not artistic, not really a gardener, like you or Lucille," he would say, as he hand-snipped the grass precisely around a stepping-stone, making of it his weekly deep-dish pie. "This is all hers; I'm her maintenance man — that's about all."

That was much. Year after year, I watched their teamwork, and, all unknowingly, I learned how to balance my own art of gardening. Their garden, you see, was a spare and sensible orchestration of some forty-five kinds of plants — trees, shrubs, vines, perennials, bulbs, annuals, and edibles — on a half-acre lot, an average garden, I suppose. Mine was a plant collector's pandemonium. At my wildest I grew about eighteen hundred and fifty kinds of plants on five adjoining lots. Comparing my darkening jungle with my neighbors' Dutch-neat surroundings, I decided that I had plenty enough of leaves — more all the time — but too few spaces, and fewer all the time. Yet I was at the height of a collector's acquisitive stage, with no intention of curbing my delight in acquiring still more plants. All right — from now on I would have to be a terrific pruner of plants and hauler away of debris. And that is the primary lesson taught me by my neighbors' garden.

I'm going to apply that lesson immediately to our garden in the making. If you'll turn to the end of the chapter, to the last photograph, which shows the garden in a fairly completed and grown-up state, you'll find, on close examination, about as many different plants in this tiny area as my neighbors had in their whole half acre. The garden is four years old now, and those plants have not grown into a photogenically balanced composition simply of their own free and all too willful will. Twice during the growing season I thin out, cut back, or train, by tying, each plant in this packed little garden, including the ankle-high edging ferns and perennials. The problem — and the reward — of gardening is that the more plants one assembles closely, the greater their interaction and the consequent entertainment value from all that life in motion — and the more pressing the need for artistic pruning. Pruning can, and must, be as much a creative part of gardening as planting. Besides, there is a bonus: Having a constant hand (one's pruning hand) in a plant community is a kind of fun, a relaxing, absorbing, and ennobling exercise, once a person gets at it.

When, after twenty-one years, I bought the house from my neighbors, they left me the juniper — a *Juniperus chinensis* 'San José,' to be precise — in the north-wall bed, a shrub that had provoked my curiosity continually over the years. The plant was a living contradiction to the plant kingdom, the first law of which seems to be "to live is to grow." But this plant stood still. For more than two decades the juniper stood three and a half feet tall by three and a half feet wide, approximately its nursery size. Typical of its clone, the San José juniper was a "leaner" (old nursery term), even a lounger, on branchy knees and elbows: The shrub had "character" (another oldy). Now, the many Chinese junipers with predominantly juvenile foliage, of which San José is one, are usually fairly willing growers in half shade or in dappled shade, as under trees. Landscape architects use them by the thousands as under-tree ground covers. But solid north-wall shade might, I thought, have overtaxed that shade tolerance and retarded the plant. It seemed healthy enough and remained reasonably ornamental, but — sure sign of excessive shade — it was somewhat thinly dressed, more twisty bare branch and rough bark than leaf. I found the shrub engaging for that very reason; it had almost the makings of a bonsai. Year after year, as I passed it when on neighborly errands, I carried on a bonsai buff's flirtation with the San José juniper, though in my more reasonable moments, I had to admit to myself that the plant was really too rangy for a bonsai pot, where it would receive fault-finding attention.

One day, more than two years after my mentors moved away, curiosity, irritation, and derring-do finally caught fire within me, like so many rags composting in a closet. Today, this very morning, I would landscape the north-wall bed. I would "do something" with the juniper — put it in a planter box, maybe. Then I would refurbish the bed by digging out a goodly depth of soil, screening it, mixing it with compost, and shoveling it back in. I would have time to plant the bed before sundown. My planting would be bold and sensitive, a jewel of its genre. Tomorrow I would rejoice.

San José, old chum, this is the moment of truth. The moment sweated on for hours while I mined the shrub from hardpan (a veneer of leaf mold had concealed the true nature of the bed). All those years I'd suspected it was excessive shade that held back the juniper; now I found the plant's suspended animation resulted from impenetrable soil. Restriction at the root had caused corresponding restriction of growth above ground. I transplanted the San José juniper, not into a planter (away from the wall it seemed too gauche even for that), but to a sunnier part of the garden, into one of my best beds of hand-mixed loam, black and fluffy. That was several years ago, and in the interim the shrub has put forth sleek leaves and has grown taller by nearly a foot. I feel decidedly avuncular about this entire episode, and if I had a recent photograph of the plant, I'm sure I would waylay you with it.

The hardpan and the consequent restraint of the shrub were only part of my shovel revelations. Six inches down, I began to uncover two lines of intersecting drain tiles. To dig the ground deeply enough for planting, I would have to dig below the tiles without disturbing them. I used an archeological technique: I left the artifacts elevated on soil trestles while I chipped away the rest of the ground to a depth of fourteen inches, as deep as I dared go without risking the collapse of the trestles. I leveled the floor of the excavation and looked into the hole, gloomily. The tiles took up a third of the space in a bed that would have been unspacious even in their absence. Accommodating the roots of plants large enough to green-up the walls seemed hopeless. (The conversion of the formidably ugly corner into a garden room would seem so out of the question that the idea had as yet not entered my mind.) I reviewed the situation, spreading pessimism, like crankcase oil, over everything in sight: There were the tiles, nervously naked in the light of day; that lid of concrete, locking up practically all the ground; those Big House walls of brick; and that loutish downspout lording it over me. I was ready to fill in the hole and cover up my foolishness. Why can't I leave things alone?

That was that. But as long as the tiles were exposed, I had better be a dutiful householder and check into the lines for clog. I pried up a couple of tiles. Sure enough, the lines were nearly plugged with the sediment left by years and years of rains carrying off the roof's normal detritus. I lifted all the exposed tiles, troweled out the gunk, and replaced the lines. Bravely done. Somehow this bit of positive action braced me as much as a shot of brandy and a boost into the saddle administered to an unhorsed dragoon. Forward! Once again in my gardening career I would override every good reason for not gardening.

The north-wall bed excavated.

While I was filling the bed with some of the old subsoil, screened and mixed with a generous amount of rotted compost, I began puzzling out the planting-to-be: simple wall covering of one foliage, or a harmony of several? And what plant, or plants? At this point I had to think carefully about the antipathy of drain tiles toward planting of any sort. The thing about tile lines is that they exude a supernatural fertility that excites the transformation of normally decent roots into a chemically crazed mob, much like the imbroglio of bristling mad (with heat? on alcohol?) angle-worms that builds up within a barnyard heap. "Manure worms," as we boys going fishing used to call them, are clearly insane, and so are drainage-fed plants. I would know better than to employ shade plants that in normal circumstances are thuggish at the root, plants such as the yews, the cane-brake polygonums, or the bamboos, all of which are useful north-wall covers wherever there is no tile line close by. But even with the "nicer" plants, known to have slow-growing, fastidious roots, I would be taking a calculated risk. I would have to be ready in some future year to dig up everything, cleanse the tiles of matted roots, and replant the battered plants. But just then such doubts were mere transitory twinges. The native optimism of the gardener was on the rise, like Dandelions in April.

Next, the real problem: Bricks, two self-satisfied walls of brick. The active colors and textures of the red brick and white mortar walls would compete mightily with plants placed against them and would limit effective planting to heavy, solid greenery — a vine, perhaps. I thought of one or another of several vines that perform well in shade, and I tabulated the good and bad points of each. How about English Ivy in one of its less gigantic, less institutional forms, such as Bird's-foot Ivy? Dense growth, moderately fast. The plant would take about six years to cover the north wall, would need bushels' worth of annual pruning during that time and forever after. Or Boston Ivy? Fast, nothing as fast, nothing so messy. Climbing Hydrangea? There's a choice vine, slow to start, never rampant; give it ten years to cover the wall. But I don't have ten days' worth of patience. Creeping Fig? A fine fabric of a wall cover that, and a novelty this far north. Should I take the hardiness gamble? I've lost that one a few times.

Which, out of this multiple choice, would be the best plant? Reader, my considered answer is: I don't know. I never know. I do know there are only arbitrary choices in plants — no panacean species that supply shade, shelter, manna, color, perfume, self-perfecting form, and four varied sea-sonal performances, all in one superplant and with never a dropped leaf or any other offal. I wasn't at all certain a vine of any kind was my answer. In the end I settled the matter by having my various mental factions debate and take a vote. My Finance Committee plumped for a vine, noting that any kind of vine would be by far the least expensive landscape treatment of the bare wall. My Corps of Engineers likewise endorsed a vine, because the alternative planting — shrubbery — would be the more difficult to re-move in case of trouble with the tiles. My Don't Fool Around Lobby, a concerned citizens' organization devoted to saving time and energy for bread-winning work, rallied in behalf of a vine; nothing else could be planted so quickly and easily. But my Art Commission argued against a vine and, with its single vote, won. (It always does.) The artistic argument was this: though a vine would in time cover the bricks better than any free-standing planting I could fit in here, providing, no doubt, an admirable walk-by wall of greenery, what I really wanted and needed was a sit-down garden where I could live intimately in community with foliages.

A planting of shrubs was the artistic solution, then — the course offering the most entertainment to mind and body. The shrubs I would plant must be large enough to cover the wall instantly, for the patience needed to stand by for about a decade while the foliages of baby plants slowly build into a garden at last, has always been beyond my reach. The difficulty, in this era of the container nursery, is in finding sizable plants. Only a few fast-growing (and for most landscape situations, fast outgrowing) varieties of shrubs are generally available in sizes taller than about three feet. If one does discover a choicer plant (such as aucuba, pieris, yew, or rhododendron, to name a few popular shade garden shrubs) that stands taller in the nursery than a kindergarten tot, that plant is considered nowadays a "specimen," a venerable oldster, and priced like a bona fide antique.

One must, I find, be philosophical when one goes nursery shopping. There are even those of us who consider the purchasing of plants for landscaping a religious experience. Whenever we buy, we involve ourselves in a kind of purifying self-denial. We give up material things in favor of the ethereal plant. In my case, a pilgrimage to the nursery may mean that I won't be getting the new chair I had my eye on; or that the painting I found to be such a soul mate in the gallery will grace some other wall than mine. Or if my garden project is a major one, then I won't be going to Bora-Bora, after all.

I thought over the financing of my shady-wall planting and made the kind of decision I always struggle against mightily: Sorry, old sport, you really haven't the spare capital to buy two steaks' worth of plants, let alone a chair's worth. You'll have to improvise your planting. Whatever large shrubs I found for my project would have to be chanced upon somewhere outside the realm of the contemporary nursery.

Here I have certain advantages, for which I ask the indulgence of my reader: I headed straight for my own garden next door (my garden still extends over several adjoining properties), a section that then dated back almost twenty-five years, time enough for quite a few shrubs to have grown into supernumeraries suitable for transplanting. My search turned up a likely candidate for the wall planting, a *Rhododendron decorum* three and a half feet tall by three and a half feet wide — as I discovered after digging the shrub from a close krummholz planting of various Himalayan rhododendrons. I set the shrub on the garden path and looked at it intently for the first time in ages. It had grown leggy, but still seemed leafy enough to be useful. The green of its leaves possessed a special olive softness. I recalled my first response to those leaves many years before, and I fell in love with the plant all over again. In my enthusiasm, I inflated its size; I believe I saw it as five, or maybe six, feet tall. Naturally I was in for disappointment. On tryout, the rhododendron spread far too little leafage over the brickwork to effect more than slight improvement. There was none of the magic I'd hoped to see. Perhaps I could fit it under the wing of some larger shrub in a companionable planting of two.

Once again I looked over my older shrub beds. No use; there was nothing available of more promising size. I would have to search farther afield. And I knew just where. Against my sense of sportsmanship and just plain tact, I suppose I've got to confess to another wholly unseemly advantage I hold over my reader: I have a secret source of old trees and shrubs full of character. I'll describe the place vaguely as a small nursery in a state of romantic ruin, off the road (no sign), along a riverbank, subject to occasional flooding. Tall, riverine weeds enmesh the visitor; riverine gumbo gloms the feet, expanding them into mud melons. Yet, for a romantic landscape stylist to whom age and sinewy character in plants are far better than symmetery of branch and fullness of leaf, this place is a forest of transportable enchantment. Here woody oldsters grow on, forgotten except by me, by a few other nursery customers as reticent as myself, and, of course, by the nurseryman. He's been gardening in this place since the 1930s. Some of his earliest stock remains in the rows, for sale at prices stationary since the Depression.

My anachronistic friend wasn't around, as far as I could see, which wasn't more than twenty feet in any direction. Threshing onward, I came to a dense row of eight-foot-tall Japanese Hollies (*Ilex crenata* 'Convexa'), apparently planted out closely as liners many years before and never transplanted. Superficially, the ilexes were thickly leaved. But I visualized that any one of them, separated from the others, would have the compressed shape assumed by a shrub that's part of a hedge: In form it would be a gigantic fan, plumy with leaves around its periphery, yet with the inside part of the limbs bare. I saw the narrow uprightness of the single shrub as an advantage in the north-wall bed — just what I needed. Now to find the nurseryman. With feet so chipper they forgot their mudpack, I climbed the steep path to his house. There he answered the door.

"Five dollars each," he said, a price I found so poetic I began at once to invent places for the ilexes in my garden aside from the north-wall bed. I ordered several. "Come back later," he said, "and they'll be ready to haul away."

When I returned to load the ilexes on my pickup, I was stunned stock-still for a moment. Those shrubs were all bare legs, four, even five, feet up from their bases. Though I had foreseen as much, my mind's eye had been biased. Now I saw the stark reality of it. Moreover, there was a nothing of a rootball at the base of each shrub. To free the ilexes from the row, he'd had to slice the ground, as if the clay-soil and the mesh of shrub roots were a meatloaf laced with carrots julienne. "They're a little rough", he said, perhaps sensing my dismay, which I was trying to conceal in stoical silence. "They'll make it, though; this is an easy mover." But I was pretty sure those shrubs were dead, just huge, hopeless branch cuttings. Even if the ilexes still clung to life, they no doubt were dreadfully wounded and would mope along for years before regaining health and resuming growth. As it turned out, I was wonderfully wrong. An easy mover, did he say? *Ilex crenata* 'Convexa' is a marvel of regeneration. Those eight-footers, impossibly poor at the root, did not even blanch. They stayed green and glossy; they even grew a little the first summer.

To go back to moving day: I reached home with the pickup-load of ilexes, selected the specimen whose branch form most suited the job, and manhandled it over to the wall (ending up rather badly shrub-handled, with a torn jacket and three or four scratches). I propped the ilex beside the rhododendron — first on one side, then, more harmoniously, on the other — and spent some time composing the two shrubs, a matter of fine but telling adjustments, such as one makes in arranging friends for a photograph. The arrangement of plants into a garden is an art I find indistinguishable from any other arrangement of objects for harmony. This most universal art seems to me a kind of sculpting of the features of

Wrong way: my first attempt at composing the two shrubs.

My best effort: I'll go ahead with this.

one's environment toward one's sense of home and accord. In this sense, a garden is a sculpture modeled, basically, out of soil, air, and plants.

There is a key to arranging plants sculpturally so that they fit together and become a garden: Find the front of each plant and face it, so that when you walk by you greet its most affable part (I'll explain that later).

Having found the front of the ilex and the rhododendron, I turned the faces of both shrubs outward. Now I stood there, working out a comfortable side-by-side relationship of the two shrubs. Bringing into harmony plants that stand close together, as I was doing, requires much fine tuning; the relating of plants that are some distance apart is less exacting.

To this sculptural beginning — the balancing of plant shapes in space — the landscape gardener adds the subtle equilibration of airy and dense plant forms juxtaposed, and of a variety of leaf sizes, shapes, textures, and colors. And finally (not first of all, as most beginners want to make it), the gardener takes up the exciting fact that plants flower, however briefly, and need to be balanced for floral color, for size, and for muteness and brilliance of bloom. Perfumes, too, ask for balance, and, with that, landscape gardening becomes sculpting with all one's senses (granting the unity of taste and smell). The very air of the garden is, to the gardener, malleable into shapes of scent, sun, and shade.

But first find the front of the plant. I suppose I could not have been more than three or four years old when I first discovered that plants have a perceptible phiz. And, ever since, the knowledge has served me as an artist's tool of endless usefulness and entertainment. From that first face-to-face meeting onward, the gardener — the pregardener in my case — recognizes in every plant, from a tree down to an alpine tuft, a frontal part that speaks to one's artistic perception and that suggests, if the plant seems gardenable, just the place for it. Ah, you ask (forgive the Kahlil Gibran rhetoric), but what are the signs, the signals, the earmarks of the frontality of the plant? First off, plants are formal or informal in aspect, and that difference varies the character of their frontage. That of the formal plant — the green column, cone, globe, or cube used in formal landscaping — is like the front of the Christmas tree: the most closely branched, regular quarter we can find. Our recognition of the rightful front of the formal plant is quick and easy, a part of the instinctive human attraction toward symmetry. But the front of the informal plant, useful in free-form landscaping, has qualities not at all universally recognized. I know this because I've watched a number of professional landscapers go through their careers planting such plants backward.

The front of the informal plant will be known by its entertaining openness of branch, an invitation to explore visually the plant's interior. Quite often the frontal branches, more than merely open, are held wide, wide apart yet somewhat forward, like the arms of a Latin posed to welcome a long-lost friend with an *abbraccio*. (The ilex in my composition displays exactly this frontal configuration, and bonsai trees are often superb examples of open-branched frontality.) Leaves, too, form an important feature of frontality, as for example in my rhododendron, whose frontal leaves faced decidedly toward me. There seems a friendly alertness about their incline in our direction, but their tilt is actually toward the sun directly or indirectly received, and is a more or less fixed habit. Some transplanted plants are able to twist their leaves toward a new source of light, but all plants dislike having their leaf orientation changed; north-facing leaves faced southward in a transplanted plant may get sunburned and drop off. In shade gardening, however, the old orientation of leaves is usually not seriously violated, even if we turn south-facing plants northward in their new bed. In facing plants northward — as in front of a north wall — we face them toward the most direct, if diffuse, daylight; their leaves are still oriented toward the sun.

Meanwhile, back at the wall, I stood wrestling those two shrubby heavyweights. I made my fanciest moves. Now I stood back to appraise my effort. Frankly, it didn't amount to much — so far. As the photograph shows, I'd managed to bring about a crude balance of two green masses against a mass of brick. Clearly, I'd need to enrich my planting with other plants.

Those two shrubs represented merely first-scale planting, a category in which I place trees, large shrubs, and any other dominant plants the eye registers as individuals. A planting made up entirely of such dominant individuals never amounts to a garden (but a great many front-yard plantings, amateur or commercial, contain nothing more). First-scale plants remain forever alone unless they are brought together. In a big, enclosed garden (bigger by far than the half-enclosed planting I was working on), the garden fence, or the hedge or wall, or the encompassing forest that goes *around* the plants may be enough to give them a sense of belonging together. In big, open gardens, something unifying must go *beneath* — a grass lawn, for instance, unites many sizable trees in a city park, and in certain temple gardens in Japan, old pines that have been pruned year after year to accentuate their individuality rise from a unifying sea of white sand. But in a very small garden, such as the one under construction in this chapter, something must go *between* the first-scale plants.

Here I had an ilex and a rhododendron standing at the edge of the sidewalk, rather like two normally self-contained people at the curb: eyes and front frontward, though at the same time aware of each other, glimpsing each other peripherally, setting up some edgewise blending of their force fields of individuality. Yet that was the end of it. A garden is a party of plants, and without assistance these two were certainly never going to spark any party atmosphere. They were waiting to be introduced — by the smaller plants that go between, by second-scale planting.

In the second-scale category let me group low-growing, yet substantive shrubbery and other plants used as fillers, en masse, all of one kind or of similar leafage, which the eye registers uniformly and serenely. In nature, the larger woodland ferns often fulfill this artistic assignment, growing as they do in great stands, filling the forest understory. In shade garden plantings, these rank among the best of blenders. And I was pretty sure I knew where I could dig some good-sized woodland ferns without committing rapine in the woods. I staged another raid next door. There were shady areas in my older garden containing decades-old Western Sword Ferns *(Polystichum munitum)* that by then crowded their beds splendidly. Here and there I found a fern I could filch without really shorting my garden. I dug up five good, big plants, lugged them to the job site, and scattered them about the bed experimentally. Ah ha! Now we're getting somewhere. I used only two of the polystichums, however, and congratulated myself on my Japanesque sense of understatement. Two ferns seemed exactly enough to unite the shrubs and tie them to the ground. Oh, I suppose with equally good taste I could have used ten or twelve ferns, filling the entire bed. I pictured the bed filled with fern fronds. Not bad, not bad at all — but I decided against it. I wanted much more action here than those peaceful fronds could provide.

I began to dream up the richest of gardens, be it ever so small, flourishing in this space. Having begun with shrubs native to (Asian) forests, I decided to build up within the bed an entire cross section of forest. Actually, I would build down, since the first-scale shrubbery already in place now took on, in my mind's eye, the size of first-scale forest trees, whereas my ferns remained ferns, the second scale of the forest. Now to build down, to make the forest floor intricately alive with a woven, tufted pattern of miniatures, a third-scale planting.

Large ferns (second-scale plants) unite the shrubs.

I deferred planting, though, while I added to the surface of the bed some weathered stones I happened to have stockpiled. Stones were an afterthought. Ideally, their placement should have come earlier, concurrent with the composing of the two shrubs, whose meticulously worked-out relationship might now be incompatible with the stones. Only the two ferns, however, had to be lifted and set aside. Without disturbing the shrubs, I managed to crowbar stones between and around their trunks, just so. Angular stones such as those I used ask for careful alignments of surfaces in order to work together visually (rounded stones, on the other hand, are easy to group because of their uniformity of form).

I had several excuses for using stones. In a garden, stones seem to me to anchor and precisely locate the atmosphere of the plant community, the mood that shimmers from leaf to leaf and enfolds us in those moments when we become part of the garden, a thing so light that it is almost nothing and therefore can do with solidification. I needed, also, some practical means of holding soil back from a below-ground-level vent in the foundation of the house. Furthermore, I could use a stepping-stone nicely at the inhuman right turn of the sidewalk framing the bed.

I had first considered brick as a retaining and paving medium. I studied, on paper, several designs of used bricks (to match those of the house), and I think brick might have worked out all right if only I could have gotten away from the Navaho or Hopi quality of all my brick patterns, quite out of place in this lumberjack part of the country. Of course, I could have encouraged the spread of carpeting plants over the jigjog Indian edges of my brickwork (as I have allowed foliages to partly conceal my stonework), but I feel better knowing a garden has good bones.

The next photograph shows the north-wall bed with stones in place. About half the soil surface remains unused after placement of shrubs, stones, and ferns. Actually, the photograph does *not* show the ferns in place. I should have restored them in time for the picture; please imagine them in place (a mental exercise that is the garden designer's first and final and only tool). My own imagination was churning like a kaleidoscope just then, visualizing patterns of little plants upon that beautiful, dark, unused dirt. My third-scale plants for this minuscule bed would have to be chosen from among the least of species, the woodland weavers and peepers.

There are probably several thousands of kinds of shade-loving minia-ture plants available to the gardener who is willing to search. They belong to "alpine gardening," the cultivation of miniatures native to every natural location, including woodland. The handy small size of alpines is, to me, ever an inducement to bring together a treasure trove of little foliages. But

Stones — a late notion. To place them, I've had to set aside the ferns temporarily.

that doesn't say it all: In fact, I go hog-wild over third-scale plants and planting. In this scrap of soil beside the walk I would have riches: detail, transition, something new to see every day — well, every week. My little garden would hold variety enough and action enough to vanquish gardeners' blahs, that disengagement and boredom one usually experiences, for example, in about ten minutes' worth of plant study in a routine city park, lacking as it is in detail and in variety of planting. I ended up adding perhaps as many kinds of little plants to my three-by-ten bed as one would find big plants in a park. A close look at the photograph on the next page will show some two dozen different species.

I watched the life of my completed planting for a spring, a summer, and a fall, and, yes, the woodland microcosm provided enough goings-on to hold my attention as a spectator. So far, though, I had only put together a wall planting — a leafy mural or high relief. I still had to make good my promise to myself and to you: a garden in three full dimensions and even a mysterious fourth.

Having done all I could do artistically with the north wall, I stared with concentrated enmity at the brick blankness of the east wall, and at that crassness of concrete paving, fused to the wall, where there should have been plantable soil. I considered renting a concrete cutter, a brute of a machine, but I talked myself out of it. I'm not good with machines, and I feared for my toes. My east-wall landscaping would have to be in containers.

I went to work at the height of spring, daringly late, with the leaves expanding. I placed five cedar boxes along the wall and planted them with shrubs of the first and second scale, plus the fullest third-scale planting I could jam-pack into the soil, actually using my fist to pummel springy roots into the skimpy dirt. Nevertheless, by midsummer the foliage bouquets in those planters equaled in verdure the fullness of flowers in successful hanging baskets. Suspecting that they would be just as hungry and thirsty, I gave the boxes the daily watering and the fortnightly fertilizing that hanging baskets require for continued enthusiasm.

Again, throughout a spring, summer, and fall, I watched my wall plantings grow. Although there was now more to see, and though I harvested a steady supply of satisfaction and even a few gems of wonderment (such as the opal-pale and fragrant flower of *Rhododendron decorum*), I still didn't have "it." I still had mere wall plantings, a pause-and-walk-by garden, and not one of live-in dimensions.

Reader, I'll own up. I sometimes begin to doubt my slow and maundering way of creating a garden for myself,* even the littlest of gardens, such as this: thinking it through; coming up with rather good ideas; rejecting good ideas for better ones that come belatedly; revising, with better ideas, plantings that were hastily begun ("The better is the enemy of the good," as an old teacher of mine used to say); adding whole beds of plants as expressions of thrilling new plateaus of thought. No, this garden can

* For a client, however, the job just has to go faster, and the mind gears up to it.

hardly be said to have popped from my brow and into place in one Jovian gesture. Still it is my only way and is more sculptural, more spontaneous, more richly woven, this landscaping by evolution instead of by adherence to a pat design on paper.

A brand-new idea came to mind. One more planting — in ground on the other side of the walk — should do it. The planting could be quite small and *would* be. With my shovel blade I outlined a patch of ground roughly triangular, measuring about four feet on each side. I dug out hardpan and filled in with good stuff. The season was summer, the year after the planter episode. The first week in August I went plant hunting in my own garden. Seizing the invitation of marvelously cool, wet, unsummery weather (O my treacherous delight, while grounded swimmers groaned at home) to transplant almost anything I might choose, I selected for the principal plant in the composition, a smallish first-scale shrub, *Lonicera nitida,* with fine twig and leaf textures that related to those of the ilex on the north wall. Lifted from a nursery holding bed in an obscure quarter of my garden, the lonicera looked so-so in its new place. I added stones to give the lacy shrub some weight, and the stones helped. Yes, in terms of a landscape assist, the shrub seemed to be doing a job of work here. Yet it appeared unsettled, not part of a functioning ecology.

Smaller plants enrich the composition. Photographed immediately after adding third-scale foliages. (left)

Shady den four years after breaking ground.

Rather swiftly (for me), after only a couple of days of cogitation, I saw that the success of this annex composition — indeed, the fusion of all the plantings into a functional garden — awaited third-scale planting as lapidary as I could make it. At the base of the lonicera I planted more of the same shrublets and miniature perennials I had used to the north and east, and added a few newcomers of compatible woodland carpet texture. When I had finished, something happened all at once. What is it they say — the whole is greater than the sum of its parts? That, I think, is the working law of the garden, when the garden works. With this tag-end planting of seeming trifles in this triangular postage stamp of ground, the garden instantly gained a soul, began to breathe. A bit of the Sistine spark passed from one to another of the separate plantings and galvanized them into one life.

If you'll turn back to the first photograph in this chapter and use the side of your hand to cover the lower right part of the picture (the triangle formed by sidewalk and foreground planting), you'll perceive the three-dimensional and atmospheric development brought about in the garden by the new planting. Hand in place, the garden is not yet a garden, merely wall plantings. Hand taken away, the garden breathes an atmosphere of its own making. The details of the third-scale planting, in combination with the strength of character apparent in the larger plants, lend the garden whatever believability you find in it as a life unit, as an ecology. But it is the small plants that bring the garden to life. *"Natura maxime miranda in minimus,"* said Fabricius. To be honest, I only read him in translation: "Nature is most to be admired in those works that are least."

There you have it: shade gardening in three dimensions, and in four. Patient reader, ready gardener, the fourth dimension of the garden is you. *Salute!*

2

Preparing the Site and the Soil

The place undoubtedly has "capabilities for improvement," to quote the signature phrase of Lancelot "Capability" Brown, the eighteenth century's best-remembered shade gardener, to whom no site ever seemed less than promising. His dauntless way of looking at a job of garden making is a pretty good attitude for anyone to adopt when preparing ground for planting.

Bare Ground: the commonest site new gardeners confront; typically, a raw plot of ground around a new building.

Seven Situations

The drainage is usually adequate, and the ground stays naturally moist in autumn, winter, and spring; in summer it tends to dryness and will need irrigation to sustain most garden plants. All in all, this is the normal condition of soil in North America (except for the desert or for marshy places, which will be discussed separately).

Wherever a building contractor has already trucked in and spread commercial planting mix or topsoil, check the soil blanket for thickness and quality. You'll need at least a 6-inch thickness of crumbly, humusy soil for most shade gardening. Six inches of soil will do for shade-loving perennials and ground covers, and for many shrubs. (In ground this shallow, taller-growing perennial species will grow less tall than is usual.) To accommodate shrubs and trees whose root masses at the time of planting exceed the depth of the topsoil, you'll need to dig into the subsoil (see chapter 3).

Where the ground has been scalped of topsoil, you will have to spread new soil, or till missing components into the subsoil to bring it to the condition of first-rate shade garden loam. The latter tack is not always practicable; the ground may be too flinty-hard to submit to tilling, or to the bite of any tool less powerful than a steam shovel. So if you are of a mind to till and improve the existing poor ground, rather than to cover it over, find out just how poor it is by plunging a shovel into it — or trying to. You may decide immediately that the ground is only suitable for burying beneath better stuff. Or you may be pleasantly surprised.

The shovel test is best made in the fall, winter, or spring, when the ground is seasonally moist with prolonged precipitation. Summer-dry ground, even with a week's watering, probably won't soften enough to give you a correct reading of how workable the ground will be when it is truly moist. Ready now? See if you can plunge a rounded or pointed shovel blade into the ground, using foot pressure alone and without having to hack at the ground.

If the shovel blade goes in easily, the subsoil will be workable. Dig out a shovelful. What have we — clay, or sand, or sand-clay? Are there rocks mixed in? No matter. The ground was, after all, diggable, and so it can be amended. In any case, what you have turned up on the shovel blade will almost certainly be mainly mineral and scantly vegetable. Subsoils lack humus, and shade gardens need a great amount.

To make subsoil gardenable, use a garden fork or a tiller to break up the ground. Then, on clayey subsoil, spread a 2-inch depth of sand and till this in with the subsoil. On top of the tilled sand-subsoil mixture, spread 4 inches of humus (vegetable matter such as compost, rotted sawdust, sedge peat, or peat moss), and till together to make up a humusy loam. On sandy subsoil, spread, and then till in, a 4-inch depth of humus and — a luxury ingredient — 2 inches of loam, if you have it available. Shade plants, however, will grow in sand and humus alone, with added fertilizer.

Here are formulas for determining the number of cubic yards of sand, humus, loam, or planting mix necessary for a given depth of any of these materials.

To determine, for instance, the number of cubic yards of material for a 4-inch depth (allowing for 10 percent settling of the material after it is spread), take the square-foot measure of the ground you're going to turn into a shade garden and divide that figure by 73. The quotient will represent the needed number of cubic yards.

Example: A 10-$\times$-25-foot area contains 250 square feet ($250.00 \div 73 = 3.42$). To cover the ground 4 inches deep, nearly $3\frac{1}{2}$ cubic yards of humus will be needed.

To find the cubic yards of material needed for a 2-inch depth, divide the square-foot-measure of the ground by 146. To find the yardage for a 6-inch depth of soil additive, divide the number of square feet of ground by 49.

Tilling by machine (instead of turning the ground over and over with a fork) is a great blister preventer and probably a mandatory time-saver when doing a larger job. Many tool rental companies offer rotary-bladed tillers. The operator walks behind the smallest of these, hands on handlebars, guiding the bronco of a machine over the ground. The hand-operated tiller will work well on loose, sandy subsoil. But heavy as it is, it lacks the weight to force its blades more than several inches deep into ground at all hard or rocky. For this I recommend a small tractor with an attachment for tilling. Even tractor work will probably not pulverize resistant ground more than about 4–6 inches deep. For maximum depth of soil preparation, till the ground before adding any humus, sand, or loam. After adding these, go over the ground again, tilling them in.

If your shovel test of the subsoil was a dismal failure, you have a choice of covering the ground with a soil blanket or excavating it with a pickax (see the section "Bad Soil Dug Out . . ." at the end of the chapter).

Established Woods: woodland with good trees, but with weedy or overly dense undergrowth.

The ground should be fairly dry when you undertake any clearing, since the crumb texture of wet woodland soil is easily lost through compression by feet or machinery and is not easily restored. Clear off unwanted bush, roots and all, using hand labor or a small tractor with a bucket attachment. If the ground is too thin or hard for planting, till it and add whatever ingredients are lacking, as detailed above.

You'll probably want to lead footpaths through the nicest part of the woods and yet leave things undisturbed as much as you can. Trailblazing by hand is the more sensitive and conserving way. However, hiring a tractor for a sizable job is usually cheaper and is often a vital time-saver: 120 hours of hand labor in the woods equal about 10 hours of tractor work. The small tractors I've used for clearing cut a swath through the woods slightly more than 6 feet wide — the width of the tractor with its bucket. So, six feet plus was the minimum width of the paths we made. That's actually a couple of feet too wide for a footpath without side plantings, taking away some of the close companionship with trees that we look for in the woods. On the other hand, a wide swath through the woods, widening in places to definite clearings — up to perhaps 18 feet wide in a large woodland — is just right for a path with plantings at its sides. The broadish clearing brings in brighter shade or patterned sun/shade, which is to the liking of shade plants.

Beneath Trees: As on a garden lot with mature trees.

To grow shade plants beneath existing trees, you'll need reasonably root-free soil and bright shade. Remove low branches to let in more light because direct sunlight up to midmorning and in late afternoon is usually beneficial to shade plants; it is the midday sun they can't stand. Test the soil by trying to plunge a shovel blade into the ground. If the shovel is repelled by a mesh of roots, the ground is unplantable as is. Spread new soil and fertilizer on top of old, root-congested ground, keeping the new soil a foot or two away from tree trunks. New soil 4 inches deep will suffice to establish a tough ground cover such as Periwinkle or ivy. A 6–8-inch depth of new soil will sustain many choicer plants. (But with water! The trees will tend to make the ground dry.)

Big, tough, drought-tolerant ferns and other tough shade-loving perennials can be established in root-congested ground, even within a few feet of the trunk of a large tree, by chopping planting holes in the ground with an ax. A vigorous tree will probably not *(probably* not) notice the loss of root. Seal any sizable root cuts with pruning paint. Plant the perennials in ideal shade garden soil *(see* below*)*, keep them moist, and fertilize them each spring.

I learned what I propose here some years ago. In an experimental moment, I chopped planting holes in a bare, dead-looking patch of ground at the base of an old pine (cutting through roots as thick as cudgels) and planted *Hosta* 'Frances Williams', the ferns *Polystichum munitum* and *Dryopteris Borreri,* and the native forest wildflowers *Aruncus dioicus (A. sylvester)* * and *Xerophyllum tenax.* All the plants grew healthily, but with leaves reduced in size. For years I gave the perennials no fertilizer (generally, I never fertilize shade garden plantings — most plants seem to do well enough without). Then, on an impulse one early-spring day, I scattered complete, general-purpose fertilizer around each plant in the unprosperous bed. They all boomed up that year, making full-size leaves at last, and a convert of me. We now fertilize annually all of our shade plants that grow in starvation soil, as beneath this pine.

Grassy Ground: garden lawn or pasture grassland to be turned into an open bed for shady plants.

Mow the grass. If you want to keep a part of the lawn, outline the shady garden bed-to-be with string or garden hose. Then cover the grass within the outline with newspapers, ten sheets or more thick. Overlap the papers so that no strips of grass are left showing (on a breezy day, weight the papers with small rocks or whatever). Use scissors to cut the papers to conform with the outline of the new bed. Spread shade garden soil *(see* below*)* or planting mix thinly over the newspapers and wait at least six months before planting. Or spread the soil thickly enough (6–8 inches) so that you can plant as soon as you wish without tearing the paper. This little trick is my own invention — no cotton gin, I realize, but the least expensive, least laborious way of getting rid of grass where you want plantings. The grass will die completely, blade, root, and runner, before the newspapers disintegrate.

Others ways of preparing ground for plants where there is lawn or wild grass: In summer, spread a heavy, lethal application of fertilizer potent in nitrogen; then wait until next spring to plant (a costly method); or, spray a quickly biodegradable weed killer on the grass and wait the requisite time while the poison neutralizes. Or dig out the grass sod (practicable only in a small area); or spade the grass under. I've tried all three methods, and recommend the third only where the grass is sparse. Thick grass turned under will come up again, about half as thick as before. Turn it under once more and you get a twenty-five percent return, with the grass hankering for full recovery. The gardener tends to give up before the grass.

---

* All Latin names given in this book are in accordance with *Hortus Third* (Macmillan Publishing Co.), which is based upon the *International Code of Botanical Nomenclature* and the *International Code of Nomenclature of Cultivated Plants.* Given in parenthesis after the Latin names recognized in the U.S. are those authorized by the Royal Horticultural Society in Great Britain.

Concrete, where there should be plants.

There still can be. You have the tame option of container gardening, or the wilder one of gardening in soil spread over the concrete (covering part of your concrete parking area with planting beds, as I have done in my New Zealand garden, is liable to gain you a reputation as a shaggy mind). An 8-inch depth of soil on concrete will sustain complete gardens of small-growing trees, shrubs, and plants; 6 inches of soil will grow small shrubs and most perennials. Retain the soil with railroad ties, stones, concrete building blocks, stove wood, boards, or ground covers (*Ajuga reptans* is a good one for this use). In a cold-winter climate, select the hardier plants for a garden on concrete.

Arid Land: dry mineral ground in a desert or prairie climate.

Work the ground in the spring when it is moist, or irrigate it deeply. Till in ruined hay or straw, cottonseed meal, sawdust, or aged feedlot manure compost, together with sulphate fertilizer to reduce alkalinity, to make a mixture of about half existing soil and half humus. You may need to add chelates to the soil to further counteract alkalinity. Foliar application of chelates to woody garden plants is a usual practice in many areas of the Southwest.

Another method of preparing ground is to cover the existing mineral soil with riverside loam or other alluvial soils, when such are available from soil suppliers in your area. Spread the topsoil at least 6 inches thick. Dirt isn't cheap any more, especially in the desert. So it is a stroke of artistic luck that areas of bare, unchanged natural ground in the garden are quite in keeping with desert surroundings. For a balanced design — perhaps both sophisticated and naturalistic — have some garden areas of black dirt and rich, shady foliages, with others left in native soil and sown with seed of native wild flowers.

Depending on your selection of plants, shade gardening in the desert will require either much irrigation or hardly any. With much water (and with shelter from wind) in desert regions of mild winter, you can grow bamboos and barberries of Asian monsoon forests and many other lush and unlikely plants. With little irrigation, your choice of plants will be curtailed, but still interesting. The following will do with infrequent irrigation, once they are established.

Trees: *Acacia Farnesiana,* Olive, Russian Olive, pines, Staghorn Sumac, Tree-of-Heaven, *Pseudotsuga Menziesii* var. *glauca* (in Arizona and New Mexico, best in the high deserts), *Casuarina,* vitexes, cypresses, junipers, *Catalpa,* Chinaberry, hackberries, Crape Myrtle (*Lagerstroemia indica*), *Morus alba, Quercus rubra,* Quercus virginiana, orchard Apricot, and orchard Crabapple.

Shrubs: *Mahonia repens,* and other natives of the same genus, ground-covering junipers, *Paxistima Myrsinites,* Correa, *Kerria japonica,* deutzias of all kinds, Winter Jasmine (*Jasminum nudiflorum*), Spanish Broom, *Lonicera nitida, Lonicera tatarica,* privets, *Nandina* (an outstanding shrub for dry shade), *Cotoneaster Franchetii*, *Styrax officinalis californicus*, and shrubby forms of English Ivy.

Perennials: shade-loving cacti and succulents, *Phormium tenax*, euphorbias, native heucheras, yuccas, *Agave*, *Aloe*, *Campanula poscharskyana*, *Rohdea*, *Cyperus alternifolius*, echeverias, *Iberis sempervirens*, *Helleborus lividus*, *Sansevieria* and *Monstera deliciosa*.

Marsh: shady, wet soil, the draining of which would be an unreasonable undertaking; a place where the ground stays soggy the year around, or half the year, and is covered with razor-bladed grass or other coarse, unwanted marsh plants.

Sound unpromising? Not a bit! The place definitely has capabilities, since many a fascinating shade garden plant enjoys wet ground, or even requires it. But I'll grant the situation sounds like work: Burn the weeds to the ground with a weed burner, or cut them down and rake them away. Then poison the ground and the plant roots in it with one of the new, rapidly biodegrading weed killers. Or cover the ground with heavy-duty black plastic sheeting and leave the plastic in place for at least a year before taking it up in preparation for planting. In a large garden area of boggy soil, walkways and living areas for people can be in the form of wooden pads or rafts.

Trees partial to wet ground: *Larix laricina*, *Metasequoia*,* *Thuja plicata*,* *Acer circinatum*,* *Nyssa sylvatica*,* *Sophora microphylla*, *S. tetraptera*, *Populus tremuloides*, *Casuarina*, *Liquidambar*,* *Betula*, *Sequoia sempervirens*,* *Hoheria*,* and *Taxodium distichum*. The trees marked with asterisks tolerate being overshadowed by taller growers, as in a woodland. Of the entire list, only *Taxodium* will grow year-round in standing water. The others withstand flood conditions up to several months and quite enjoy bottomland or waterside soil that stays moist or saturated with fresh, percolating water in all seasons.

Shade shrubs for wet ground: *Vaccinium corymbosum* (Highbush Blueberry), *V. Vitis-idaea* (Lingonberry), *Leucothoe*, *Rhododendron viscosum*, *Spiraea*, *Zenobia*.

Perennials: *Cyperus*, *Hosta*, *Caltha*, *Iris Douglasiana*, *I. siberica*, *Zantedeschia aethiopica*, *Phormium tenax*, *Gunnera*, *Lysichiton*, *Tolmiea*, *Carex*, *Alocasia*, ferns (*Osmunda*, *Athyrium Filix-femina*, and others), baby's-tears, *Astilbe*, *Calocasia*, and *Rodgersia*.

Bamboos: *Sasa Veitchii* (stand back for this one, but the following two are moderate in growth), *Arundinaria viridistriata* (*Pleioblastus viridistriatus*), *Pseudosasa japonica*.

Ideal Shade Garden Soil

Most shade plants are woodland flora by nature, with an inborn preference for the kind of fluffy, woodsy soil out of which you can steal a fern, with a stick as digging tool. That would indicate their liking of a garden soil lighter than the loam that sunny garden plants prefer. The shade garden ideal is a mildly acid soil, rich and light and moisture-monitoring by way of a generous component of humus, lighter still with sand content, and made nutritious by a minor amount of clay. Such a soil can be blended by hand, using two parts humus (such vegetable matter as garden compost, leaf mold, sawdust,* particulate tree bark, sedge peat, or peat moss), one part builder's or riverside sand, and one part loamy soil. Blended, these ingredients make up a soil salutary to virtually all shade plants that can be grown in open ground.**

Before the blending, any soil components that contain roots, clods, or rocks larger than bantam eggs should be run through a soil screen. One I knocked together some twenty years ago — a wood butcher's job that has served me well — is a 3-×-3-foot square frame of 1-×-6-inch lumber nailed into a crude semblance of a deep picture frame. For screening, 1¼-inch mesh hardware cloth stapled over the frame.

To use the screen, I place it flat over the top of my wheelbarrow (a large-sized construction worker's model that I recommend for any home garden larger than a tablecloth), on which the screen fits as an overlapping lid. After shoveling loam or humus on the screen mesh, I scrape them through with the shovel used blade-edgewise into the wheelbarrow.

Now for the blending. Dump the screened materials in three piles on hard, dry ground, canvas, or a stretch of concrete (a garage floor is perfect for soil-mixing — garages, as most gardeners come to realize, are too good for cars anyway). Mix the three ingredients by shoveling them into one pile, two shovelfuls of humus to one of sand and one of loam.

The above recipe produces soil ideal for our kind of plant. The majority of shade-loving plants, however, are not exacting. Primulas, ferns, rhododendrons, and, in fact, most of the world's colossal catalog of shade plants will keep healthy and will grow (with added fertilizer) in soils as far from the ideal as four parts sand to one part humus, or nine parts humus to one part sand, or in a clayey soil that is workable enough to be turned and broken up with a garden fork. For famous results, though, give shade plants humus, sand, and loam in a 2-1-1 blend. This ideal soil will provide everything they need for thrifty growth balanced with a goodly show of flowers.

Though shade plants growing in ideal soil won't actually need fertilizer, they'll enjoy it, all right, in the same way a human being will gladly top off an already fine dinner with a thousand-calorie dessert. Human result: supergrowth in all directions but up. Plant result: the same, but with upward growth as well. With fertilizer, shade plants in any root medium will be stimulated into growing faster, with longer stems and larger leaves and flowers. A "complete fertilizer" (see below) supplied in early spring, and

---

* Sawdust in the rotted, humusy condition that plant roots enjoy is not often obtainable, but fresh sawdust (or tree bark) is usable, with the addition of fertilizer to the soil mixture to compensate for the consumption of the nitrogen in the wood by the bacteria that cause its decay.

** Exceptions: Epiphytic orchids and bromeliads, though usually grown in pots, can be grown as open-ground plants in a mounded bed of orchid mix consisting of lumps of bark or tree fern trunk, pumice, and scant leaf mold.

again in high summer, will provide the stimulus for a season's super-growth.

The usual commercial "three-way" planting mix (one part sand, one part loam, and one part half-rotted sawdust, bark, sedge peat, or sphagnum moss, with added fertilizer) is adequate for shade gardening. A two-way mix of sand and sawdust, or some other form of humus, with added fertilizer, is usable. Shade plants growing in prefertilized commercial mixes usually need no additional fertilizer the first year. But even a three-way mix, containing natural loam, is less likely to maintain fertility over the years than is the home-blended ideal shade garden soil described above. In the home product, true (bacterial) fertility begins quickly and becomes self-maintaining. The chemical fertilizer in commercial mixes disrupts, in some measure, the processes of natural fertility. Plants growing in mixes tend to become chemical dependents requiring feeding in the spring and summer of their second year, and every year thereafter. (Annual shade plants grow best with more frequent fertilizing, as discussed in chapter 14.) Fertilize with a complete fertilizer containing added trace elements — "complete" meaning that the product contains nitrogen, phosphorus, and potash, the three principal elements of plant growth. The proportions of these three ingredients vary from one kind of fertilizer to another, yet the differences are of small importance, or none, in shade gardening. Any complete fertilizer gotten up for general garden use, or one for vegetables, flowers, rhododendrons, evergreens, or roses, will do nicely for shade plants. I've tried all of them, experimentally, on shade plants, with the same results: taller growth, bigger leaves and flowers.

Dry fertilizers dissolved and much diluted in water are safe to use on shade plants; the gritty liquid will clog some spray apparatus, but not a watering can. Store-bought liquid fertilizers are safer than either dry fertilizers or homemade liquids (and more expensive). It is not easy to burn plants chemically with liquid fertilizers, even in overdose, but dry fertilizers will be safe enough if one immediately washes off the fertilizer dust that almost inevitably settles on plants. Shade plants growing in containers are easier to feed with liquid fertilizer than with a dry fertilizer, and are fed the liquid stuff with greater certainty than with the newer, slow-release fertilizers that are encapsulated in tiny plastic globules. (I was sure I was finding slug eggs when this invention, unknown to me, first came out. I would buy nursery plants and carefully brush off and stamp upon the evil little gift pearls of my tormentors — so I thought.)

Commercial planting mixes are much lighter than real soils, even airier, as a rule, than one's home blend of humus, loam, and sand. As growing media for plants in containers, the mixes tend to be too fast-drying; plants may need more water than is practicable for the gardener to provide. I suspect the greatest killer of plants in container gardens is not any insect or disease, but the commercial planting mix. In the small confines of a container, the fluffy mix may give up available moisture, from the condition of full irrigation down to the plant's kill-point, in a single, windy, moisture-extracting day; and twice-daily watering is too much to expect of most gardeners. An unfulfilled need in home gardening is a better light-weight planting medium, a substance that would remain airy yet moisture-retentive without becoming soggy. For the present, container plants are probably safer in ideal shade garden soil *(see* above). A mixture of one part screened garden loam and two parts planting mix is good, too — superior to straight mix in moisture retentiveness.

Planting mixes have yet another shortcoming, in that they invite frost more deeply down into the root level of the plants — with consequent more rapid freezing and thawing — than do natural soils. Where winters are severe, frost-sensitive plants such as rhododendrons are at a disadvantage planted in mix. Compensate for this by mulching the plants heavily and covering them with boughs or cloth.

Bad Soil Dug Out, Ideal Soil Filled In: A Case History

In an area of my garden where I wanted to grow such small demurrers among shade plants as *Soldanella,* Trailing Arbutus, *Trillium rivale,* and Gold-Thread, the property had been bulldozed down to a subsoil layer of hardpan. There I excavated by hand to a depth of 14 inches and filled in with ideal shade garden soil, in this instance a mixture of two parts woodland leaf mold, one part builder's sand, and one part pasture loam; no added fertilizer. I screened and blended the three ingredients, shoveled the blend into the excavation, filling in higher than the rim of the bed, and then trod upon the fill to quickly gain the effect of natural settling of the soil. Hand-preparation of a ground area of merely four hundred square feet required full weekends and spare hours over a couple of months.

That was thirty years ago. Today, whenever I dig into that bed, I gloat. It's a thoroughly chummy piece of ground, never becoming sodden or cloddish even in wettest weather. Here, with fingers alone, I can dig out a plant with a proper root ball, and have done so, in a rush of enthusiasm, with no tools at hand. Without the addition of fertilizer, the bed remains amply fertile, not to say rich. The plants have made steady, unforced growth year after year.

The soldanellas and other small shade plants for which I originally made up the bed grew and flowered improvingly here for perhaps a decade, or until I carelessly let larger plants *(Hosta, Pulmonaria, Epimedium,* trilliums, dicentras, ferns)*, planted later, overgrow them and shade them out. I probably would not confess that if the circumstance were rare and inconsequential. But it is most usual. Being grown over is the commonplace demise of choice little shade plants in gardens. They won't take being doubly shaded by both trees and taller plants.

Of the larger plants that have pre-empted the bed, the trilliums alone have almost made me forget the lost miniatures. The quarter-century-old clumps of eastern America's white *Trillium grandiflorum* and maroon *T. erectum* growing here open scores of flowers in late April and early May. With these and with the other spring woodlanders, and with the naturalization of ferns that has taken place here, I count this bed a piece of shade gardening at its most rewarding.

Plantings in new soil, spread over the old, enliven this small space. The added soil is only one brick deep, but adequate. White gravel heightens light intensity within full shade. Plants include ivy, trillium, Christmas Ferns, and Hydrangea, all quite young. With several years' growth, the garden will fill out and improve. (GEORGE TALOUMIS)

Yet I wouldn't prepare a bed the same way again — I wouldn't bother to excavate. New soil could have been spread over the top of the hardpan that the bulldozer left me, and it could have been retained with railroad ties (twenty-five cents each in those days). I know now that the good soil really wouldn't have to have been deeper than eight inches to sustain all shade plants; even a six-inch depth would have sufficed, as I may have said too often already.

Spreading new soil over the old is the easiest way of preparing shade garden beds wherever the existing soil is too hard to till or is too poorly drained to grow your favorite plants, or in places where there are established trees. Capabilities for shade gardening exist here and practically anywhere.

3

Planting

A few plants such as willows, bramble fruits, and Ocotillo are able to witch themselves up from sticks stuck in the ground. Aside from these, the planter deals with roots. Knowledge of roots, finesse in digging and filling holes, and dedication to watering are the main things. Plants come with roots bare, or they are held in containers or are balled and burlapped (swaddled in gunnysacking), and each root style requires a somewhat different planting method.

Ball and Burlap Planting time: a day in autumn, preferably, or in winter or early spring. Where the soil is good and deep, the planting hole needn't be more than about 15 inches wider than the root ball, and no deeper (you'll need the extra width of excavation solely for working space when filling in soil around the plant). Where the soil is poor, dig a hole at least twice as wide as the root ball and half again as deep. (In the case of a very young, small specimen, the hole should be even larger in proportion to the plant's roots.)

Lower the root ball, still covered with burlap, into the hole. The plant (unless it is a rhododendron, camellia, or another of the family Ericaceae) should rest firmly 1–2 inches lower than it grew before. Partly fill in the hole with the native soil (if it is good) or with ideal shade garden soil (*see* p. 28) and press the fill with your foot to firm it beneath and around the plant. Cut the rope away from the top of the root ball and peel back the burlap until the root package resembles a tangerine attacked by a child of fickle appetite — skin opened at top only. Let the rest of the burlap remain in place. Roots will grow happily through it, and in a year or two the jute will decay into root food. (But examine the material to make sure it is

34

indeed burlap sacking and not plastic; if it shines, remove it entirely.) Fill the hole up to the top of the root ball and compact this second addition of soil. Water the plant, the filled hole, and the soil around the hole to saturation. Top-dress the root ball with 1–2 inches of loose mulch, such as sawdust, compost, or presoaked peat moss.

Rhododendrons and other Ericaceae are placed in serious jeopardy if planted deeper than they grew before. Set any of these shrubs or trees so that the top of the root-and-soil mass lies even with the surface of the hole. Some specialists in Ericaceae plant high — an inch or so above ground level — with the idea that the specimen planted in loose soil will settle.

Newly set-out plants need bathtubs of water the first summer and an extra plenty the second. The third year, watering can be as for the rest of the garden.

Bare Roots

Planting season: early autumn (the best time) to earliest spring, while the plant is out of leaf and before leaf buds loosen their chitonlike covering to show the beginnings of spring green.

While you are digging the hole, keep the roots of the plant moist by wrapping them with wet cloth or newspapers. In planting, avoid forcibly bending the roots. Let them point easily in their former directions, in a hole deep and broad enough to accommodate old root habits. In good soil, the hole needn't be more extensive then the plant's roots; in poor, hard soil, dig a hole about twice as wide as the roots and half again as deep. But if the tree or shrub you're planting is small, with a root system perhaps no longer than your hand, dig a hole at least three times wider and twice as deep.

Stand the plant in the hole 1–2 inches lower than it grew before. The plant probably bears signs of its former depth in the soil: slightly paler, smoother bark on its roots and trunk base, up to the exact point the growing plant met the soil surface and daylight. If the plant lacks such demarcation, simply plant it deep enough that the topmost parts of the roots lie about 2 inches below soil surface.

Throw in a few shovelfuls of good dirt to half-fill the hole, flood with water, and jiggle the plant to settle the soil in among the roots. Now fill the hole, reserving an inch or two for mulching. If the plant is more than 4 feet tall, it will probably need to be staked.

Container Plants

Container-grown nursery stock, plantable in all seasons, is the great gardening innovation of this century. The container technique has partly, or in some areas of North America almost totally, replaced that of plants grown in open soil and dug for sale with roots bare or balled and burlapped. The container plant is less prevalent in the East and in other cold-winter climates, where the roots of many plants are uncertainly hardy when contained above ground. But nurseries in our milder western and southern regions now containerize nearly all plants: large trees and shrubs in boxes, smaller trees and shrubs in cans or plastic bags (the latest method and in several ways the best to date), small plants in pots or pokes. I wish

I could tell you that all is perfect with the container system of dispensing plants. Certainly it is highly efficient, but there are also a few glitches to be known and taken into account when buying the plants.

Those demon cans! They catch many a plant by the root and won't let go. To free the plant, the can must be cut down the side in two places, transforming the metal into ragged straight razors, open and springy, that sneak a flick and a swipe at the gardener. Nurseries that sell canned plants usually have on hand an enormous, foot-operated can opener designed especially to cut the sides of cans in which plants are stuck. Before going home with canned plants, test them for ease of lift out of the can. Hold the container down by pressing your feet against the sides of the can's base. Then grasp the tree or shrub by the trunk and pull. Or have an assistant (in this feat of legerdemain) pull on the can while you pull on the plant. If it comes out, congratulations. But let the plant slide back into the can, for the protection of the roots and for the cleanliness of your car, when you take your purchase home. If, however, the plant won't budge from the can, have the can cut and removed at the nursery. Then wrap the liberated plant with the paper and string that you've brought along for the purpose.

The container-grown plant reaches peak condition at the end of its first full growing season. By then, vigorous new roots will have grown spoke-wise from the hub of the plant and will have met the inner surface of the container and begun feeling their way along the walls. These are roots at their best — new, but not too new, pliable, capable of finding their way into garden soil when the plant is set out.

Container plants still unsold toward the end of their second summer begin to grow tired of confined life. The roots that reached the perimeter of the container now coil round and round until the plant becomes root-bound or pot-bound (synonymous terms). Branch growth becomes slow and shortish, and the newer leaves open smaller. Bonsai fanciers might begin to eye the plant, but for most garden purposes the nursery item that has been too long in the container is one of lessened value. Pot-bound roots usually slow the plant's growth in the garden; new roots break away tardily from the old dense mass, and the plant may never attain normal size.

Container plants are also sold prematurely at times — freshly "potted up." Turn such plants out of their containers, and the soil mix will fall away. Any brand-new roots that have formed will be easily broken. The too new plant is recognizable by the freshly shoveled look of the mix in the container, by the absence of moss, and by the looseness of the plant.

Ah, but the convenience of container plants well contained and poised for planting. Planting time: anytime. With the advent of the container plant, every month, spring to fall and on through the winter (as long as the soil remains unfrozen) has become at least reasonably suitable for planting. Even so, fall and spring remain the high seasons, times of rains and mild weather that assist the new plant. Summer planting is perfectly possible, but disadvantageous. On a hot, dry summer day, water each plant as you set it out, and after the planting session, water the vicinity to increase humidity; repeat the overall watering daily while the heat continues. (According to a widely held belief, watering plants from overhead on a hot day is apt to burn the leaves. Yet farmers pour water on lettuce and other leafy vegetables all during the dog days. Having observed this, I've never held off watering the garden in the hottest shade and sun. No harm done, except for the demise of a few alpine cushion plants with downy leaves.)

Planting technique: Remove the plant from the container, and after that, all else is as detailed above at "Ball and Burlap" (except, of course, that there's no bothering with burlap). In synopsis: Where the soil is good, the planting holes can be smallish. If the soil is not so good, dig a big hole, set the plant slightly low, firm the soil with your foot, and top with mulch; be generous and frequent in watering throughout the first summer and early autumn. As for pruning on planting day, do this only if the plant is an Ichabod Crane in its proportions — that is, impossibly leggy in relation to its root mass, gawky, and floppy (as a result of having been given massive doses of fertilizer to force it up quickly). But since container plants lose no roots in the planting process, a properly grown specimen requires no pruning for above ground–below ground balance.

Planting soil: porous, not clay-heavy. An airy soil, readily penetrable to the roots, is especially important to container plants. They've been grown in a light planting mix uncommonly comfortable to their roots, conducive to quick, uninhibited root growth. Set into heavy soil (roots still within their cozy mix), the container plant is reluctant to get out of bed, so to speak, and put its feet into the cold clay. Plant it in a large pocket of ideal soil (*see* p. 28) or a well-worked loam. Counsel for the perfectionist: Before planting in clayey soil, work the entire planting bed to as close a semblance of ideal shade garden soil as you can manage.

Follow the planting scheme that suits the tree's roots, with these minor variations:

Trees in Hard Ground or a Grassy Area

For many years, probably for centuries, the accepted method of planting trees in a harsh, hard clay area not to be improved overall, has been to dig the planting hole a good yard wide and about half a yard deep; and to fill the hole with some of the native soil (screened or chopped fine with the shovel blade, if it is lumpy), mixed with sand and humus, or with planting mix of the sort that may have come with the plant.

Lately, many North American arborists have begun to advocate using the native clay soil of the planting site without amendments — merely digging out and filling in with what is there. They say that the old way of filling in with an amended, lightened growing medium creates in many cases a bathtub of a planting hole, which fills with water in the rainy season and remains mucky to the detriment or loss of the tree.

And in fact, the repeated advice in garden writings about digging a water outlet deeply down into the ground from the bottom of the clayey planting hole has never worked for me in any of the several properties where I've tried it. The hope is of reaching a freely draining, sandy or pebbly stratum beneath the clay. The result for me has always been a deeper water hole. But do attempt at least one such hole within a hole if you're keen on a certain tree that won't take wetness. You may have the luck of encountering just the right soil profile. Consider, as well, planting your trees in raised, retained soil. The 8-inch rise of a railroad tie set on edge will provide enough depth of drained soil to grow trees (but to a height much dwarfed if the water table stands very near the natural soil surface).

Where drainage is suspect, make a percolation test: Dig a planting hole ahead of time and fill the hole with water. If water remains in the hole next day, choose a wet-tolerant species for this location.

Where the tree is planted in a meadow, keep the grass away for the first several years by edging it along the perimeter of the planting hole, or even farther from the tree. If the meadow were allowed to grow closely about, the tree would stay stunted for perhaps ten to twelve years, until it slowly formed roots deeper and more determined than those of the wild grass.

Lawn trees are another matter. As long as the lawn area is deeply irrigated, grass neighboring the tree trunk won't seriously impede the tree. For a restful appearance, grass (or a ground cover) should indeed cover the ground up to the tree trunk; the tree that rises from a patch of bare ground within a lawn looks tense.

Staking After planting and watering (all done according to the root style), stake the tall plant to keep it from blowing over. But leave out stakes for any specimen that really doesn't need support. Recent studies prove that unstaked trees and shrubs form stouter, stronger, more wind-resistant wood.

For the guying of each plant, you'll need three sharpened stakes — 2-×-2-inch lumber — or sections of old water pipe (junkyard stuff); strong

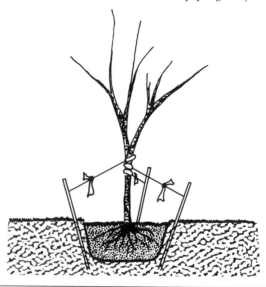

Tree planted, mulched, staked, and flagged.

wire — ¹⁄₁₆-inch wire should be adequate; wire cutters or wire-cutting pliers; strips of rag to attach to the wires to warn pedestrians; 1-foot-long sections (three of them) of old, outworn garden hose; a sledge hammer or, in a pinch, a good-size rock.

Pound the pipes or stakes into the ground at an angle away from the tree until they are firm enough not to wobble when you give them a test kick (the staking needn't show higher than tent stakes). Next, hold one of the hose sections against the tree or shrub trunk — at a level 4 feet or more above the ground if the plant is as tall as a beanpole, but 6 feet and upward if it is as tall as a flagpole — and bend the hose into a U-shape. Run the end of the wire through the piece of hose and knot the wire to hold the hose section in place. Loop the other end of the wire around one of the stakes, pull it taut, and secure it with a few python coils and twists. Repeat all this for the other two stakes and then attach the rag flags. Keep the stakes and wire in place for a year (for two, if the plant grows but little the first summer).

A more glamorous method of staking plants (and a safer way to stake curbstrip trees, in consideration of the pedestrian) is to use two 7½-foot-long milled pieces of 2-×-2-inch lumber stained a woodsy brown or soft green. Place these good-looking stakes on either side of the plant so that they stand straight about 5 feet high. The wiring is done the same way as in the other, rough-and-ready staking.

Cut the slope into terraces and plant on levels, or form a terraced planting hole for each plant. Whether tree, shrub, perennial, or bit of ground cover, the plant will establish itself far more easily on leveled ground. In digging a terraced planting hole for a solo tree or shrub on a steep slope (20° or more), build up the lower rim of the hole with excavated soil. Retain the

Planting on a Slope

Terraced planting hole for a single shrub on a slope (about 20°).

built-up rim with stones or shingles, or take a chance and leave it unretained, counting on the plant to become established before the rim erodes away.

Perennial Ground Covers from Divisions

A single plant of a shade garden ground cover that is grown in ideal soil (*see* p. 28) for a summer can usually be divided into dozens the following spring or into hundreds the spring or summer after that. Divide pieces of waldsteinia, lamium, creeping jenny, oxalis, carpeting sedums, campanulas, and other divisible ground covers from the mother plant and set them directly into a well-prepared shady bed, from about May 1 to September 1 (hold off the operation when the weather is hot and dry, unless you can be on hand to sprinkle the planting twice a day throughout the hot spell).

The ground at the time of planting should be moist but not sodden. If planting in newly spread topsoil, roll it or tramp on it beforehand to firm the ground. The object is to press away excessive airiness that would cause the shallow-rooted ground cover divisions to dry out. Plant each start in a slight hollow, with the soil surface around the plant roots a half inch lower than the planting bed itself. The plant should rest in its place at a low angle, with the underside of its stems touching the ground. Take care not to plant too shallowly; about half of the young plant — including some of the rootless stem — should go below ground.

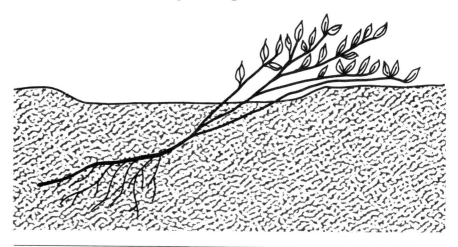

Start of ground cover planted in a slight hollow to aid watering.

Mail-Order Plants

Here, if anywhere, your author knows his onions (and mossy saxifrages and maidenhair ferns). During the 1960s and 1970s I operated a small mail-order nursery, The Wild Garden, specializing in uncommon hardy perennials and wildflowers. Allow me, then, to give an insider's interpretation of catalog assurances that plants will be shipped at a mythic "right time for your area": This usually means "when we get around to it." It is better to overrule the sweet-talking catalog by requesting shipment in a specific month of spring or autumn — the earlier in either season, the better for hardy plants.

September to early October is the choicest planting season for most hardy mail-order plants (miniatures excepted). By September the top growth of plants becomes less active and the cell walls tougher, in anticipation of winter. Now in semidormancy, the plant will ship with less likelihood of becoming battered or etiolated; yet the roots remain on full summer alert, ready to respond to autumn rains on still warm soil and to grow and provide anchorage against winter frosts that might otherwise heave the plant out of the ground. Early-spring shipment is, however, preferable for the many miniature shade garden perennials and shrublets one can obtain from mail-order nurseries (and usually in no other way). These would like to have a summer's growth in the garden to beef up for winter's trials.

Mail-order plants should be unpacked and cared for the day they arrive. If that can't be done, place the package in the refrigerator or in a cool place completely out of the sun. That way, the plants will hold for a weekend, if they arrive on Friday and you happen to be going out of town. But early processing saves the plant.

The larger mail-order plants — trees and shrubs, stalwart ferns, perennials, and trilliums and other shade garden "bulbs" — can usually be planted directly into their permanent places. Miniatures, however, should be planted for a time (a few days or two weeks, or until good color and a perceptible stir of life returns to their leaves) in a velvety-perfect little shade garden bed or in specially prepared containers. After refreshment from its trip, the miniature can go into the garden proper. But at first the plant will need to be kept away from the crises it would surely confront in the relative wilderness of the open garden, where a strolling caterpillar, an erupting and depositing angleworm, a scratching sparrow, or a drying breeze would be to the unestablished plant as simoom, bulldozer, avalanche, or rhino.

Locate the special bed in a place that is warmed by filtered sun or part sun, but not made hot by sun for too long a period of the day. A bench-bed in an airy greenhouse (the building having been whitewashed or otherwise tempered against sun) would be nearly perfect; a bed under lath shade or lightly foliaged trees is virtually as good. Other workable locations are the east side of a fence in morning sun and afternoon shade or a place that is in warm shade all day. Eschew making the bed in a chilly, densely shaded area, because the roots and leaves of convalescent plants will need warmth from tempered sun (or a heating cable) to resume growth.

Make the bed with ideal shade garden soil (*see* p. 28) that hasn't been recently fertilized — no fertilizer, please, during the plant's convalescence — and keep it not wet and not dry, but just moist (the bed should drain quickly and remain airy). These rather exacting specifications are easy to meet in a raised bed, which need be only an inch deeper than the roots of the plants it is to accommodate. The bed can be as simple as a blanket of soil spread atop a level area of open garden or upon concrete. Mail-order plants can also be potted up in unglazed clay pots or lodged in a soil-filled wooden box. Plastic pots, however, are dangerous to the travel-weary plant: the imperviable plastic may cause rotting by holding too much moisture around the plant's crown. Whatever the accommodation, there is prudence in making it up ahead of time rather than having the newly arrived plants standing about gasping until the gardener has time to put something together for them.

Digger's Delight Having arrived at the end of a chapter that deals superabundantly with the fine points of digging holes and heaving dirt, I suspect that you and I have both reached a certain rote numbness of mind best cured by an ocean cruise far from terra firma. Before embarking, there is one more species of hole to be dug, and I hope it doesn't fall to you to dig it: the planting hole in stony hardpan or in actual stone. The irony is, the less penetrable the ground, the larger the planting hole should be, because the plant's roots will be contained here as in a pot. Dig or blast a hole big enough to bury a wheelbarrow with dignity and plant the plant instead.

4

Creative Pruning

Landscape gardening is sculpture in a medium that won't stand still. Untamed, plants will creep, climb, run, sneak, and otherwise get away from the gardener. Those of us who have ever poked about in an abandoned, overgrown garden have come away stunningly aware of the part that pruning plays in gardening. It is, perhaps, gardening's most sculptural phase — the actual carving of plant forms and of spaces, a clarification of branch lines by removal of excessive portions. With pruning, we lighten plants, lower them, heighten them, and keep them out of our way and out of one another's way.

Winter is the traditional pruning season. It is then that orchardists and gardeners most easily have time for the job, whereas in the growing season their schedules are crowded with other duties. Summer pruning, however, offers a different advantage, that of immediate healing: Cuts made in the plant's time of fullest growth will partly close over with new bark before plant growth ceases in autumn.

A Few Tools

Few tools are really necessary for this work. Pruning a young garden usually calls for only three: pruning shears, a folding handsaw, and a dropcloth (an old tablecloth will do nicely) in which to collect the cut branches and carry them away. For carrying, a lightweight dropcloth is better than canvas or a wheelbarrow and is, in fact, one of the handiest of all gardening tools, useful in lawn edging, leaf raking, weeding, and flower grooming.

Pruning shears are of two types, one of which is damaging to the bark of the plant. The blades of this unrecommended tool meet edge to edge. Pruning shears of this design mash the bark of the portion of the branchlet that is to be retained; bark that is mashed dies.

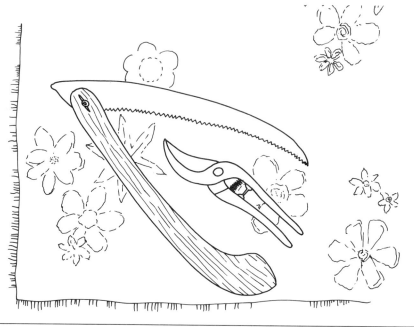

A Handiest of pruning tools: shears, folding saw, old tablecloth.

Drawing A outlines a superior, cleaner-cutting sort of pruning shears. The blade action is that of household scissors, one blade sliding against the side of the other. You'll need a heavy-duty model with blades about 2¾ inches long. To cut flowers for a bouquet, you may want to invest in a smaller, lighter pair, as well).

I've been somewhat dictatorial about pruning shears, with good reason: This tool is probably the third most important in all gardening, next only to the shovel and the spade, which it follows only because pruning follows digging and planting. Many gardeners (I among them) practically never prowl the garden without pruning shears in hand or pocket. There is always some plant in need of an improving snip.

Pruning shears are the correct tool for cutting twigs and branchlets up to about 1 inch in diameter. For larger work, use a folding handsaw (drawing A shows one partly unfolded). Usually the least expensive of pruning saws, the folding handsaw is unbeatably fast among muscle-powered saws for cutting limbs about 1–4½ inches in diameter. It is a cheap enough tool that one doesn't feel too many twinges of conscience about throwing it away when it gets dull (getting it sharpened would probably cost substantially the price of a new one). Folding handsaws come in several sizes. I find those with blades about a foot long to be right for a great range of limb sizes. The garden, until it grows up, will probably need no other saw.

Garden loppers may begin to prove handy some year in the first decade of your gardening, if not at the start. I use them in thinning, at soil level, canes of bamboo and raspberry and stems of forsythia and viburnum. The tool consists of pruning shears — with blades somewhat longer and heavier than in hand models — at the end of long handles. The best size for the work I described has handles about 2 feet long. An ax is also useful in soil-level pruning.

Hedge shears, a big scissors with handles that are held in both hands, are the requisite tool for clipping formal hedges and ivy.

In pruning tall trees, a saw on a pole will somewhat save the pruner from climbing ladders and walking limbs (a certain amount of ladder work is probably unavoidable, however). Some polesaws are sold poleless, merely a saw with a hollow neck extending from the blade. Into the hollow you fit — after whittling it to size — whatever pole, grape stake, or straightish tree limb you can find. An orchardist's pruning shears (pole, pull cord, spring-operated jaws) are also valuable when working on big trees.

These pruning tools, in addition to a ladder, may be all, or more than all, you'll ever need. Home gardening is still possible without the use of a chainsaw, that rage of the age, of TV commercials, of early Saturday mornings.

For Control, for Enhancement

The commonest reasons for pruning are to control plant size or to enhance branch structure. The two objectives require utterly different approaches to the plant. For control, prune from the top down and from the outside in. For enhancement, prune from the bottom up and from the inside out. Formal hedges, formalized evergreens, and ground-covering ivy are typical plantings pruned for control. Witch-Hazel, viburnum, forsythia, and nearly all other deciduous trees and shrubs are pruned for enhancement, or should be. Sometimes control and enhancement figure equally in pruning, as with apple trees and garden hydrangeas; such plants need thinning of branches year by year, and eventually, control at the top and sides.

Pruning purely to control the plant is routine work. Using hedge shears, one clips away at the puffed-up plant until it is reduced to the desired size, and the job is done. The dense, finely textured surface we admire in formally pruned plants is achieved by clipping branch ends frequently to induce twigginess and predetermined form in the plant during the years it is growing toward an ideal size. To keep the plant from outgrowing the ideal once it gets there, clip it at least once a season, twice if you are a hedge hobbyist — once in early summer, once again later on. The developing of a formal hedge or the geometrizing of a free-standing evergreen can be a relaxing subhobby in gardening.

Pruning to enhance branch structure is quite another matter. In this task we have one of gardening's higher metaphysical mysteries. Appraising each branch and twig by turn, the pruner must decide whether to prune or not to prune, basing each decision on the artistic merit or the defect of the branch to the human eye, and on the structural value or superfluity to the plant of every limb and digit. The pruner tries to visualize the effect each cut will have on the direction of the plant's growth in years to come. The task evidently seems so beginningless that most gardeners shy away from it. Trees and shrubs that should be thinned of branches are, in common garden practice, lopped back at top and sides. Stopped short, they grow thickety. (I'm thinking especially of spring forsythias, pruned into laundry bundle shapes the year before, flowering in a pinched way.)

With a little practice, pruning for enhancement loses its frightfulness. Most people catch on quickly. I've given lessons in the art, and I find that branch butchers often turn into creative pruners in one session. Having analyzed one complex branch and thinned it out attractively, a person can, I daresay, look at any branch and see the structure to be brought forth cleanly by removing the clutter.

Drawings B, C, and D provide a lesson in pruning for enhancement. The subject is a badly cluttered branch. The pruning approach will be from the bottom up and from the inside out.

B. The numbers 1 to 18 appear beside branchlets and twigs to be removed. For readability, I've tried to have the numbers progress in an orderly fashion from left to right and from the bottom of the branch upward. I would like to be able to tell you that this is exactly the sequential way I would make the cuts 1 to 18. But knowing my shuffling entrée to a job of pruning, I would probably *not* begin with 1, which is a major cut. To get my pruning hand started and my courage up, I would, typically, start by cutting away small stuff, obviously expendable twigs. I can see myself beginning with cuts 2, 3, and 4 — not necessarily in that order. Then, encouraged, I would surely attack 1, an ingrown branch that does nothing for the tree. The rest of the cuts would, or could, go by the numbers.

C. Job half done. I've stopped with the cutting of 8 to call your attention to branches 9 and 10 — a close choice. Though both have their merits, both can't stay, jammed together as they are. One or the other — but which? After study, I will elect to give 9 the coup de grâce and will then remove the innermost branchlet of 10 (drawing D reveals the results). The ingrowing direction taken by branchlet 11 is obviously untoward: adios to it. The remaining cuts, 12 to 18, are all minor to trifling. By now I may have said enough for you to have gotten the why and wherefore of each cut to be made.

D. Pruning completed, but only according to my own ideas. In pruning there are stylists and stylists. I like to leave the tree or shrub with much detail intact — that is, with many twigs full length. Other pruners would prefer thinning or cutting back still more twigs and branchlets, leaving an even clearer, sparer branch pattern. I admire this other style when I see it well carried out. The only pruning of deciduous plants I'm uncomfortable with is the pollarding* of trees (a medieval tree torture fortunately rare nowadays) and the ever so common lop-lop pruning, which I described earlier, of deciduous plants such as forsythias.

* The term was formerly applied only to the annual decapitation of a tree to induce it to form a broomlike head of the same height as the year before. More recently, pollarding has also come to mean the annual pruning back to main limbs of all the tree's new growth. Branches that are cut back to the same point year after year become clubbed, as if afflicted with elephantiasis. To prevent this monstrous effect (considered ornamental by many pollarders) cut the branch a little longer each year. Probably the most famous stand of pollarded trees in North America is the Sycamore grove outside the Shedd Aquarium in San Francisco.

Pruning to enhance branch structure.

E

F

Pruning for enhancement satisfies everyone's Japanese sense that trees should be readable branch by branch. Other benefits are gained simultaneously. The same pruning (from the inside out) directs the tree toward its future, because we retain the branches that point the way we want the tree to grow. This same pruning (from the bottom up) also opens headroom for ourselves and for plantings beneath the tree.

Drawings E to K show all these results brought forth in the enhancement pruning of a young tree. The principles of pruning for enhancement that are illustrated here fit any tree and many shrubs. First pruning (E to I) takes place all in one day. It induces the sapling to grow into a well-balanced juvenile (J), and on into a graceful young-adult tree (K).

E. Unpruned seedling or graftling tree newly planted in the garden. Problem: Find the branches that will best build the tree. Method: enhancement pruning, from the bottom up and from the inside out.

F. Off with the two lowermost branches. If they were left to grow, the tree would develop as a shrub, and there would be no walking or gardening closely beneath it. What's next? Pause for a minute to study the tree. (In pruning a real tree, one literally and repeatedly follows the footsteps of an artist backing up to appraise work in progress.) We see two branches crossing, locked in combat like swords or stags, disturbers of the peace. Besides which, they are both would-be leaders in competition with the branch to their right, the one that would seem to be the true leader of the tree.

G. Half the X is gone, a good cut. Before taking the other half, step back mentally to verify the rightness of the supposed leader (the tall branch to the right).

H. Indeed, it is the true lead branch. Now only one suspect branch remains on the tree, to the right of the leader, paralleling the leader and wanting to take over. If this pretender were left in place, the tree would

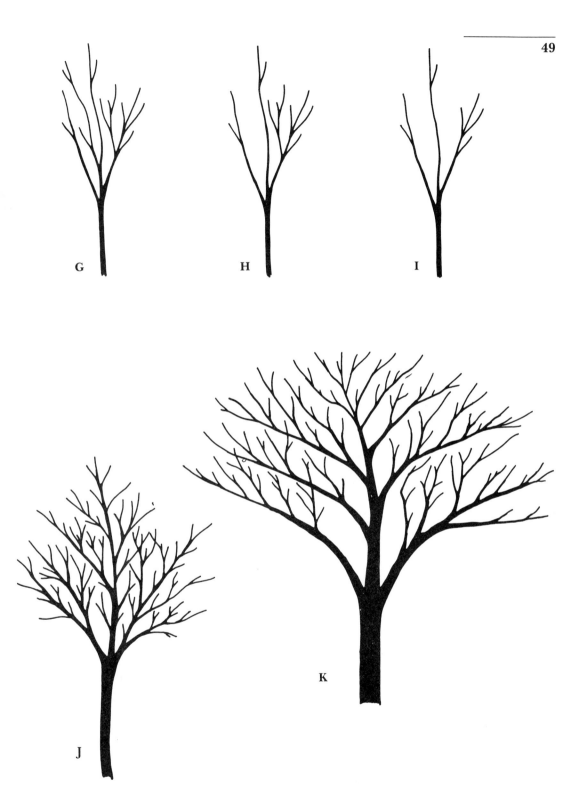

G

H

I

J

K

develop two trunks with a narrow V-shaped crotch — a structure apt to split. (Furthermore, the branch just doesn't look right.)

I. The sapling tree reduced to a trident, to the only branches that seem fit to carry the sapling treeward. The three-branch structure of the baby tree is less than exemplary, but it is typical. In my estimation, this was an average tree in the nursery row, and it is now an average garden tree newly planted and given the best headstart that the first pruning can provide. Would that the tree had had side branches higher up on the trunk. But there were none higher than the ones that were kept, and those two are probably too close to the ground to be retained in the maturing tree. I visualize the branches being three or four feet from the ground. They will become expendable when the tree grows taller and forms new branches higher up. Five to eight feet from the ground is a usual and practical range for the height (measuring at the juncture of branch and trunk) of the lowest branches of a maturing garden tree in its twenties. Later in life, taller-growing trees usually appear at their best "limbed up" to at least eight feet.

J. Two or three years later, the tree has developed into this youngster. The trident form of the sapling tree remains readily visible, although somewhat internalized by new growth. New side branches have developed higher up on the trunk, where they were wanting. After an initial heavy pruning such as this tree received in one day, some trees will grow on in an uncluttered way to the present stage entirely on their own, without any touch-up pruning. Other trees require an annual going over in their early years, without which they'll turn into a chaos of branches. Imagine that our young tree has received no pruning at all since we left it in drawing I. Now there is work to be done, approaching the job of pruning as before, from the bottom up and from the inside out (you know my refrain by now). Perhaps I should turn the pruning over to you at this point. Before I leave you to it, I'd like to consult with you about the main branch on the left side of the tree. This one has divided into two equals — a close and debatable choice. What's your opinion, Doctor? Retain the upper or the lower half of the bifurcation? All right, that's just what we'll do. And what's next?

K. Same tree about five to eight years later. Light pruning biennially (working always toward a taller clear trunk and an airier spacing of branches) has helped the tree develop into a graceful teenager. The lower branches are still those retained in drawing J, but they no longer grow at the same angle, for accumulating weight of growth has arched them downward. Just above them, left and right, the next two branches have attained nearly enough size and presence to serve as the tree's lowermost branches; with another year's stoutening, they'll be ready. Then the present lower limbs can be sawed off, giving better clearance beneath the tree. One might even do it now — what do you think? — and save having to make larger cuts next year. Even now, in taking branches as heavy as these, one should first notch the limb on the underside before cutting it through. The idea is to avoid ripping the bark from the trunk as the branch drops

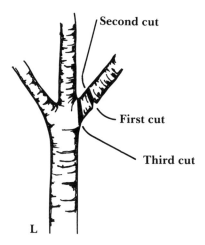

Second cut

First cut

Third cut

L

away. Following the pruning of any branch that is the diameter of a garden hose or larger, use pruning paint to cover the wound. I find tree paints in aerosol cans far easier to use than spread-on preparations.

Over the years, shade garden trees growing in most locations should be progressively relieved of their lower branches to keep the garden open beneath the tree and to control shade density. The height of summer (June or July) is the best time of the year for the job; winter is second best. But retain lower limbs that give privacy or shelter from wind.

Raising the Roof

In a temple garden in Kyoto, many years ago, I stopped dumbfounded to watch a pair of gardeners standing on branches in a full-grown pine tree, thinning its needles cluster by cluster on limb after limb, using small sickle-bladed knives — days of work, no doubt, the object being to reveal the tracery of the tree.

That was Japan at its most Japanese. The country as an objet d'art depends much on pruning. If all the patient pruners were to go into factories, we would have to look for Japan in boscage.

Pruning for Tracery

M

N

Head too low, raised by taking off bottom branches.

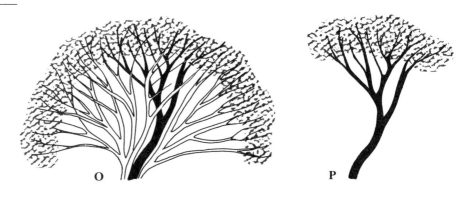

O   P

Within this fat, 12-ft.-wide shrub is a thin tree trying to get out.

The forests of Japan contain many understory trees and shrubs that grow thin and twisty in the shade, among them the native maples, mahonias, *Enkianthus*, nandinas, azaleas, and *Kerria*. Garden-grown and pruned to emphasize their specialties, tracery plants have long been a characteristic feature of Japanese gardens, as well as an influence on the classical spareness of other Japanese arts. There Nature has taught art, which has returned to instruct Nature. In the high shade of the gardens of Japan, plants that would be thin are coaxed onward and upward into lines like fine curly smoke.

The Japanese have no patent on elegantly thin shrubbery. In North American forests grow such spindleshanks as Witch-Hazel, azaleas, vacciniums, Vine Maple, and viburnum for the gardener to add to those more sveltely limbed plants from Japan (all of which are widely cultivated in our gardens). Shade garden vignette: a tracery plant against a wall or behind a translucent screen (making even plastic personable). Planted there, the naturally thin shrub is further reduced to the least number of branches that will carry the artistic message. Use the enhancement technique (drawings B, C, D), sparing terminal twigs on the branches you keep.

Arborizing a   The hugely overgrown shrub, beyond transplanting, lapping over the
Shrub   walk, perhaps, or standing in front of a window so solidly that "something's got to be done," can often be turned into one of the garden's best features (and a fine patch of ground for shade gardening brought to light and air) by making a tree out of the plant. Tall lilacs and rhododendrons are often good for aborizing; some of the many others are English and Portuguese Laurel, *Photinia, Viburnum, Aucuba, Banksia, Bougainvillea* (wear leather gloves when you wade into this spiny monster), old Mugo Pines and shrubby junipers.

No outsize shrub of any kind should ever be chopped down without first being given this test for artistic talent: Part the branches and peer inside; there in the interior of the gross shrub may be a graceful tree, to be released by pruning. Select for the keeping one or several fairly upright trunks (but if the shrub is a leaner growing on a steep slope, you may be able to turn it into a romantically leaning tree, remindful of those in old Chinese scrolls). It is usually safe to remove as much as four-fifths of a shrub's trunk and branch structure in pruning for arborization. The trunk(s) you select to retain should at best provide a spreading canopy of branches at the top (see drawings O and P). Prune away the shrub's side branches and cut off unwanted trunks at ground level — I find garden loppers and an ax useful here — until the tree you have spotted stands forth. No branch stubs, please; leave the selected trunk or trunks clean up to a height that suits you and the plant. Shrubs 8 feet or more tall can often be limbed-up to a height that will let you step right up without stooping and place a hand on the trunk: ancient greeting of human and tree.

Beneath the tree you've created (is the gardener, at this juncture, Dr. Frankenstein or Luther Burbank?), prepare the ground for planting according to the methods given in the "Beneath Trees" section of chapter 2.

Curbing Rhododendrons

Rhododendrons are somewhat the sacred cows of shade gardening. Once planted, they are usually allowed to grow their own way forever. Woodland paths become barred by their growth, household windows darkened. Any pruning of the plant would be regarded as sacrilegious sacrifice by the majority of gardeners, those in Japan excepted. There they routinely shear small-leaved (Kurume, Kaempferi) rhododendrons, rounding them into puffball shapes that contrast with taller, lankier plants pruned for tracery. Performed annually immediately after the plants flower, Japanese-style pruning of rhododendrons takes some of last year's wood and some soft new growth; the pruning is never hard — never back into two- or three-year-old wood.

Hard pruning of rhododendrons is, however, quite possible. Commercial collectors of wild rhododendrons in North Carolina are not in the least reluctant to stump back lank woods-grown plants of *Rhododendron catawbiense* and other Appalachian species. They will lop the branches of a tall plant back to nearly bare, 18–24-inch sticks and grow it on in a half-sunny nursery bed until it forms new shoots and healthy leaves in a compact, bushy mass — a prime horticultural porker, such as one sees in the rhododendron section of any nursery. (I'm a tepid admirer of large-leaved rhododendrons as landscape material.)

Having seen and been emboldened by this operation, I have since had occasion to practice the same kind of severe pruning on an 8-foot-tall rhododendron 'Cynthia', a robust, large-leaved hybrid growing in a friend's garden. The shrub's branches blocked a living room window, yet the plant had no upright trunk suitable for arborizing. We cut it back to 3½ feet tall. Nearly all the shrub's foliage went with the pruning. There was really no other way. Transplanting seemed out of the question. The rhododendron's roots were in a clinch with those of other shrubs, making a neat job of digging impossible; a large rhododendron whose roots are injured or bared in transplanting usually mopes and looks poorly for years afterward. As I put the case to my friend, we had the alternative of stumping back the plant, with a good chance it might regrow, or of chopping it off at soil level, which would afford the shrub only a small chance of regenerating. And so we stumped back the thirty-year-old 'Cynthia'.

For years afterward leaf production became almost the sole business of the shrub. Hardly any flowers appeared until the third spring after the stumping back. That season, the shrub opened a goodly show, and it has done so ever since. The new shape of the rhododendron is that of a leafy ball, of a rich shade of green.

But that was a risky piece of work. Large-leaved rhododendrons are better pruned selectively, branch by branch, in late spring, when the new growth is still soft. Each season, take away half the new branches at the point where they fork from the old wood. The next season, take the branches skipped the year before. To remove them, cut back into two-year-old wood.

Sound like the voice of experience? Indeed it is. In the garden of another friend, I planted as a hedge a bunch of young plants of large-leaved rhododendron hybrids my friend had rooted from cuttings (my main object was to make some use of propagules to which said friend was emotionally attached). In the seventeen or so years since then, the hedge has grown to seven feet tall by nine feet wide. In recent years, rhododendron branches have constantly intruded on a path beside the hedge, and, feeling somewhat responsible, I have been pruning them back from the path year after year (a favor that's good for a home-cooked meal every time). Working at this, I lean into the hedge, selecting for removal two-year branches way inside. Meanwhile, the shrub pushes at me with springy limbs and big leathery leaves. In my ongoing training of the rhododendron hedge, I think of myself as an elephant handler, leaning into the beast, trying to get into its head the idea "back, back."

I'm delighted to have discovered that the late, famed landscape architect Thomas Church made the same error in one of his gardens — that of planting big-leaved, big-growing rhododendrons too close to the path, on both sides. The rhododendrons totally erased the path and solidly interlocked their branches to nine feet above the place where it had been. But gardeners have turned this accident into one of the most refreshing features of Church's garden, by cutting a tunnel through the rhododendrons to reopen the path. They used the shrub arborization technique, but cut only the pathward side of each plant.

Open-Ground Bonsai

In my Seattle-area garden I grow a variety of trees and shrubs as open-ground bonsai, among them maples of several species. The treelets are lifted and root-pruned early each autumn, all the current year's roots being cut back to about the same point I cut them the fall before, to form a root ball about a foot wide. With yearly root-pruning, the height of open-ground maples (and many other shade garden plants) can easily be kept just where you want it, anywhere from 1 to 8 feet, not a bonsai if much above 2 feet, but a petite tree or shrub for a small space.

The root pruning will greatly tame the plant's power to grow: from feet to inches. A minor amount of branch pruning, however, will still be needed for enhancement and for control. Almost any woody plant that can be dwarfed in a pot can be dwarfed in the open ground. Root pruning every year is essential.

The Great Over-achievers: Garden Hydrangeas, Bamboos, Ivy

These three need much control. Cut out old branches of garden hydrangeas at ground level. From the branches that you retain, cut off branchlets that hold fading flowers. This is summer work. A garden hydrangea can also be cut tidily (but temporarily) to the ground, if you get fed up with the aggressiveness of the plant. It will *usually* come back smartly, but probably won't flower until late next summer.

The tall, root-running, grove-making bamboos (timber, golden, and others) best display the famous qualities of bamboo when they are thinned so that one can see through the grove. Cut at soil level as many canes as you wish, at any time of the year. Then cut off (or snap off while they are in soft growth) as many side branches as you wish from the canes you leave standing; a plume of leaves at the top will be enough to sustain the plant. It is difficult — I'm almost ready to say impossible — to overprune a lustily growing bamboo. Too tall? Cut the canes off at whatever height you wish while they are in soft growth. Those canes will never grow taller.

Root pruning can be as good a method of stopping running bamboos as the more usual one of surrounding the plant with a two-foot-deep subterranean wall of concrete. As a preliminary pruning, first dig an 18-inch-deep trench around the plant. Fill the trench to the top with a fluffy, leafy mulch (the bamboo, a great litterer, will help you there) or with peat moss. In early June and again in late September, use a garden fork to remove the mulch from the trench and expose the rhizomes of the bamboo, which will almost certainly be growing into the mulch. Take the lopping shears to them. Clump-making bamboos, on the other hand, can be curbed by running the lawn mower over the soft new shoots as they come up.

Ivy that is to be kept low to the ground can be sheared in late spring and again in late summer, if need be — or even mowed, if you have a hefty enough mower. Many tool rental companies offer the right machine for this. Shear in spring and summer ivy that is to be kept flat against a wall.

Ivy planted at the base of a tree loves to climb the trunk and coil about the limbs. Ivy on a living tree is unsightly, as well as weakening to the host, and it eventually kills the tree by overshading its leaves. It's best and easiest, of course, to rip the ivy tendrils off the tree trunk before they've climbed the first foot.

Thicket Thinning

Forsythia, Philadelphus, Deutzia, Ribes, Flowering Quince, and many other natural woods' edge shrubs have the bad garden habit of turning into broad thickets, taking far more space than they merit. These are plants that one has to keep after annually, pruning out branches freely. The best

Q   R

Thickety shrub (about 9 feet wide) overdue for thinning.

time is when the plant is in flower (or soon afterward; or even winter pruning will be perfectly acceptable to the plant). Pruning in blossom time, one can be generous with armload bouquets for oneself and friends. Withal, the thicket-forming shrub is still an overdoer. Completely remove unwanted new trunks where they ramify from the crown of the plant.

When Transplanting   Trees and shrubs dug from the woods or the garden usually lose some — or much — of their root system when transplanted. The remaining roots will probably be inadequate to supply the plant's complete above-ground structure with water and food. The solution is to prune away branches to a degree corresponding with root loss. A lightly damaged root system requires the removal merely of some twigs and minor branches. Heavy damage (more or less half the roots gone) will necessitate major pruning. Use drawings E to I as a guide: Let the sapling tree shown here be a stand-in for any plant you are working with.

But if your plant comes out of the ground with only stumps of roots, stump back its branches and hope for the best. The stumped plant should somewhat resemble the sapling in drawing I, yet the sapling should be pruned even further than you see it done in the drawing — back to the lowest twigs on all three branches. Perhaps the pruner should save those three twigs and so keep their leaf buds, which are ready to open leaves that will feed the plant. If stumped back to budless wood, the plant may not muster the strength to strike new growth. Then again, it may strike readily even if cut close to the ground.

"Perhaps . . . may . . . or may not . . . then again": These uncertain terms are the best that can be applied to a plant badly root-wounded in transplanting. Torn stubs of roots should be pruned off cleanly — back an inch or so, to a point where the bark is unmashed and untorn. The neatened root stubs should be sealed with pruning paint.

Some woody plants — *Ilex crenata*, mountain ash, maples (except for grafted ones), sumacs, and raspberries — are notably easy movers. Even with roots much bobbed at the time of moving, these plants will usually take hold and grow in their new locations without being heavily pruned.

Other plants are hard movers that seldom survive a rough job of transplanting. Magnolias, dogwoods, grafted maples, English Hollies, mature rhododendrons, and sourwood are among those I have found to die easily when transplanted badly. (I had tried to work alone on plants that were too heavy, and couldn't move them with a broad enough root pan. Should have corralled a couple of friends to help.)

Nursery trees and shrubs grown in the open ground are usually root-pruned yearly to keep the root system rounded and manageable. As a result, the properly root-pruned specimen can be dug for transplanting with its roots scarcely nicked, and hardly any pruning will be necessary for purposes of strengthening the plant. However, at the time of transplanting, one does seem inclined to give the plant's branches a shrewd examination, with an eye toward determining what is good and what is bad, and how the plant should be faced in its new location. Since it may be a while before one again sharply focuses on the plant, consider this a golden moment for creative pruning.

5

Shade Garden Pests

Shade gardening has its own bugbears in the form of slugs, snails, and root weevils, but here's the good part: The great variety of sunny garden pests seldom attack seriously in shady places. Usually, the shadier the garden, the rarer the aphids, caterpillars, mites, and scale insects. But at times a shrub growing close to a shady wall of the house, where the eaves prevent cleansing rain from reaching the foliage, may become host to a crowd of mites or to scale. Hosing the shrub with plain water is valuable as a preventive measure. Systemic poisons and contact poisons give a high degree of control if applied repeatedly; springtime spraying is the most effective.

On the uncommon occasions when aphids and caterpillars hatch out in the shade, they are usually found bunched on one or two plants of some rare, shade-inhabiting relative of the insect's customary sunny food plant. The chosen shade plant is in for thorough ruin unless the gardener takes quick action. That seems to be the very action some of us are not quite up to — one of us at least. When I discover an attack upon a plant in my own shade garden, early in the month of June, let's say, I may not get around to doing anything about it until July, meanwhile walking by the plant daily during the crucial month when I could have saved it. Pest control seems to be the gardening job I put off longest and like least. When and if I do get out the spray rig, I spot-spray only to the infested plant, splashing as little as possible on the garden around it. Spot-spraying is the only kind I ever do, and that most reluctantly. At times I'll cut down a bug-eaten plant to avoid spraying it. The infested branches are then burned or buried, or sealed in a plastic bag and garbaged. I count on the plant to restore itself from the root.

Kinds of spray? Spraying schedules? I'm hardly qualified. May I refer you to the labels on the bottles in the garden store? I do own a single bottle of insecticide (malathion — generally effective, horrible-smelling) whose cap is going rusty with age. Better a few bugs than a lot of poison.

Root weevils (now we're getting down to the hard-core pests of the shade garden) are a chronic low-key affliction on the West Coast of the U.S. and Canada and, from place to place, eastward to the Atlantic. The root weevils are of several similar species: small, slow-moving, dark beetles with anteaterlike or tapirlike snouts. The adults eat only the edges of leaves, biting out crudely scallop-shaped portions. Their soft, white or pinkish larvae attack the roots and underground bark of the plant. The adults merely ruin the plant's appearance; the larvae often kill it.

Within the insect's range, nearly all topsoils and plant communities harbor at least a few weevils. At times, in a single garden or in a city neighborhood, the root weevil population builds up into an epidemic. They are apt to be especially troublesome in a newly planted shade garden that features one or more of their food plants. Most new gardens are sparse environments, with smallish plants and open soil spaces. In this desert vastness (to reduce our perspective to that of a beetle), the weevil will be drawn directly to any available food plant as toward an oasis. Without protection, the plant won't stand much of a chance.

Peculiarly notched leaves are one sign of root weevils. Another is when an entire shrub suddenly goes limp and browns off in dry weather. If weevils are the culprit (simple neglect of watering may, after all, be the cause) they will have left underground marks on the plant.

The brown and brittle shrub is dead, all right, and ready for plant pathology. Pull it up, shake the soil off, and hose the root system clean. Weevil larvae, if culpable, are probably long gone, but they will have left their traces — bare wood visible on the bark of main roots or a girdled underground trunk. In losing its bark, the shrub fatally lost the cambium siphon system that enabled it to deliver water and minerals to the leaves. Maddening! Months too late to do anything for this victim, and high time to protect other susceptible plants.

Weevils sprayed with any soluble contact poison (malathion or others) will die if the spray hits them, but their underground larvae are hard to reach. For the best control possible, soak the poison into the soil beneath and closely around the plant; dousing the plant itself is of minor help as preventive medicine. Repeat the application every several weeks from spring to fall. Repeated soaking of the soil directly beneath shrubs and perennial plants vulnerable to weevils will save most of the plants. Complete control of the pest is not feasible. Some of the larvae, eating away in sheltering root crannies, escape the poison and live to complete the destruction of the plant. They then inch away a short distance, and become still; metamorphosis transforms them into adults that will carry on the chronic presence of the insect.

Root weevils are partial to a wide variety of vegetation, including important shade plants: primroses, coralbells, strawberries, and viburnums; all shrubs of the heath family, such as rhododendrons, azaleas, *Pieris,* and blueberries; *Bergenia,* saxifrage, *Cyclamen,* and *Astilbe;* tall sedums such as *S. spectabile; Corydalis, Doronicum, Francoa,* and others, no doubt. I've only named those that figure in my own experience with weevils, the plants I had to fight for in the early years of my shade gardening. Weevils were then rampageous in my garden, but never since.

Over the years the garden, on its own, has gained a measure of self-protection. Maturing shrubs have become largely immune to weevil damage at the root. Rhododendrons, for example, that were in their first years tender prey to the grubs' jaws have become thicker of bark and more resistant every year. I can't recall having lost to weevils any rhododendron or other shrub (except *Pieris japonica*) that was eight years old, or older. (*Pieris japonica* is perhaps the most weevil-prone of shrubs and can be killed even when it's in its twenties.)

And, with time, an overall protection arises in the shade garden that is its only lasting defense against insect pests: It is a balance of nature that grows within the garden as the garden becomes established. It may never equal the complete balance one observes in a healthy woods, but it will be enough to keep down the weevil population, along with other harmful insects. The garden's balance of nature begins with the development of shade and of leafy shelter close to the ground. To this cozy shelter come the eaters of insect pests — the birds, predatory beetles, centipedes, toads, salamanders, lizards, and garter snakes. Parasitic flies and wasps — obscure, incalculably valuable insects — come, as well, in order to lay their eggs on certain garden pests. These good agents are attracted to the garden's burgeoning plants, not for shelter, but as likely homes for their prey.

From the time such natural helpers begin to work in the garden, any spraying for weevils or other pests should be kept to a minimum. Spot-spraying a few plants probably won't greatly upset the garden's biological balance, but spraying the entire garden with any contact poison will knock out whatever equilibrium there is in it. Not only will the insect pest die, so will any of the pest's natural enemies that are touched by the poison. In the ensuing years, the rarity of the pest's enemies (they are comparatively slow breeders) will make the sprayed garden more favorable to the prolific pest and more dependent on doses of poison. Elementary ecology, all this — facts apparently too widely known to need announcing on insecticide labels.

Root weevils can be a hard blow to the shade gardener, especially when they attack the garden during its tender beginnings, the very time the gardener most needs to experience success. Later in one's gardening career — to repeat an encouraging prognosis — the problem lessens.

The garden slug never lets up, nor does the garden snail. The garden slug, black or tan or reddish brown (same animal, different color phases) is the horticultural plague of North America, east to west. In a poll taken for this book, American shade gardeners over much of the country named the slug garden enemy number one. Only gardens in California and in western deserts and prairies largely escape this prolifically breeding pest.

But the garden snail, brown-shelled with subtle blackish markings, abounds along California's Mediterranean-like coast, where it takes precedence over the slug as the worst of pests. Long summer droughts in California act as a deterrent to the shell-less slug, but when hard times come to the snail, the animal has only to withdraw into its shell to literally seal itself from the world.

The garden snail is increasing its North American range by riding on plants exported from its adopted state of California. This creature is not native to North America, and neither is the garden slug. Both came from Europe, along with rats, mice, roaches, root weevils, and a hundred other noxious insects, plus a hundred or so grievous weeds, such as Dandelions, sorrel, and thistle. Europe would seem to have been lying in wait for North America, the biological innocent. Nearly all our floral and faunal infections came over as stowaways on sailing ships in centuries before the present one. The Pandoran gift was unreciprocated by America, very few biological sorrows having gone in the other direction.

North America had its own slugs and snails, and still has — rather nice animals that were probably never overly abundant. And now they are becoming scarce. They seldom trouble gardens. Less aggressive than the imported mollusks, they retreat as the interlopers advance and proliferate. Our native snails and slugs usually live in the woods or at the woods' edge, but they will readily venture forth for a meal of exotica just beyond the woods. *Garden* slugs and snails keep mainly to the garden, the farm, the city park, and the weed lot, seldom venturing into the deep woods.

Garden mollusks are controlled by being lured to poisoned bait or to a fatal alcoholic binge, or by being hunted. The hunter goes out during the mollusks' feeding time, in the cool of the evening or on a moist, dull day. A heavy foot is the handiest weapon against snails; or collect them in a tin can and pour boiling water over them. For a slug, a stab with a sharp stick is sure death, and kills humanely fast. But the gardener who relies solely on the hunt as a control measure will have to spend more than one evening at this. Garden mollusks seem to breed almost as fast as one can destroy them. Every snail or slug the gardener misses is a potential egg layer (it is both male and female), capable of depositing a score or more of relatively large, pearl-like eggs in one cluster. Look for and destroy these eggs in their hideaways beneath stones, duff, or rosetted plants.

The hunter who is also an adventurer with food might like to consider going out on a pot-hunt for garden snails. They are perfectly edible, being none other than the escargots of Europe, available to us in cans at fancy gourmet prices, but free — and much tastier — when gathered in one's garden. I've tried shade garden escargots and can recommend them.

Here's my own recipe. Before cooking the snails, confine them in a jar with lettuce leaves for a couple of days, time enough for them to clean the grit out of their craws. Kill the snails before cooking. First tap on their shells to induce them to retreat inside. Then drop them in boiling water for but an instant. Now they are ready for broiling. If you have no escargot pan (as I have not), potato slices will serve as supports while the snails are broiled. Cut thick slices of potato and boil them until they barely reach the mealy stage. Carve hollows in these slices and nestle a snail on each one, with the shell opening upright. Pour over the snails a simmering mixture of butter, minced garlic, and parsley (the garlic should be cooked through). Place the snails on their potato rafts under a broiler for several minutes, or until their juices simmer with the butter. Voilà: shade garden escargots.

Shade garden slugs I have not tried, but determined experimenters at the University of Washington have; recipes on file at the university proffer slugs with Italianate sauces. As survival food, if nothing more, the garden slug offers a ready source of protein; but the name would need euphemizing. *Limace* — French for "slug" — gives the animal a certain lift and lilt; it might do even more for the culinary slug than *escargot* does for the snail. However, for the purist who objects to Frenchification of our language, how about *garden sausages?*

Our next lesson comes regrettably soon after dinner: the drowning of slugs and snails in beer. For this you will need only a bottle of beer, a soup bowl, and a trowel. Scoop a depression in the soil of the garden, place the bowl in it with the rim close to ground level, and pour in the beer. During the night, mollusks will be drawn to the volatizing alcohol and grain factors in the beer. Coming from as far away as some yards downwind, they imbibe, get drunk, and drown. (You can increase the drawing power of the beverage by adding about a tablespoon of rum, the darker and more heavily fragrant, the better.) The allure of the cocktail, unless cut short by rain, will continue through several nights, after which the gardener is in for a dismal cleanup job. The best way is to dig out a shovelful of dirt beside the bowl, tip the contents into the hole, and cover with dirt.

Boozing them to death is an effective control (you may need to set several bowls in several locations) and fairly narrowly aimed at slugs and snails. True, there are a few harmless or valuable forms of insect and other arthropod life that may come and drown, together with the mollusks, but birds and animals won't be harmed by the brew even if they lap up the entire contents of the bowl.

Dry baits provide an easier means of controlling garden mollusks, but are not entirely without risk to higher animals. The active ingredient in slug/snail baits is metaldehyde, a polymer of acetaldehyde, as vicious as it sounds. It comes either in a grain mixture (pellet form or meal form) or soaked into dried apple pomace (the sweet-smelling leavings of apples squeezed for juice). The poisoned pomace has the consistency of coarse sawdust. The sweet cidery smell of it will bring slugs and snails from at least three yards away, making this the best of dry baits. The others are less alluring and shorter-lasting in rainy weather; shortest-lived of all are the mealy baits.

Scatter or place the bait in the garden in moist weather, spring to autumn. In dry summer weather, the pests sleep and are not to be tempted. The bait is probably most effective when placed in small heaps of about a half a cup each, at intervals of every few yards in the garden. Caution: Some dogs will eat the bait if they find it, most poultry certainly will, and a preschool child might. It may be safer to scatter the bait so that it will be lost beneath foliages.

Rained on, the bait loses its allure and killing power in a couple of days. To prevent this, make a little house for the bait. Thus protected, it will last for weeks, or until consumed. An open-ended box of shakes or scraps of board, nailed together, will be just the thing. The pests will die nearby, and the carcasses can, if you wish, be left to sink into the ground as fertilizer.

Shade plants vary in their attractiveness to garden slugs and snails. Some plants excite the appetites of these molluskan sharks and barracudas to a pitch that will make maintaining the plant in open ground nearly impossible. Toward other plants, the creatures seem, for a while, to be more blasé. For months they'll ignore a plant or merely nibble it, and then one night they may eat it to the ground, apparently for a needed change in diet. Still other plants are almost never eaten.

By specializing in shade plants that mollusks don't like, you can forget about controls. But the tactic won't work perfectly if there is a sunny vegetable or flower garden nearby. Slugs and snails hiding in the shady garden by day will descend on open garden areas by night.

Shade Plants Usually Slug and Snail-Proof: *Agapanthus, Alocasia, Anemone japonica, Anemone memorosa, Arum italicum, Galium odoratum* (Asperula odorata), *Aspidistra, Astilbe,* Baby's-Tears, bamboo, bedding begonias, *Begonia* 'Cleopatra', bleeding-heart, bromeliads, *Campanula Poscharskyana,* coral-bells, *Cyclamen, Dichondra, Duchnesea, Epimedium* (the taller species), Evergreen Candytuft, ferns (most large-growing kinds, including Lady Fern, *Osmunda, Polystichum*), foxglove, *Gaultheria, Hedychium, Impatiens,* ivy (usually left alone by slugs, but snails may riddle it), juniper, Kenilworth Ivy, *Linnaea,* London Pride, *Nandina, Oxalis oregana, Sansevieria, Endymion hispanicus* (Scilla campanulata), sedums (most species; *S. maximum,* however, is on the menu), *Sempervivum,* Solomon's Seal, *Taxus, Thalictrum, Thymus Serpyllum, Viola hederacea, Viola rupestris,* Wandering Jew *(Tradescantia fluminensis).* These are merely the ones I know about through my own experience. There must be a parcel of others, to be discovered by test.

Shade Plants Relished by Slugs and Snails: Constant baiting is usually necessary to keep these from being eaten to tatters.

Asarum (wild ginger), *Athyrium Goeringianum; Campanula carpatica, C. isophylla* and most of the other low-growing campanulas; primroses (the flowers), Daffodils and narcissuses, *Doronicum, Erythronium,* gentians (autumn-flowering), *Helleborus niger, Hepatica,* lettuce, lilies, *Lobelia* (perennial species), *Parochetus communis,* strawberries (fruit of the commercial varieties is quickly eaten, but the small fruit of the Alpine Strawberry is much less attractive), tuberous begonias, trilliums (sometimes a quick snack, sometimes — curiously — left alone), *Viola sororia (V. papilionacea).* I fear this list is far from complete.

In country locations, the gardener may have to take steps against deer, squirrels, rabbits, mountain beavers, gophers, or other herbivores. Bambi can turn out to be the terror of the woodland garden, and a troop of bunny rabbits can trash one's homemade woodlet in the manner an elephant herd will waste a jungle grove. The gardener may need to put up a fence — or trap the lesser animals — in order to maintain a garden of exotic plants. The appetites of plant-eating animals are definitely stimulated by unfamiliar foliages placed in their environment. There is shrewdness (but nothing, I hope, of sour grapes) in deciding to grow no exotics at all, only plants that are native and abundant in the area: The gardener thereby bores the animals. "Same old stuff," they'll think, after a bite here and there. "Might as well pass it by and see what the next place has on the menu."

And then, when a plant in the garden turns out to be manna to slugs and snails, scale or mites, or to some other pest that leaves the plant skeletonized or palely vampirized year after year, despite one's efforts at control, it may make more sense to get rid of the plant than to keep on trying to get rid of the pest.

Above all, the best means of dealing with garden pests is often the practice of tolerance: accepting the fact that a certain portion of the garden is going to be eaten. We see this easy attitude in trompe l'oeil paintings of flowers and herbage by old masters. There are the flowers with perfect foliage, and there, also, is the occasional leaf with holes, and, nearby, the insect that ate the leaf. Compare the gardener's harvest as it is represented in the painting with the tithe taken by the pest: The loss seems trifling. The seventeenth-century artist who grew those flowers relied, perhaps without knowing it, primarily on the pest's natural enemies to keep it from taking the whole garden. We of the twentieth century have relied up to now on increasingly potent applications of poisons. By the inadvertent poisoning of controlling species as well as pests, we end up losing more of the garden with our use of chemicals than our ancestors did without them.

To repeat a banner phrase: better a few bugs than a lot of poison. However, I'm no zealot in this matter. If the bugs begin to take over, better a little spot-sprayed poison.

6

A Great Lawn in Shade

You're sure, now, this is what you want — a toe-inviting carpet of grass in the shade? There is an alternative: the moss lawn from which one eradicates the stray grass blade (as described at Mosses in chapter 11). Not for you? All right, let's see what is in the photograph on the next page.

Beneath mature oaks, velvety green lawn sweeps up to the very bark of the trees' boles. The oaks, *Quercus rubra (Q. borealis maxima)*, were planted forty-two years ago; they and the lawn have gotten on together beautifully throughout the years. Just how shady is this scene? About 95 percent so, I would estimate, having subtracted from the preponderant shade the wraiths of sunshine we see on the grass and tree trunks. All around the lawn are magnolias, azaleas, and rhododendrons that shield out the low sun of morning and evening. This is a garden virtually in full shade, but shade that is light and wholesome. The lawn has not been fussed over for its photograph. The grass is about due for a mow, and the beginning leaf fall of October dots its surface. Never mind. I believe you'll get the picture: serenity, seclusion, shrubbery possessing that special floatiness of leaf that develops in shade — all in all, a spacious shade room with a soft grassy carpet on which to laze.

This is the garden of Elizabeth M. Hopkins, who has cared for it from the start. Beth Hopkins keeps a garden record and has, in our behalf, looked up the seed recipe for her lawn.

Ingredient	Percent
Creeping Red Fescue	44
Chewing's Fescue	30
Kentucky Bluegrass	15
Highland Colonial Bentgrass	10
Inert material	1

Velvety grass beneath oaks. (HOLLY HOLLINGSWORTH)

That blend has turned out to be first-rate in shade. But there exist about as many lawn seed blends as there are recipes for chili. The "shady lawn" mixture carried by your local seed store will no doubt grow a shady lawn just as fine as the one you see here, as long as you'll give yours the amount of care this lawn receives.

Mrs. Hopkins mows her lawn every three or four days in the spring months, once a week in summer and fall. The grass is mowed short — less than 1 inch high — a practice contrary to the advice of a major grass seed company, which holds that shady lawns are best kept longish. Their idea is, the longer the grass, the more blade surface available for the absorption of chlorophyll-inducing, life-giving daylight. But judging from the results of the Beth Hopkins method, a thick carpet of short grass presents more leaf surface than a thinner stand of longer blades (grass thins somewhat if left long of blade).

The Hopkins lawn grows on deep sandy soil deficient in clay and native minerals. The grass is fed once in spring and once in summer with a liquid "lawn tonic," a product that is a complete fertilizer, in combination with ferrous sulfate (15 percent of the total), which kills moss and so encourages thicker grass. Beth Hopkins also spreads dolomite lime on the lawn once a year, or less often — whenever the surfaces of nearby plant beds become mossy, her clue that the soil has become too acid for the health of grass.

In the summer, watering is done only about once a week, the grass being soaked for an hour or more. Deep watering through September on into early October, or until rains come and mean business, is necessary for the continued greening of the grass. Deep watering has the additional effect of keeping the oak leaves overhead green for a longer season. Fall comes later to these trees than to the unwatered oaks elsewhere on the property.

In recent years the lawn has been mowed by an electric mower with a vacuum that takes up acorns, acorn cups, and fallen leaves. (In the old days there was much picking up of fine debris by hand after a bamboo rake had cleared off the bigger stuff.) A lawn in shade will quickly weaken beneath fallen twigs or leaves that are left to block out the light. The lawn in shade restores itself more slowly than a sunny lawn, once the cluttering bit that was left too long is finally removed.

Yet, over the years, the success of a tree-shaded lawn owes much to the bonhomie of the tree. One kind of tree differs greatly from another in the matter of friendliness toward lawn grass and other underplanting. Deciduous trees are generally better natured toward competitors than are evergreen trees. Among deciduous trees, oaks rank among the best of boon companions for shady garden and lawn. Other especially companionable trees are hackberry (*Celtis*), European Ash (*Fraxinus exelsior*), jacaranda, flowering crabapples, orchard apple, pear and lemon, and Japanese Pagoda Tree (*Sophora japonica*). Of evergreens, palms are notably easy on grass, and Douglas Fir, limbed high to admit sidelight, will encourage grass to grow to golf course perfection right up about its trunk.

Happy days on your shady lawn!

7

Season by Season

Winter Watching the snow fall on the garden is one of gardening's finer moments, savored to the fullest when standing at a window with a mug of steaming coffee or hot buttered rum in hand. The cottony flakes blanket, in their beds, the leaves and buds of primulas, ferns, and all low plants. They'll sleep easily now beneath the snow. The deeper the better, for snow is the great saver of the garden, the surest insulation against repeated freezing and thawing, against the winter sun that sets up that harmful alternation. So don't hesitate to shovel snow from the drive or walk onto garden plantings.

In snowless, freezing weather, check perennials planted late in the fall to see if there has been frost heaving. Replant any that have been prised out of the ground. If the frost-heaved plant has been merely half-ejected from the frozen ground — held fast by earthy ice clutching the lower parts of its roots — pack evergreen branchlets or some other insulation around the plant until the ground thaws and you can take proper care of it.

Nearly all the water the wintering garden requires will be provided by rain and snow and will be conserved by slower evaporation during this season. But outdoor plants in containers and plantings beneath the eaves of the house will probably need occasional watering, particularly in windy, sunny weather, with the ground bare of snow. Water no later than midday, if you expect frost at night.

Winter is the conventional season for pruning. Branches of evergreens taken in December are good for Christmas decorating. Several Decembers I've given Christmas swag-making parties, for which I've provided boughs of firs, hollies, and pines (with cones attached); I schedule some of my pruning in time for the party.

Branches of forsythia, witch hazel, and cherry can be forced (persuaded, I'd rather say) into flowering indoors. Cut them after the first of the year and keep them in water. The flower buds will explode in a bunch, like popcorn kernels — a spring preview.

Spring

Remove protective boughs or other covering from beds of shade perennials early, to prevent their stretching for light. Best do this as soon as you feel in your bones that the last big freeze has come and gone (I truly believe the gardener who reads soil, sky, and plants daily gets to be a better weather prophet than the meteorologist, who reads instruments and doesn't even look at the sky). But don't burn up those boughs just yet, in case your bone-instinct about the weather proves not quite equal to that of an Indian shaman. In an on-again, off-again kind of spring, it may be necessary to replace the winter protection. Light frosts, however, won't hurt early shade flowers.

This is clean-up time, time to clear away all brushy brown foliage left about the bases of plants as a natural mulch. In earliest spring, cut back to the ground last year's deciduous and evergreen fern fronds, as well as the carexes, luzulas, and other grassy-leaved shade plants. Before their flowers and new leaves arise, cut back epimediums and other evergreen perennials still in last summer's tattered leaf. Cut them as near to the ground as can be done without damaging the still sleeping crown of the plant, with its tightly clutched buds.

Apply fertilizer to plants that are growing in soil mix, to shade plantings that compete with the roots of mature trees, and to container plants that have overwintered.

Watch for the awakening of big bear-hungry slugs and snails that have hibernated; the spring hatch-out of their eggs will take place any time now, too. Time to give the wretches their first comeuppance of the season.

Pick fading flowers from camellias, and from rhododendrons, azaleas, enkianthus, and others of the family Ericaceae. At the base of each flower is a newly forming seed pod, the part that actually wants removing. Ericaceous plants that are kept from going to seed often double or triple their flowers next year: true of western American irises, as well.

Summer

Apply fertilizer again to plants beneath robber trees and in containers.

Water the shady garden enough to keep the soil moist. It will require only about half as much watering as the sunny garden — except for the shade planting beneath a big, thirsty tree. That spot will tend to be a shade desert in summer, requiring deep, frequent watering.

Water in unstinting amounts is crucial to a newly planted garden, but next summer you can be a bit lax and get away with it. And in later years an established shade garden in a forest region (all North America aside from prairies and deserts) may need watering only infrequently, in time of drought. But at first, water.

I hate to be a nag, but have you lined up somebody to water the garden when you go out of town? Give that friend a demonstration of the fine art

BENEATH DOGWOODS

Season by season pictures of the life of a shade garden community beneath a Dogwood grove; any trees that take to underplanting could be used.

Spring. Dogwoods open white flowers followed by pale new leaves. Ground planting of shade-loving perennials and shrublets includes *Trillium, Primula, Jeffersonia, Saxifraga, Andromeda, Daphne, Sanguinaria,* and small-leaved rhododendrons. (DON NORMARK)

Summer. Columbine in flower, and behind it, Dogwood boughs ripe and weighted to the ground with the fullness of dark summer leaves. (DON NORMARK)

Fall. Inside the grove, backlighted by late afternoon sun. The leaves have taken on persimmon colors and a certain translucency. Many leaves have already fallen, and all will be left there for the winter as a mulch for the perennials and shrublets. The ferns (*Polystichum Andersonii*) will brave the winter in full leaf. This side of the tree has been cleared high of limbs over a number of years, but the limbs on the other side have been allowed to grow down to the ground, forming a full shady curtain.

Winter. First snowfall. For the garden's sake, let's hope it piles up — the deeper, the better. Snow provides the best winter protection for the shade garden. All the spent brown foliages of the shade-loving perennials have been left in place as a natural blanket for the plants' sleeping buds.

of watering. Most nongardeners have no idea how much water plants really need; usually, they underestimate. With your apprentice Aquarius looking on, actually apply the garden hose to each of your prized plants for one, two, three, four — and more — seconds, demonstrating how you water and for exactly how long. Then hand the hose over and let your pinch hitter show you that he or she has got the idea. If you expect certain plants to be watered daily, say so. All this may sound overbearing, but better a fussy owner of live plants than a gentle soul who returns to a crispy garden.

Autumn   Now is the top of the year for the planting and transplanting of trees, shrubs, and flowers. In earliest autumn, divide and replant polyanthus and Juliana primroses, epimediums, saxifrages, and other divisible shade garden perennials. Early planting brings the best flowering of crocuses, snowdrops, fritillaries, and the other shade-tolerant spring bulbs. They perform well beneath deciduous trees in spring sun–summer shade.

Keen shade gardeners (I among them) seem predisposed to plant specimens that aren't rock-hardy in the gardener's region: Asiatic gaultherias in Connecticut, for example. In a hard-winter climate, mulching gives the unsure plant its best chance. On or about November 1, apply evergreen boughs, or harvested autumn leaves held down with chicken wire.

Except in California and other mild climates, the shade garden prefers to be left shaggy for the winter. The browning leaves of perennials that bend to the ground are protection to winter buds and roots; the dry seed capsules that remain standing on stems — what case can I make for them? — are autumn architecture, feeding stations for birds, winter sculpture against the snow. All the drying parts of the plant have their art and practical science and should be left for the winter. Do I hear "Poppycock!" from gardeners neater than I? I'm not surprised. I recall not being able to convince my mother of the point of shagginess one autumn day as she was cleaning up the garden I'd planted for her. I trailed after her, protesting, as she made hay shocks from place to place on the garden path, of all dry foliage, all dry seed structures — now they were destined for the compost heap.

"Not *that* one," I remember pleading, the defendant being *Centaurea macrocephala* in seed. "Those seed cups will last all winter. They'll catch the snow and turn into long-stemmed ice-cream cones. Fantastic show." Snick-snick went the pruning shears. Her only verbal reply was, "As long as you're standing there, how about picking up those messes," which I did.

I've always thought of gardening as a kind of détente between the artistic and the practical mind . . . And being of two minds, here I blithely contradict remarks I made in chapter 1.

8

Shades of Shade

How many hours of shade do violets require, a gardener asked me once, and what exactly did I consider to be optimal shade time for the other plants that I, a consultant, was recommending? "Not too much shade," I said brightly; "not too much sun, either. About half-and-half. Dappled shade is the best sort."

This chapter dates from our little colloquy and is an answer to the deepening look of disappointment, distrust, and dismissal that greeted my advice. Can't blame him. There I was, addressing dappled English to a mathematical mind. For us, shady ground — always terra somewhat incognita — happened to be the poorest of meeting places.

How much shade for the plant? The answer depends on the weight and measure of a shifting nonsubstance that varies in intensity. In fact, we garden in shade with sketchy knowledge of the ambience we work in. We get by on intuition, old gardeners' tales, and trial by shade. Some of us are known for digging up plants and moving them to more shade or less shade until we find just the right shade.

Shade gardening will remain a nice little body of folk lore unless and until the stern eye of science focuses on our fun. Indeed, I think we can expect the coming of an umbratonomist, a scientist of shade, born of this age of specialization, who will repeatedly hold a light meter in various shady places and will note there the effects of differing degrees of indirect light on growth and flowering, coefficient with varying amounts of water, nutriment, and warmth, and who will then feed all these data into a computer. The forthcoming masterwork on garden shade, a ten-pounder studded with math and graphs, will undoubtedly be of service to plant breeders and horticultural scientists, and certainly to my former client. For the rest of us, it will not make good bed reading.

Part shade, with moist streamside soil. Humidity, soil, and shade are here exactly suited to the growth of nearly all shade plants, including the more fastidious gentians, primulas, and meconopsises. In this garden, blocky patches of fairly solid sunshine are balanced throughout the day by patchy shade (with some dappled shade on the lawn in the foreground). Christmas Ferns and Periwinkle (*Vinca minor*) fill the bay at lower left. Garden of Helen Van Pelt Wilson. (GEORGE TALOUMIS)

East-wall planting in morning sun–afternoon shade, with some valuable morning shade provided by overhead boughs (reflected in the windows). Japanese Anemone *(Anemone japonica)* in flower, with a carex (grassy foliage) at lower left, and *Vaccinium Vitis-idaea* (oval foliage) at lower right. (DON NORMARK)

Yet the only measurement of shade I have for your consideration is the same one I offered my ex-client — dappled shade — and other terms just as shifty. Perhaps the fairly discursive glossary of the terms used to describe shade that you will find below (and in other garden literature) will help pin down the shades of shade.

In reading all that follows, please keep in mind the role of moisture in the air. Humidity plays a part in shade gardening as important as that of shade itself. Humidity acts on shade, altering its values. For plants, shade is strengthened by accompanying moist air, and weakened by dry air. Due to differences in humidity, the life-giving powers of shade vary from one garden to the next. A mile down the road, in a sheltered garden where the air is moist, primroses planted in the sun grow as lush as leaf lettuce and flower magnificently. A mile up the road, in an exposed garden where the air is dry, primroses planted in part shade, where all the world knows they should be, and watered well, remain little dry dabs resembling lichens.

The variations that humidity works on the values of shade in garden microclimates it also works in the climates of different regions. In a bright, dry climate shade plants need more shade, and even sun plants welcome shade during the hottest part of the day. In a cloudy, moist climate shade plants prefer less shade and sun plants want no part of it.

Now for the shades of shade.

Light Shade (Thin Shade)

A lightly shaded area receives full shade for about two or three hours during the part of a summer day when the sun stands high and hot — between 10 and 6 daylight saving time. Or a lightly shaded area receives a sparse, spotty pattern of shade throughout the day, shade such as that cast by saplings or the laciest of mature trees. Most plants recommended for full sun also perform well in light shade. Many shade plants that would really prefer richer shade will adjust to light shade with some reduction of their usual stem length and leaf size. By means of somewhat risky experimentation, there is something to be gained: The more sun you can give a shade plant without burning it, the greater its flowering. But pick off flowers as they go over, to keep the plant from setting a debilitating quantity of seed.

In a moist, humid garden, light shade may be the best of shades for nearly all shade plants. But in the average garden, lightly shaded ground really belongs to the sunny garden.

Dappled Shade (Filtered Shade)

The sun/shade pattern cast by trees not too dense to admit rays of sun between their leaves. Dappled shade encourages normal flowering of shade plants and fosters shapely, upright plant growth. A dappled pattern of equal sun and shade is ideal.

Half Shade (Part Shade, Medium Shade, Semishade)

Shade for about four to five hours of the summer day between 10 and 6. In half shade, plants receive masses of full sun alternating with masses of full shade. Half shade stimulates fuller than usual flowering and compact growth in shade-loving shrubbery. Many wildflowers that naturally grow tall, slim, and fragile in dappled woodland shade will adjust to garden half shade — as they will to light shade — by shortening their stems, reducing their leaf sizes, and increasing the numbers of their flowers and rhizomes: Trilliums, bleeding-hearts, Lily-of-the-Valley, Wood Anemone (*Anemone nemorosa*), Confederate Violet (*Viola sororia*), and that toughest of America's terrestrial orchids, *Epipactis gigantea,* come to my mind at once as plants native to dappled woodland shade (nature's best and liveliest shade) that will spread and strengthen year after year in half shade. Other wildflowers, such as shooting-star (*Dodecatheon*), Bloodroot, and Trailing Arbutus, are often eventually unsuccessful in garden half shade. These plants decline slowly over a period of years when they are forced into premature dormancy by exposure to only a couple more hours of sun than they can

High shade, provided by Douglas Firs that have been limbed up to about forty
feet. But at the far side of the grove, limbs protective against street, sun, and wind
have been left in place. The small deciduous tree at the right is a Japanese Maple.
(GEORGE TALOUMIS)

absorb. But in a cool, sheltered garden where the sun is softened by evaporation from ground constantly moist, these same plants will probably grow happily wild in half shade. Even a maidenhair fern will luxuriate in a half-shady place if it is cool and moist.

Full Shade A healthful shade served up the whole of the summer day; a more substantial shade than that provided by trees whose leaves are divided and sun-sifting (mountain ash and others). Full shade obtains beneath the boughs of mature, spreading trees whose leaves are solid and sun-blocking (oak, dogwood, hawthorn, and most kinds of trees).

Dense Shade The ground beneath old, lolling evergreen trees or jumboizing shrubs is
(Deep Shade, often densely shaded, as is the area well back beneath decks or steps. These
Heavy Shade) ground areas are usually too dark, and often too dry, to sustain plants higher on the scale of life than mosses (and then only those mosses that will withstand seasonal drought). Here you might place ferns and other sculptural plants in containers, temporarily. Garden areas in shade impossibly heavy for growing plants may be fine display areas for plants in rotation — a month or two here and then remove for R & R.

Cold Shade Dank, dark garden spaces, anathema even to mosses. Consider textural treatments: sand, pebbles, paving. Or how about limbing up the trees or thinning their branches, or eliminating the trees altogether, if they are the cause of the condition?

Morning Shade in the morning won't keep shade plants in health unless there is
Shade afternoon shade to go with it. A west wall, shady in the morning and sunny in the afternoon, absorbs the afternoon sun and radiates heated air that is dehydrating to plantings in a wall bed. An area shaded by *trees* in the morning but exposed to sun in the afternoon is also not cool enough for the needs of shade plants. Exposed west-side places make unsatisfactory locations for shade gardens.

Afternoon Shade cast by the east sides of buildings, fences, walls, trees, and tall
Shade shrubs. Afternoon shade comes to east-wall plantings no earlier than about 1:30 during high summer (when shade plants need shade most). Dry heat radiating from the wall may be a problem for the more tender plant: A fern planted against an east wall may fry; a few feet out from the wall, in the same sun and shade, it may thrive. Yet, unless there is some augmentative tree shade or shrub shade near the wall, this location may not provide *any* shade-loving plant adequate life-support. Even a little extra shade helps a lot: Together, an east wall and a few shady branches can turn the area into good shade garden ground.

Afternoon shade cast by trees is more effectively cooling and nurturing than the afternoon shade of heat-storing and -radiating structures. But most annuals and perennials flower less fully in the afternoon shade of trees than that of east walls or fences. Afternoon shade, structural or vegetational, is welcomed by many evergreens — among them bamboo, *Buxus,* and *Azara* — and is often necessary to their well-being in a hot, dry summer climate.

Sun strength, of course, increases during the day. We feel it; plants feel it. Shady plants growing in east-side locations will tolerate more hours of sun than they would if set out in west-side places. The postmeridian sun is stronger than the morning sun because humidity usually drops in the afternoon. In hours of low humidity, leaves and flowers transpire heavily, cooling the plant. (Transpiration in plants is like perspiration in animals.) Afternoon loss of tissue moisture causes the plant to flag and leaves it sensitive to sunburn — if it is a shade lover inadequately shaded. (Certain shade plants register a day's drop in humidity dramatically, yet harmlessly. An *Acanthus mollis,* standing full flush in the morning, may lie flat on the ground by afternoon; but then night revives it totally.)

North-Wall Shade (Northern Exposure)

The shade cast by north walls or by the north side of either a fence or a solid tree screen. Many shrubs and perennials perform beautifully in these closely related shades. North-wall plantings in locations otherwise open to the sun receive sunlight briefly in the early morning and again in the early evening during high summer, and that low, temperate sun is eagerly absorbed by shade plants, to their betterment.

North-wall plantings tend to lean away from the wall. To the south, their light source is blocked by structure; available light sifts in over the top of the structure and around its sides, and the plants lean toward the average source of this sifted light, the north. If your viewpoint is toward the wall, as, for example, from a parallel walkway, the list of your plantings will be toward you, which is all to the good: you'll be seeing more than usual of leaves and flowers. However, this same planting, viewed through a north window, will be facing the wrong way. Wherever it appears awkward, the leaning tendency of a shrub can be corrected, and the shrub kept neatly close to the wall, by formal (or more casual) espalier pruning once or twice a year (with, of course, a plan in mind for the future form of the shrub). Shrubs that will not readily espalier can be wired to walls branch by branch — tedious work. A better idea, where there is space to indulge it, is to plant several feet out from shady walls. Plantings that stand that far out, although still in shade, lean less and usually require little compensatory pruning.

High Shade

Shade beneath trees that have been limbed up 20–40 feet above ground. Air circulation is usually good in high-shade areas, and often a considerable amount of reflected light locates here — both aids to growth in most plants. But there are possible disadvantages. Ferns and other tender foliages may suffer dehydration if hot, dry breezes enter from sunny areas. In a high-shade garden that is drafty, specialize in the tougher kinds of underplantings such as Lily-of-the-Valley and *Campanula Poscharskyana.* Yet, where the garden is sheltered, one can make singularly effective use

Lath shade. In this plant collector's retreat, we see many ferns, including platyceriums, hanging from posts. Outside are cold frames for the wintering of the alpine plants in the foreground (in scree-filled pots). Summering in a half-barrel is a favorite indoor-outdoor shrub, *Rhododendron* 'Fragrantissimum'. (DON NORMARK)

of high shade by planting small, graceful trees such as Japanese Maples or *Styrax,* as well as the full parcel of shade-loving shrubs and flowers hardy in one's area.

Lath Shade Here gardeners can improve on nature: In the woods, dappled shade is the shade of shades most generally sustaining to plants; lath shade is even better. Lath shade is the sun/shade pattern within a lathhouse, a pattern created by spaced laths or other lightweight lumber nailed to a frame. Orchids like it here. Shade-loving alpine plants of garden uneasiness — that snark, the *Shortia soldanelloides,* and that holy grail of cupflowers, *Primula Reidii* — are at last to be beguiled into flowering in the perfect shade of the lathhouse (or the garden frame covered with lath panels). Thousands of species of collectors' plants of all kinds will prosper in lath shade, species that will grow under practically no other garden conditions.

Lathhouses are especially helpful in growing lush green plants in hot, arid climates. Skillful gardeners in the San Joaquin Valley and in our western deserts grow ferns and flowering Himalayan rhododendrons in lath shade. In Phoenix, Arizona, a house of aluminum lathing, the metal white-anodized to repel 120°F desert heat, protects shade-loving cacti that would roast outside. On a treeless shoulder of a mountain in Brazil stands a split-bamboo lathhouse sheltering some 200 varieties of philodendrons (the world's largest collection). The trough of each halved bamboo cane that forms the building's roof faces upward. Roberto Burle-Marx, the collector, has the roof hosed daily to fill the bamboo troughs and cool the philodendrons by means of evaporation and dripping water.

Lathhouses with earth floors work best when they are located in the open away from trees, without the competition of their roots in the soil. If trees stand close by, *raised* beds within the lathhouse will be free of tree roots for only a year or two. To elevate plants completely out of reach of invading roots, grow them in containers or on soil-topped tables (which must be built massively strong). Design your lathhouse with the laths stretching north to south on the roof, up and down on the walls. These alignments give the greatest movement to the sun/shade pattern within, as the sun progresses from morning to evening. A fifty-fifty spacing of lath and gap is best.

Lathhouses have garden values beyond plant sustenance. With a book and a chair, and a fern or two beside you, a lathhouse is the finest of retreats on many a summer afternoon.

Warm Shade

Warm, that is, in winter. In the tropics and subtropics, virtually all shade is warm shade. In the North, garden areas in warm shade are uncommon, usually small, and always precious: Protected courtyards and atria are the chief locations of warm shade in cold-winter climates. When we in the North plant in warm shade, we treat plants to life in a resort. Here we can grow shrubs that are marginally hardy in our region, such as *Daphne odora, Choisya ternata,* Sasanqua camellias, and evergreen azaleas. And here we can lose them — here in the gardener's gambling den, during a hard-luck winter. But what grower can resist a gamble on hardiness? The rules of the game were succinctly put by a crusty old Seattle-area nurseryman, on a hand-lettered sign staked beside a batch of little eucalyptus trees he'd grown from seed:

EUCALYPTUS

NOT VERY HARDY BUT LOTS OF FUN

(IF IT DIES YOU'VE HAD YOUR FUN)

PART II

The Plants

9

Trees

Shade for people, shade for houses, shade for plants, privacy, shelter from wind, shelter for birds, purer air: Living trees provide all these practical benefits. Esthetically, trees stand as great works of curvilinear art, the main form containing the smaller artworks of flowers and seed structures, bark patterns, buds and leaves. In cities and suburbs, trees are an herbal remedy for visual ills: They cushion the hard, colliding geometry of architectural landscapes. In the country — they are the country.

The best trees for shade gardening are, for the most part, deciduous. The house enjoys the winter sun admitted by leafless trees. Most shade-loving plants prefer the lighter summer shade of deciduous trees; few will live in the densening shadows cast by maturing evergreens.

Actually, the shade of most trees in cultivation, deciduous or evergreen, densens as the trees grow and gradually impairs the vigor of shade garden plants. Gardening beneath trees is best understood in the light of knowledge of communities of wild plants in woodland shade. Plants in woodlands seem transitory to a dramatic degree when compared with wild plants growing in the constant sun of prairies and deserts, where plant life may change almost imperceptibly over thousands of years, for changes among woodland plants are often measurable each year. As the woodland roof grows thicker and shadier, green plants beneath thin out because fewer and fewer kinds will endure the dimming light. In deep woods, hardly any flowering plants abide. Ferns take their place and flourish for two or three decades. Then, as shade deepens into day-long twilight, even ferns give up, to be replaced by an apotheosis of mosses and mushrooms, with an occasional materialization of that flowering ghost, the Indian Pipe. The progress from the half shade of young trees to the mossy deep shade

Life in the high shade of maples and Douglas Firs. Foreground planting: Sword Fern (*Polystichum munitum*), tellima (big, soft leaves), Bleeding-Heart (lacy), Oxalis oregana (shamrock leaves), Sweet Woodruff (foamy white flowers), *Mahonia nervosa* (pinnate leaves above Woodruff). Garden of Ellen Martorano. (DON NORMARK)

of the mature forest measures roughly fifty years. The garden planted in the shade of most kinds of trees would, if allowed, follow the same schedule of diminution. We can, however, forestall nature by first removing lower limbs, and later, thinning upper limbs or topping the tree, or even taking it out altogether.

All trees have roots that compete to some degree with underplanting. But a few remain throughout their lives as solicitous as a broody hen (in polite feeding competition with her chicks) toward plants growing at their bases. They shelter smaller forms of plant life dutifully, it seems, never robbing them of food or light. *Plumeria rubra* and Japanese Snowdrop Tree (*Styrax japonicus*) are two of these.

Some other trees behave as out-and-out thugs in most garden locations, especially in shade gardens where other plants are growing within about twenty feet of their trunks. Beech, Horse Chestnut, and White Pine *(Pinus*

Strobus) come first to mind, but there are at least a couple dozen terrible trees in gardening — many of them unaccountably popular. These are the ones that keep the ground bare by weaving into it roots that repel all competitors, by shading the ground blackly, and by smothering it with slowly decaying fallen leaves or highly acid needles.

The powerful shade cast by a huge old tree may be beyond mitigation; I don't seriously propose that you thin those thousand-pound limbs to bring in more light. It has been done, but on the whole it is better to cut down an outsize tree if it can't be lived with or, if it is valuable, to leave it alone and garden with it on its own terms. I wonder if coarse sand would fit into your garden as a cover for the bare dirt beneath a blackly shady old tree? The porous sand could be spread thickly and any eruptive roots smoothed over without harming the tree. Sand can be raked clean of leaves, and if light-colored, the sand will increase daylight beneath the tree and form an effective base for plants in containers. But if the tree is to go, cut the trunk as close to the ground as can be done: A skillful sawyer can get it down to within an inch of the soil surface. If the tree is of a stump-sprouting kind, obtain a hate potion from the apothecary shelves of the garden store and pour it over the cut base. Now, if you will spread at least an 8-inch depth of new soil over the trunk base and around it, you'll have a planting bed for new trees and for a garden in their young shade, all without having to get rid of the tremendous roots of the cut tree.

Portable Shade Any tree can be grown in a container, with several benefits. If small, the tree will probably become at once high enough to sit under. You will also have better control over its eventual size, and can, without digging, move it at any time. In addition, the roots will always be nicely separated from shade plants outside the container. On the other hand, trees in containers need to be watered more frequently and are less hardy at the root than those in open ground. Below-zero temperature is a trial even for most hardy trees grown in containers: If possible, move the tree to an out-of-the-way corner of the garden for the winter (a small tree in a tub is as portable as a refrigerator; you'll probably need a hand truck or a dolly) and shovel sawdust around the container and over the top 1 foot deep, or use fallen leaves held with netting. Among the root-hardiest shade trees for container gardening are pines — those that are hardy in the open ground region — and Amur Maple (*Acer ginnala*). Many others will no doubt prove serviceable. As yet, little testing has been done to find winter-proof trees for containers. The most probable success will be with the toughest trees, such as *Elaeagnus angustifolia* (Russian Olive), *Acer negundo* (Box Elder), *Ailanthus altissima* (Tree-of-Heaven) and *Robinia pseudoacacia* (Black Locust). The latter two trees are reviled by some for their sometime habit of spreading out in a thicket. But that problem is curtailed when the tree is grown in a container.

Tree tubs at least 24 inches wide, 13 inches high, of at least 1-inch-thick lumber, pressure-treated or brushed with a copper-compound preservative, will last about twenty years and will grow a 10-foot shade tree in health as long as the box holds together; a 15-foot shade tree will require a container at least twice that size and thickness of lumber. Life in a container will restrain a tree's growth — not at all unattractively. In a container a tree that would grow fast and large in the open ground can be kept smallish. Use ideal shade garden soil, (*see* p. 28), water every day or two in summer, occasionally in winter (during thaws in cold-winter areas); and fertilize the tree once in early spring, once again in high summer.

Bad Actors

No tree is perfectly behaved, but most kinds are of such praiseworthy character over all that one or two minor annoying habits are forgivable. Certain trees, however, are of such bad social behavior in most garden locations that one is usually better off without them. And a few trees are a poor garden risk through no fault of their own, but because they are prone to ruination by an insect or a disease. In the following list, a black mark (●) in front of a tree's name signifies the tree is a troublemaker or is given to troubles. A half-eclipsed circle (◐) means the tree is bad for most uses but can be wonderful in special situations.

The Best (and Worst)

Each tree described has been given code letters to indicate the regions in which it grows well.

NE: Northeastern quarter of the U.S., including New England and the mid-Atlantic states, westward to all states touching the Great Lakes, and including adjacent Canada
S: Southeastern states
GN: The Great Plains, the Great Basin, the high deserts, and all northern or mountainous or interior regions of coldest winter, including Alaska
NW: Pacific slope of British Columbia, Washington, and Oregon
C: California's mild areas, north to south
NC: Northern California, including the Bay Area
SC: Southern California
SW: Palmy low deserts of the Southwest
T: Nearly tropical southern half of Florida and tropical Hawaii

Trees recommended to northern California will grow and perform reasonably well in sheltered, shady southern California canyons, but less than well in open suburban and city neighborhoods, where the cool-climate tree would be affronted by extended periods of low humidity combined with hot, leaf-browning winds.

A note to my fellow gardeners in New Zealand: The trees (and all the other plants in the book) I recommend to the regions C and SC will acclimate to the North Island; all the trees and plants I assign to the NE and the NW will be hardy on the South Island; indeed, the majority of these species are already thriving in the Country. And wherever in the book you read of shade gardening on the north side of the house — patience, please. I know how irritating it is for Australasian gardeners to confront such

Northern Hemisphere chauvinism. One shade gardens on the *south* side of the house, of course.

The trees:

Acer (maple). The larger species, such as Norway, Sugar, Big-leaf, and Red Maples, are fast growers (2–3 ft. a year), quickly building shade for a country lane or a large woodland garden of easy lines. For street planting and home gardens, oaks would be a better choice: They deliver big shade nearly as fast as the large maples, are less ready to drop limbs during snow and ice storms, and don't have the maples' dense, shallow, competitive roots.

The small *Acer* species listed below are first-rate suppliers of intimate shade. They can be used either as minor shade trees or as shade plants beneath forest trees.

Acer circinatum (Vine Maple). NE, S, GN, NW, NC. Northwest native. As a garden tree, Vine Maple usually matures at 30 ft. in as many years. In full shade it is green-barked, has trunks that partly trail on the ground before arising tortuously, and leaves that are yellow in autumn. In sun it is upright, gray-barked, and red in autumn. The majority of Vine Maples sold in nurseries have been collected in the wild. Collected trees with green bark will sunscald unless planted in a shady place; plant trees with gray bark in sun or shade. Use the rugged Vine Maple for naturalistic shade garden effects. Grows as well in ground saturated with seeping water as in well-drained upland soil (where it will withstand a couple of months' drought, once established). This and all other small-growing maples make excellent container plants.

Acer Ginnala (Amur Maple). NE, S, GN, NW, NC. Chinese and Japanese. To 20 ft. tall at 1 ft. a year. Several-trunked, and more a shrub than a tree unless trained out of it by pruning off side branches. Glowingly red in autumn.

Acer griseum (Paperbark). NE, S, GN, NW, C. Native to China. Neat. More oaklike than maplelike, with its columnar trunk, regular branches that form an oval head (rounding with age), and three-part leaves, each leaflet of oakish form. Fall colors are orange and red. Bark peeling ornamentally, shows terra-rossa new bark. To 30 or 40 ft. in about 30 years. For street, lawn, woods, terrace, or tub planting.

Acer palmatum (Japanese Maple). NE, S, GN, NW, NC. A short-trunked tree with expansive branches that swing upward near their tips; with age, the crown becomes about as wide as the tree is tall. Seedling trees have leaves green or bronze-tinged green, grow a foot a year early on, then more and more slowly until they mature at 20 ft. Of the many grafted foliar forms, the popular *A. palmatum* 'Atropurpureum' (Red Japanese Maple) grows vigorously. The leaves come out liver-red in spring, a detracting color amid spring's other, fresher foliages, but the red later fades to taupe. Japanese Maples color best when grown in full sun, as is true of virtually all autumn-coloring plants.

flowers in upright racemes, the flowers resembling Lily-of-the-Valley. Performs well in full shade and is valuable for that rare ability.

Cocculus laurifolius. s, c, t. Himalayan. This is usually a hedge plant, but with pruning to discourage shrubhood, it will form a free-standing evergreen tree, a moderate grower to 20 ft. tall. Performs well in full sun or in full forest shade, equally well as a mural tree near a north wall, or espaliered flat against it, or as a tub tree pruned from the outside for formal effect, or from the inside for informality. Leaves are this plant's fame: dark green, brilliantly shiny leaves, 7 in. long, in outline like a cocoa pod, a papoose, a papaya (*lanceolate* is such a lackluster term).

Coffea arabica (Coffee). t. Ethiopian. Small, slender, glossy evergreen tree, 8–15 ft. tall, with languidly graceful drooping branches and leaves. Coffee berries, red when ripe, begin to appear in about the tree's fifth season. Coffee grows readily in filtered shade, or in full sun (in humid tropical areas); as underplanting, episcias and begonias suit it well. In a cold climate, coffee makes an easy indoor-outdoor container tree. If you take it outdoors for the summer, place it in shade.

Cornus florida (Dogwood, Eastern Dogwood). ne, s, gn, nw, nc. America's favorite small-growing garden tree, all-over white in spring, before the leaves come out; red berries and leaves in fall. Gives the most flowers and the brightest fall color when located in full sun, yet most at home in part shade beneath tall, clear-trunked trees: In the wild, Dogwood is a tree of the woods' edge. Best transplanted from a container or as a ball-and-burlap production; slow-starting when planted with bare roots. Give it ideal shade garden soil (*see* p. 28) and keep it moist in its early years. When established, the tree will withstand summer drought. Grows 30–40 ft. tall in 40 years. To establish an underplanting in successful root competition with the shallowly rooting Dogwood, plant everything at the same time.

Cornus florida 'Rubra' (Pink Dogwood). ne, s, gn, nw, nc. Grafted salmon-pink form, usually smaller-growing than the white parent. *C. florida* 'Cherokee Chief' is a selection with slightly darker salmon-pink flowers. These trees will war with a spring garden that features violet- and rose-colored flowers. Neutral white will cooperate with the tree, as will coral-toned Mollis azaleas, pale narcissuses, and coral or green heucheras.

Cornus Kousa (Kousa). ne, s, nw, nc. Japanese and Korean. Select and encourage one trunk by pruning away all rivals in this naturally shrubby species, and it will grow as an upright tree to 20 ft. in 20 years. The crown is narrowish, or sometimes fan-form. Large, clear white bract-flowers in early summer; hot-red autumn leaves; globular red berries. A Chinese subspecies (*C. Kousa chinensis*) has more ample flowers; if grafted, it may need staking in its early years to get it off the ground.

Cornus mas (Cornelian Cherry). ne, s, gn, nw, c. European. Spreading-branched tree, 15–25 ft. tall. The flowering is a burst of yellow puffs (effective only against a dark background) from bare twigs in late winter. Leaves red in autumn, accompanied by ½-in.-long, edible red berries in clusters. Birds love them, but if you can get to the fruit in time, it makes a delectable conserve — nothing like it. The tree is at home at the woods' edge or against an east-facing fence or wall.

❍ *Cornus Nuttallii.* NW, NC. The splendid Pacific Dogwood occurs naturally on well-drained ground that is dry during summer. As a garden tree, it is often attacked by either a blight or a mycelium, encouraged perhaps by summer watering. Or the vector may enter the tree through untreated pruning cuts or through bark scalds caused by a garden position that exposes the trunk to an amount of sunlight unnatural to this tree of open woodland. Plant Pacific Dogwood in light, dryish soil, in a mutually protective cluster of several trees, and leave the tree with branches dressed as low as it wants them — and keep your fingers crossed.

Crataegus (Hawthorn). Many species and hybrids in cultivation, most with densely bushy branches. Common English Hawthorn is one of these, a corrupt thing for landscaping. There are far better offerings in the genus, small trees with uncluttered branches that are suited to street and terrace uses as well as to informal tree-and-shrub shade gardening. The hawthorns are berry-bearing and berry-dropping — and because of that, a minor annoyance when planted near pavement. Two of the best for landscaping are described below.

Crataegus × *Lavallei (C.* × *Carrierei).* NE, S, GN, NW, NC. To 35 ft. at about 18 in. a year. Strong, stout, well-spaced branches. White flowers in spring. Smallish, blunt leaves that turn russet in fall; the coloring leaves hang long on the tree, together with scarlet fruit, the size and shape of small orchard crabapples.

Crataegus Phaenopyrum (Washington Thorn). *See* regions, above. Open-branched, with a rounded head, to 25 ft. tall. White flowers; little maple-toothed leaves, turning orange and scarlet; small fruit, shining lacquer-red.

● *Cupressus macrocarpa* (Monterey Cypress). Given to gigantism, apt to blow over.

Delonix regia (Poinciana regia; Flamboyant). T. From Madagascar. A crooked trunk branching into a broadly flat crown; to 40 ft. tall at about 18–24 in. a year. Leaves like large fern fronds, giving medium shade. Summer flowers scarlet, extravagant, yet not too much for torrid regions. The Flamboyant is to the flowering trees of the world what the carnival in Rio is to festivals. Out of flower, one of the best tropical shade trees.

Elaeagnus angustifolia (Russian Olive). NE, GN, NC, SW. Gray, Olive-like tree, to 20 ft. Valuable in Atlantic seaside gardens and in the interior of North America. Thrives in the coldest, hottest, driest, windiest garden climates, where few other trees will do more than survive. Bears small, pale, fragrant flowers. The fruits that follow are sweet and mealy — cloying to the human palate — but good bird food. For people shade, plant the tree in the lawn or on the terrace and limb it up. For a garden background or a windbreak, plant it closely and let the branches shag.

Eucalyptus. Useful in shade gardening when planted at the side or at the back of the garden; keep plants well away to avoid root competition.

● *Eucalyptus polyanthemos* (Silver-Dollar Tree). In Australasia and in California, one of the more popular neighborhood street and front yard trees; much too big and coarse for such use.

Euonymus europaea (European Spindle Tree — long ago the hard wood was used in making spindles). NE, S, GN, NW, NC. Created by pruning, a little bumbershoot of a tree; left alone, an upright shrub. Moderate in growth, maturing at 10–15 ft., taller with age. Softly rose-colored autumn leaves. The bare green twigs of the winter plant display bright red, four-part capsules that finally burst open to show shiny orange seeds. Spindle Tree is a ready grower in either acid or alkaline soil, sun or semishade. Effective against stained wood with *Polystichum,* dwarf *Mahonia,* and other forest plants.

❍ *Fagus* (beech). The eastern American Beech *(F. grandifolia)* and the European Beech *(F. sylvatica,* with several horticultural forms) are friendly garden trees in their youth, monsters in age, with their dark shade and chain mail roots that repel all others; only mud grows in their vicinity.

Ficus benjamina (Benjamina Fig). SC, T. Tropical Asian evergreen, uncommonly airy for a tropical tree. The trunk is slender, smooth, and upright; it diverges high, into branches that arch and then cascade in showers of small, pointed leaves. Shade or sun. To 25 ft. in as many years. Graceful as an entry plant or against a shady wall.

Fraxinus (ash). A group of tree species fast-growing in deep soil, acid or alkaline; poor, shallow soil will slow, but not defeat, them; they are also tolerant of wet soil. Their broad heads of divided leaves make big shade. Ash trees are among the last trees to leaf out in the spring. Planted to provide summer shade for the house, the ash lets in welcome spring sun.

❍ *Fraxinus americana* (White Ash). Any climate. Female White Ash sows myriad seedlings that seem to hide until, when finally discovered, they are already well-anchored. The male tree is safe to plant, but the species can't be sexed until of flowering size.

Fraxinus excelsior (Common Ash). NE, S, GN, NW, C, SW. Not for the small property: Grows 100 ft. tall in 35 years. Gets along well in various soils, including clay that stays mucky winter and spring. Given adequate moisture in summer, the Common Ash makes an outstanding lawn tree, welcoming the grass up to its trunk base. The form *F. excelsior* 'Aurea' is a smaller grower, with leaves lime-green in summer, yellow in autumn.

Fraxinus Ornus (Manna Ash). NE, S, NW, C. A 50-footer offering, besides shade, opiately scented off-white panicle flowers and manna, a sweet made from the sap.

Fraxinus oxycarpa. NE, S, NW, C. The several named selections or hybrids of this ash provide rich autumn leaf colors, gold and vinous red. Of these, *F. oxycarpa* 'Raywood' (Claret Ash) is slender when young; later the tree becomes an inverted pyramid to 40 ft. tall. The finely divided leaves turn claret-red. 'Raywood' is so popular as a street tree that it is in danger of joining those plants that come to vulgarity by way of excellence.

◑ *Ginkgo biloba* (Maidenhair Tree). Asian forest giant, thin and gawky when young, and when grown-up (and noble), too big for most places.

Gleditsia tricanthos (Honey Locust). NE, S, GN, NW, C, SW. Feathery-leaved tree of fast growth. Trunk and branches are armed with horrendous spines up to a foot long; perhaps the best value of the species is as a bird tree attractive to shrikes, but a proven and popular lawn tree in Texas. There are safely unarmed forms, such as 'Ruby Lace' (new leaves red, aging olive drab) and 'Sunburst' (new leaves gold, ripening leaves green — a contrast that continues through the growing season as new leaves open). Both are broad-crowned, 30–40-ft. trees that give dappled shade. If grown in containers to curb the roots, these trees could have great use in shade gardening as the living equivalent of lathhouses. Dependable gold autumn color; then, in falling, the tiny leaves sink and disappear in most garden places. But this is perhaps the shortest-lived garden tree: 15–20 years.

Grevillea robusta (Silky Oak). C, SW, T. Australian. Evergreen in a sunny place, deciduous in shade; fast-rising — rocketing upward as a sapling, later moderating; a 25-year-old stands about 50 ft. Silky Oak forms a smooth gray-tan trunk easily and early to be pruned clean for overhead shade, and soon after, pruned higher for high shade, if desired. The leaf is remarkably fernlike, a long deep green frond, finely cut into slender pinnae and recut into pinnules. Beginning in its teens, the tree flowers a showy orange-yellow in early summer. Silky Oak will grow in half sun or less but likes hot sun better, and there it will become a provider of fast shade that is not heavy. A grove planting of silky oaks set out at about 10–20-ft. intervals will soon form a shade roof that will sustain a complete garden of woods' shrubs, begonias, caladiums, ferns, and all shade seekers.

Halesia carolina (Snowdrop Tree). NE, S, NW, C. Narrow at the base, branches arching; a shrub unless trained into a small (15–20-ft.) tree. Carolina native, related to *Styrax*, with styrax-like (yet larger) white pendant flowers in spring. Appreciates woodsy soil and lighting; native plants look at home under it.

Hamamelis mollis (Chinese Witch Hazel). S, NW, C. Low — 10 ft. in 20 years — broadly open tree, attractive in winter, with its angular bare branches, and in earliest spring, with its heavily fragrant little hydralike flowers poking forth tentaculiferously from leafless limbs. Plant Chinese Witch Hazel beneath tall trees or as a tracery specimen against a wall or fence. Performs best in half shade. Needs aborizing — removal of excessive trunks and low limbs — or it will grow bushy.

Harpephyllum caffrum (Kaffir Plum). c, t. South African. Evergreen and ever-shading; in about 20 years, 40 ft. high and rounded. Compound leaves, coppery when opening, later dark glossy green. A tree that conveys the richness of tropical rain forest; full shade for a hot, sunny garden. Bearer of little red "plums," good in breakfast jam.

Hoheria populnea (Lacebark). c, t. New Zealander. Lance-blade leaves that miniaturize in their outline the slenderly upright tree. Fast 3–4-ft. annual growth, to 30 ft.; eventually twice that (with age, growth slows). Buoyant evergreen tree, easy to grow in various soils. In youth, gentle as a young birch — and birchlike in maturity, with roots that become soil-grabbing and destructive of plants close by. Special uses for Lacebark: as a screen or grove planting on an unimproved clay bank that is dry in summer, or in marshy ground.

Jacaranda mimosifolia (Jacaranda). c, t. Brazilian. Quintessentially graceful tropical tree, to 40 ft. in about 60 years. Soft-violet summer flowers. Ferny, nearly evergreen leaves, in a crown that is an open umbel (but in a location where it is heavily fed and watered, *Jacaranda* may need pruning for line). The big compound leaves slowly fan in the trade winds, making caressing shade for the gardener (seated in an arabesque white iron chair, sipping a silver fizz) and for all of the garden of ferns and tropical forest plants.

Koelreuteria paniculata. c, sw, t. Broad-headed tree, moderate in growth to 35 ft. or more. *Koelreuteria* bears a large leaf divided into a few leaflets, concentrating the sort of deep, aqueous shade one especially welcomes in the desert; the leaves hang on the tree until late autumn. Bright yellow summer flowers in upright panicles, followed by papery orange-scarlet globes that suggest the Chinese Lantern-Plant. For any reasonable soil.

Leptospermum laevigatum (Australian Tea Tree). c, t. Despite its origin Down Under, this seems eminently oriental, even recognizable in old paintings of Chinese gardens. A low, wide tree with heavy, ropy trunk and branches and raining branchlets. Small leaves, grayish evergreen; little white spring flowers, like miniature cherry blossoms. Plant it on a steep bank or in a rock wall, good tub plant, as well. To 30 ft. tall, and as broad, in about 30 years. Drought-tolerant.

❶ *Liquidambar Styraciflua* (Sweet Gum, Liquidambar). ne, s, nw, c. Grows 2 ft. a year, to 100 ft. A tree of handy size and seeming tameness in its early years, perhaps irresistible for its apple-red autumn colors, forthcoming even in mild climates. But in a garden it becomes rather much after relatively few years — densely shady and with hoggish roots. Widely

Magnolia × *Soulangiana*
'Alba'. (DON NORMARK)

planted as a curbstrip tree in West Coast cities, some of which are beginning to discover this tree's outstanding abilities as a sidewalk wrecker. Better used as a tub tree or a woods' edge tree; shade-tolerant.

Liriodendron Tulipifera (Tulip Tree). For all climates. Fast-growing giant for an acreage of planted forest or as a sentinel out by the mailbox. Tulip tree is one of the really exciting fall colorers — rich yellow.

Magnolia. Various species fit the several garden climates. Fully hardy, and carried by nurseries across North America, are such deciduous kinds as *M.* × *Soulangiana* (white, pink, purple), *M. heptapeta (M. denudata),* and *M. Kobus* (both of them white); specialists stock several others, either equally hardy or less so. Deciduous magnolias offer the winter viewer clean, open, upswinging branches topped with huge promissory buds. In the spring, these open as huge tulip- or saucer-shaped flowers. Plant magnolias in a goodly depth of ideal shade garden soil (*see* p. 28) and mulch them. They ask to be kept moist and they hate being transplanted. Deciduous magnolias perform well in part shade or (with unfailing moisture) in full sun. Bold, naturalistic branch patterns suit magnolias to woodsy border plantings, in the company of rhododendrons, azaleas, Solomon's seal, ferns, bleeding-hearts, and many other shady things. Yet these trees are equally in keeping with formal gardens.

The evergreen *M. grandifora* is something else: at ground level, a wide tarn of black shade, and a summer litter of big leaves in ones and twos over a long period. To my eyes, this handsome tree has little place in home gardening.

Malus (crabapple). For all regions except T. They are not as showy as the flowering cherries, and that may be their best point. Crabapples are more in tune with spring, a season less loud than much of horticulture would have it. Crabapples are small, refined ornamentals, creators of circumspect shade in well-drained soils, heavy or light. For company, primroses and spring bulbs, not too close to the crabapple trunk, but a few feet in front, in the jaggy shade and sun imparted by the tree branches. Directly beneath the tree, plant a low filler such as *Pulmonaria,* Oregano or Geranium.

The only bad habit of grafted crabapples is that of sprouting suckers at the base of the trunk; these should be pulled off or pruned to the ground yearly. Of the many cultivated varieties, old and new, *Malus* 'Eleyi' remains pre-eminently useful and reliable in landscaping. It is a moderately fast-growing tree (nearly 2 ft. a year), forming an open pattern of fairly few spreading branches. Leaves are bronze, flowers wine-red; the purplish-red crabapples are good for jelly. *M. Halliana* is an especially small-growing, rose-flowered species, a wildflower straight from nature (Japanese mountainsides). The species proper is less commonly sold than its close variety, the semidouble-flowering *M. Halliana* 'Parkmanii', which grows as slowly as 6 in. a year and matures at 10–14 ft.

Mangifera indica (Mango). T. To 60 ft. tall in 30–40 years, a broad, dark-leaved tree, darkly shading. Mango can be limbed up to admit comfortable light and some direct sun around its base, making it an excellent terrace tree. Use the Mango's trunk nobs and branch nooks as perches for epiphytic ferns, orchids, and bromeliads.

Maytenus Boaria (Mayten). C, T. For people shade or house shade, a Chilean evergreen with boat-shaped leaves and weeping branches. A willowy cascade of a tree, it needs lifting (by enhancement pruning from beneath) when young. Fast-growing — 3 ft. a year — for the first decade, afterward slowing; eventual height 40–60 ft. Requires well-drained soil, acid or alkaline.

Melia Azedarach (Chinaberry, Bead Tree). T, SW. Fast provider of hefty shade. A spreading crown topping at 20 ft. and, with age, twice that height. Honey-scented, early-summer flowers in a lilaclike panicle, white in the species, lilac-colored in the variety *M. Azedarach* 'Umbraculiformis'. Yellow berries hang on the tree for months after the leaves fall, or until birds take them.

Metasequoia glyptostroboides (Dawn Redwood). NE, S, NW, C, SW, T. The recent discovery of this tree, hitherto known only from fossils, is probably as valuable artistically as the recovery of Tutankhamen's trappings, and it may rank in time-warp surprise with the finding of a plesiosaur in the flesh. In 1941, a forester chanced upon a single Dawn Redwood growing in a remote village in central China; subsequent searches turned up a few more in surrounding forests. Collected seed, sent to England and the U.S. in 1947, sprouted readily, and so the Dawn Redwood entered the Western world. A deciduous conifer soft to see and soft to touch, with light green and feathery frondlike branches. Grows 3 ft. a year to 100 ft. and more.

Use this tree as a background grove or screen planting or as a woodland in itself. The young Dawn Redwood will accept underplanting and, with its ferny easiness on the eyes, will make beautiful compositions with shade plants. But the maturing tree is no more easy on underplantings than most other conifers: Plants close to the trunk will have a declining future.

Morus alba (White Mulberry). sw. This tree has its aficionados among desert landscape architects and home gardeners. One of the best large trees for the Nevada desert. In Arizona it has been much used as a street tree by suburban developers, to provide, in marvelously short order, something big against the sky and cool beneath. Growth rate 6 ft. a year in the low deserts, to 60 ft.; to 35 ft. in northern Texas. As a desert tree, White Mulberry tends, however, to become senescent when young. A tree for quick shade, with perhaps the oncoming problems of overgrowth and of decaying main limbs to be removed within 10–15 years after planting. Any desert soil.

Nyssa sylvatica (Tupelo, Sour Gum, Pepperidge, Beetlebung). ne, s, nw, c. Eastern American native. Grows a foot a year, or somewhat faster, to 100 ft. Spar-trunked, with a broad crown of horizontal or down-sweeping branches. A tree with a look of quality in all seasons; in autumn it's a dazzler, with its glowing yellow, orange, and red leaves, often all on one branch. A Tupelo in my garden has grown vigorously for more than twenty years in sandy soil, never watered after the second year, on a hot hillside that goes prairie-dry in summer; but this tree is as tolerant of wet soil as of dry. Shade for people and for shrubbery.

Olea europaea (Olive). c, sw, t. Ever-gray tree. In dry hillside soil in Italy, centuries-old Olive trees stand a mere 16 ft. tall. In a California suburb, in or near a green lawn, an Olive tree may grow to 40 ft., at a foot a year. The open-ground tree that receives abundant water forms a dense head, to be improved by thinning. A tub-grown specimen pruned for line becomes, with years, dramatic for its display of heavy, twisty wood.

Oxydendrum arboreum (Sourwood). ne, s, nw, nc. Slow-growing upright tree, narrow when young, broadening with age; a 20-ft. tree may be 25, or even 50, years old. Eastern American native, a woods' edge tree at its best in cool, moist, humusy soil (a dwarf tree in summer-dry ground). Sourwood belongs to the rhododendron clan and, like the rest of its family, the tree needs careful planting, with a soil ball around the roots. Once it is planted, provide the shallow roots with a mulch or let a shady lawn of the thinly grassy and healthily mossy kind spread beneath the tree. Transplanting an established Sourwood is a dire project that will probably stop its growth for years. Summer flowers are white bells in racemes at the branch ends, like amplified Lily-of-the-Valley. Long elliptical leaves turn from green to brilliant red — none fierier than this. One of the choicest trees for a partly shady place.

● *Paulownia tomentosa* (Empress Tree). Something close to a total mess: coarse and fast in habit, it drops squishy flowers and smothering leaves. The roots are robbers, the shade a tar pit.

Pinus (pine). For strength in the young garden composition, for a rapidly gathering sense of age and dignity in the garden, these are the trees. When topped and pruned for line, such naturally spreading pines as *P. Thunbergii, P. nigra, P. densiflora, P. Coulteri, P. halepensis,* and *P. Montezumae* begin to appear patriarchal when as young as 12. Young pines make serviceable shade garden roofs; maturing pines — 20 years old and more — will progressively overshade, and finally shade out, underplanting, unless the trees can be limbed up high and retopped occasionally to let in light. Pine roots are not as dense as those of some other conifers, but the soil in their domain becomes too dry in summer for many kinds of underplanting; meantime, falling needles cover and smother shade plants. To maintain plants beneath pines, supply extra water and rake pine needles from the foliage of the underplanting (needles can be used as a mulch *beneath* plants). Especially troublesome for its fall of needles is the Eastern White Pine, *Pinus Strobus.* I've not been able to keep any plant alive beneath it, but I must also say that its beautiful tan-colored mulch of fallen needles six inches deep beneath the tree has its uses: I steal it from time to time to spread on dirt paths in the garden.

Pittosporum eugenioides (Lemonwood). C, T. A New Zealand broadleaf evergreen of malleable nature. To 40 ft. in about 30 years. A tall screen plant or hedge plant (at planting intervals of 3–5 ft.), responsive to formal or light pruning, remaining leafy close to the ground; or, when limbed up, a free-standing tree about a third as wide as tall, one that will bend without breaking in a high wind. Lemonwood is sun-loving but shade-tolerant, carrying foliage on limbs that receive only 2 or 3 hours of sun daily. Leaves 4 in. long, light lime-green, wavy-edged, lemon-scented when abused. Bark gray-white, finely textured. As a shade garden plant, Lemonwood provides welcome color variations from the predominant dark greens of shady environs. Spring flowers greenish yellow, quiet in color but intensely fragrant. One drawback is that some of the roots grow immediately below the skin of the soil.

Plumeria rubra (Frangipani, Plumeria). T. Central American tree, long a favorite of gardeners throughout the tropics. The roots are deep and do not snake over the soil surface — a rare feature in tropical trees. To 20 ft. in 20 years or less, forming an open crown of thick, blunt branches amply dressed with handsome, rather rhododendronlike leaves a foot long. Flowers of five waxy petals, white, rose, or yellow; their perfume is seductive enough to make a northerner sell his passport and stay on forever. Give Plumeria a place in the sun or in part shade, in good soil, with moisture and drainage.

Populus tremuloides (Quaking Aspen). *Populus* = the poplars and Cottonwoods, trees with terrific roots that rule them out of garden planting, except for the use of Quaking Aspen in western mountain and intermountain gardens within the native range of this tree. Here it is in harmony with the land and with other natives. It is, as well, a unique tree: Nothing in treedom offers quite the refreshment of a Quaking Aspen shimmying

A grove of Quaking Aspens (*Populus tremuloides*) fills this quasi atrium garden in the cove of a U-shaped building. The trees are natural to the site (the decking has been pierced to accommodate two of their trunks). Trees that can be planted in a close grove include small-growing maples, alders, birches, Coffee, Benjamina Fig, Lacebark, Katsura, kauri, Dawn Redwood, larch, Sourwood — many more. Closely planted trees grow tall and gracile of trunk, specialties to be brought forth by pruning away side branches. (DON NORMARK)

in a light breeze; the effects are best in autumn when the tree is shining gold, but good anytime.

Prosopis (Mesquite). sw. Small, pinnate-leaved trees casting filmy shade. While in the Mojave and Sonoran deserts in blistering weather, I've sought refuge beneath these native trees and have mentally complained to them about their skimpiness as a sombrero. But other shade bathers find Mesquites ideal. Our Arizona consultant Catherine H. Irwin places Mesquites at the top of the list of shade trees for the low deserts (followed, in her order of value, by Little-leaf Palo Verde, fan palms, and Desert Willow).

Mesquites (*Prosopis*) in winter. The floor of this desert garden is the native beige-yellow earth, packed hard and swept clean. The garden's ground surface must be kept entirely clear to reveal visiting rattlesnakes. The eucalyptus in the background grows in a meticulously formed soil basin, which helps in the watering of the tree. Garden of Mr. and Mrs. Will Rogers, Jr. (DON NORMARK)

Prunus cerasus 'Montmorency' (Pie Cherry, Sour Cherry). NE, GN, NW. Small shade, white flowers, showy red fruit. Jolly little tree for terrace or lawn planting or in a row along a drive; other named forms of Pie Cherry are just as serviceable and ornamental.

With artful pruning, most orchard trees — Pie Cherry, apple, pear, quince (of rugged character and little in need of pruning), apricot, plum, and the citrus (especially the charmingly small lemon) — can supply intimate shade on a lawn or a terrace. Less suitable is the stiffishly branched peach. And the sweet cherry, a big tree with coarse branches, usually seems out of place as a garden shade tree.

There is no fine gardening beneath bearing orchard trees; as underplanting, only grass, dichondra, *Veronica prostrata,* Periwinkle, or small-leaved kinds of ivy will withstand the trampling involved in harvesting the tree's crop.

Prunus subhirtella; *P. subhirtella* 'Autumnalis'; *P. subhirtella* 'Whitcomb'. NE, S, NW, NC. Singularly graceful Japanese cherry of several varieties. Japanese horticulture, which has taught the world a sense of slimness in plant and flower form, also dotes on fatness in flowers such as cherry blossoms, peonies, and chrysanthemums. But this tree, in the three rather similar kinds I've named, remains a wildflower not gussied, not clobbering the ocular sense with those clubby masses of flowers brandished by so many of the hybrid cherries. All three of these simple-flowering cherries fit readily into naturalistic compositions with shady shrubs and flowers. They stand 15–25 ft. at maturity, with a crown broader than it is tall. Branches are low-angled and dramatically cantilevered, forming a rather flat treetop. Pink cherry blossoms in spring (in the semidouble form, *P. s.* 'autumnalis,' flowers open sporadically fall to spring). Favorites for planting under and sitting under. Their roots are moderate, and so is their summer shade.

Pseudotsuga Menziesii (Douglas Fir). NW, NC. Tall, pyramidal conifer, dominant native tree of the Pacific Northwest. Within its range, the Douglas Fir shades more gardens than any other tree. The extraordinary luck of it is that Douglas Fir is perhaps the most wholesome conifer for shade gardening. Many conifers are no good at all, but this one can be great. Limb it up where necessary to let in more light. Topdress the native ground beneath the tree with ideal shade garden soil (*see* p. 28), keeping the topping a foot away from the base of a young tree, 3 ft. away from an oldster; spread the topping as shallowly as is practicable for planting. Most of the hardy shade garden shrubs, shrublets, ground covers, and forest perennials thrive in the shade and shelter of Douglas Fir. *P. Menziesii glauca,* the Rocky Mountain variety of the tree, will take the hard garden climates of the mountain and intermountain regions and will even grow (somewhat gnarly) in prairie and high desert gardens.

Quercus (oak). A majority of our shade garden consultants located in different states have named oaks as premier, or at least among the best, of large-growing trees. Truly, the oaks are unsurpassed as creators of beautiful shade for people, buildings, and gardens.

The western states (especially California) are the native home of many species of oaks that grow as trees wherever the soil is deep and as scrub in rocky upland terrain. Whatever their size and shape, wild oaks are eminently worth incorporating in the garden. Yet western oaks don't much like civilizing. If possible, leave the soil unaltered for several yards around the trees' bases. Though one sometimes sees western oaks tamed as lawn trees, with sophisticated grass running up to their trunks, the amount of water needed to keep grass green all summer is a hardship to these trees. They would rather have no water other than rain or snow. A supportive sort of landscaping for a property rich in oaks is a garden of native shrubs planted several yards distant from the trees. The shrubs will need watering the first two summers, but none after they get their roots down. During those first two years, the oaks will find and take up some of the irrigation water, despite your efforts to keep water out of their vicinity. But two years of watering at a little distance will not be enough to wreck their form and their lives by changing their habit of making healthy and disease-resistant, slow, dry growth (as would quite possibly happen in a green-lawn type of garden watered over a number of years).

The equally numerous eastern American oak species, born to moist soil, thrive in lush garden conditions. Several of them, especially the Red, the Scarlet, and the Pin Oak, perform so magnificently in gardens in a variety of soils and ecological conditions, that they've become basic garden trees throughout North America, Europe and Australasia.

Quercus acutissima. NE, S, NW, C. From China, Japan, and Korea. Slow grower, to 40–50 ft. Leaves oblong, shiny green. Roots nicely deep.

Quercus agrifolia (California Live Oak). C. An oak on the Michaelangelan plan, with heroic, dynamic limbs that will extend as broad as the tree is tall and with roots that will eventually stand out like a weight-lifter's veins. An old tree newly incorporated in a garden would rather have the soil beneath it left as is — usually barren except for the salubrious litter of leaves. Garden away from the trunk. Young wild trees up to several decades old and perhaps 25 ft. tall, growing in fast-draining soil, will accept an underplanting that does not require heavy watering. If you add soil, keep it thin and keep it several feet away from the trunk. As with most young evergreen trees, the shade of the young Live Oak is not yet immoderate and the power of the roots is not yet known.

Quercus alba (White Oak). NE, S, NW, C. Deciduous species from eastern America, a 100-footer within 70 years. The massive broad crown of the maturing tree closely resembles that of the English Oak. Prospects for gardening beneath the American tree are the same as for its British counterpart — especially good.

Quercus coccinea (Scarlet Oak). All regions except T. Grows 18 in. or more a year to 80 ft. The head of the young tree is nearly as broad as it is tall; with age, the crown grows wider still, with branches held straight out. Roots are deep and benign. Fall color a long-lasting scarlet; the best oak for autumn red and one of the best of all autumn trees.

Quercus Garryana (Garry Oak). NW, NC. Northwestern American native inhabiting dry, stony upland soils. Blessed is the gardener who moves into a property where clumps of Garry Oaks grow; one gains thereby a headstart of a century or two on the slow art of gardening. An oak with tortuous, open branches and with roots that own the soil close to the tree trunk. Keep any new soil and plantings a couple of yards away from the communities of trunks. One can, however, garden closely — even within a foot of a small Garry that stands some feet from the main group. In nature, Garry Oaks often rise clear from sparse grass and meadow flowers. The picture is perfect and is only to be diminished by adding garden plants. Wild Garrys grow about 6 in. a year. Young trees transplanted into a garden readily accept summer watering, their growth rate becoming twice that of wild trees; to keep them in health, drainage must be pluperfect.

Quercus nigra (Water Oak). S. Found wild in wet soil, but an easy grower in upland garden conditions. Valuable street tree in the South, where it is native. To about 80 ft. tall in 50 years, with a symmetrically rounded head. The small oval leaves hang on the tree until midwinter.

Quercus palustris (Pin Oak). All garden regions except T. *Palustris* means "marsh-inhabiting," but the tree will take dryish ground as well. Grows approximately 16 in. a year to 80 ft. Roots are well-behaved. Autumn leaves peach-pink or watermelon color at first, finishing leather brown. A lone, free-standing Pin Oak becomes, with age, as broad as it is tall, with down-sweeping branches; left to their own bent, the branches of many Pin Oaks touch the ground at the tips. To maintain openness beneath the tree, limb it up high, then shorten the remaining lower limbs annually — or relax, let the limbs have their way, and think of the closed space within the cloche of branches as a secret room.

Quercus phellos (Willow Oak). For all gardens except T. A dome-headed tree; grows to 80 ft. at a rapid 2 ft. a year. Roots not bad. Leaves willowy-slender, lively grassy green, turning mahogany red or yellow in autumn.

Quercus prinus (Chestnut Oak). Of eastern American origin; growable everywhere except T. To 70 ft., at a moderate pace; wide of branch. The serrate oval leaves compose easily with those of companion plants in a shade garden, turn deep crimson before they fall. Especially recommended by our Georgia consultant.

Quercus robur (English Oak). NE, S, NW, C. A tree from the more muscular side of the family. The true and original oak in the thinking of many gardeners. At age 100, English Oak stands about 80 ft. tall and 90 ft. wide; the species grows moderately fast in its sapling years, more slowly as it matures (true of most trees). The form *Q. robur* 'Fastigiata', of quill pen outline, is useful in line plantings in narrow spaces where few other trees will fit; this oak grows somewhat broader, yet has a far smaller crown and decidedly less rampageous roots than that better-known quill-form tree, the Lombardy Poplar.

Quercus rubra (*Q. borealis maxima;* Red Oak). For all regions except T. Grows about 2 ft. a year to 100 ft. Limbs are horizontal, broadly out-thrusting. Roots are deep and out of the garden's way. Autumn leaves russet, then walnut. Certain individuals of this tree hold some of their leaves until February — a disreputable sight in the eyes of many gardeners. To avoid it, buy clean-limbed trees in winter.

Quercus Schumardii All climates except GN. A Texan and Southeastern tree, 75 ft. tall in maturity, yellow to red in autumn. In mature form it resembles Red Oak, but offers a great advantage over that tree early on. *Schumardii* usually forms a full, symmetrical crown by age 10; Red Oak, meantime retains a gangly adolescent look until age 20. *Schumardii* will grow readily in any reasonable, well-drained soil. A workhorse tree to add to the easygoing troika formed by Red, Scarlet, and Pin Oaks.

Quercus velutina (Black Oak). NE, S, NW, C. Deciduous tree, to 100 ft. tall, growing moderately fast. Lower limbs atrophy during the tree's early years, exposing a clear columnar trunk.

Quercus virginiana (Live Oak). S, C, SW. Arguably the most handsome of evergreen oaks, to 70 ft. tall and broader than it is tall. This is a massive southern tree, famed for its beards of Spanish Moss as much as for the ponderous shade of its lane-covering limbs (shades of Tara). A tree that adapts well to the desert and that has been used dramatically — dark tree against bright grass — in golf course landscaping in the Southwest.

Rhus lancea (African Sumac). C, SW, T. An outstanding small shade tree and screen plant for gardens in low deserts; to 20 ft. in about 15 years. Leaves dark evergreen, divided into three narrow fingers.

Rhus typhina (Staghorn Sumac). NE, S, GN, NW, NC. Fast-growing, to 15 ft. tall (usually), with a slender bare trunk or colony of trunks; on each trunk, a flat crown of divided leaves, tropically luxuriant. Altogether, a tree rather like Bracken Fern grown arboreal; rich green in summer, in autumn brightest red. The variety *R. typhina laciniata* has leaflets deeply and elegantly serrated; mature specimens stand as shrubby trees 8 ft. tall. Staghorn Sumac's virtue of virtues is its ability to prosper in subsoil of pure clay or of sand or gravel. Growing in the last two media, the tree will sucker about and create a grove. It is completely drought-tolerant when established. Provides cooling shade and refreshing greenery in terrible soil conditions. Not one of the better trees under which to garden, except, of course, when it stands in a container. Smooth Sumac (*R. glabra*) is a similar tree, usually smaller in growth.

Robinia pseudoacacia (Black Locust). Growable anywhere. A weed tree sowing itself into dry soils in Rocky Mountain states and along the West Coast. If you find yourself in possession of a wilding patch of Black Locusts (the tree usually exists in patches), consider sparing the trees on their merits as ready-made shade and garden structure: They may not be choice, but there they are. To establish plantings beneath and near large Black Locusts, cut off any thin suckers at ground level. Spread on top of the existing ground a ½-in. thickness of newspapers (optional) and, over that, ideal shade garden soil (*see* p. 28). Then plant your garden, including, perhaps, some small trees as eventual replacements for the black locusts. The first season of gardening will be free of the locusts' roots; the second season, their interference will be minor. And during those two years, the trees and shrubs you plant will grab enough of the soil for themselves to stake out their place and defend it against the oncoming horde of Black Locust roots.

Robinia pseudoacacia 'Frisia'. A yellow-leaved form with a broader and lower crown than that of the parental Black Locust. Though not yet mass-produced, 'Frisia' seems destined to join Weeping Willows and White-barked Birches as one of the most popular of all garden trees. One bright gold tree in view is nice, three may be the visually digestible limit, and ten of them to the city mile might be damaging to the nervous system. Trees gold all summer are not like those that turn in autumn, whose act has crescendo and who afterward get off the stage.

⟩ *Salix babylonica* (Weeping Willow). Hungry, thirsty, overly big, and brittle. In no wise is this a garden tree. Still, the Weeping Willow is the most romantic of vegetation. Plant it in a riverside or lakeside pasture, overarching the water; on the pasture side, a philter of shade to make even a Clydesdale and a Guernsey gaga for each other.

● *Sassafras albidum* (Sassafras). Too many volunteers from the roots of the parent tree.

⟩ *Schinus Molle* (California Pepper Tree, Peruvian Pepper). c, sw, t. Small evergreen tree growing about 2 ft. a year to 40 ft. or more. Leaf, fresh green, in form like the long, side-feathered tail of an archaeopteryx. The young tree has a broad head, rather dense, yet gracefully weeping at branch ends; a tree 35 years old and older develops a trunk and limbs as impressive as those of old oaks, or of cypresses and pines on coastal cliffs. Since the early twentieth century, *S. Molle* has maintained its place as one of the most popular street and garden trees throughout the Mediterranean climates of the world, nowhere more than in California. As seems axiomatic with trees of great popularity, the California Pepper has serious faults: The tree develops huge concrete-wrecking roots as it matures, and it is a notable messer, dropping leaves and all sorts of parts during a long season. On the good side, California Pepper will supply abundant greenery and shade even in poor, dry soil.

Schinus terebinthifolius (Brazilian Pepper Tree). C, T. Divided leaves, dark evergreen. A cleaner tree than the other pepper, smaller (commonly to 20 ft.), and with roots less gross. Best used in a raised bed in an outdoor living area or as the shade giver in a shrub and fern garden. An added feature is its bright red berries in autumn and winter, good for Christmas decorating and as bird food.

Sequoia sempervirens (Redwood). NW, C, T. This colossal evergreen tree happens to be, in its cherubic early years, one of the better conifers for shade garden use. The shade and the roots of the young Redwood make good company for all shade-tolerant plants. The darkening shade of the tree that has grown up to two or three times house height — in astonishingly few years, it will seem in retrospect — remains wholesome only to a few ground covers, notably *Oxalis oregana* and *Hypericum calycinum*. Redwood planted in moist soil grows especially fast — 3 ft. or more a year.

Sophora japonica (Japanese Pagoda Tree). For all regions except SW; NW, not the easiest of trees — here it does best on raised ground, above excessive soil moisture. Small, neatly rounded tree of the pea family, to 40 ft. in about 25 years. Leaves pinnate, dark green, casting medium shade; deciduous. Summer flowers cream-colored, in clusters. A mannerly tree for all small shading; good with plants, good in a paved area or in a lawn. Used for a thousand years in the landscaping of pagodas.

Sophora secundiflora (Mescal Bean, Frijolito). C, SW, T. A 25–40-ft., darkly evergreen tree with pinnate leaves and late winter flowers, violet-scented, violet-colored in racemes. A Texan and Mexican native built to withstand desert sun, severe drought, and alkaline soil. Shade values are those of *S. japonica*.

Sorbus (mountain ash). The sapling grows 3 ft. a year; growth later moderates, and in 25 years, the tree will be about 40 ft. tall. Mountain ash is an upright grower, with one or several shafty trunks readily cleared of limbs to any height that suits the garden. It is equally presentable standing singly, in a line, or in a grove. With the limbs cleared high enough to admit sun until midmorning and again after midafternoon, Mountain Ash makes one of the better parasols for deciduous azaleas and the many other shade shrubs and flowers. The pinnate, airy foliage of the tree gives moderate shade. Other features are white umbellate flowers and showy autumn berries. The following entries include two mavericks: As noted, they are slow-growing species.

Sorbus Aucuparia (Rowan, Quickbeam). NE, S, GN, NW, C. The only common Mountain Ash, an old-fashioned garden tree with bright red berries. The species includes a seldom seen yellow-berried form, *S. aucuparia* 'Xanthocarpa', and the lacy-leaved *S. Aucuparia* 'Laciniata.' All three forms turn orange-red in autumn. Easy in any well-drained soil.

Sorbus hupehensis. NE, S, NW, C. A white-berried Mountain Ash whose autumn leaves take on violet tints. The form of the tree is like that of *S. Aucuparia*. Grow in well-drained soil.

Sorbus scopulina (Western American montane), GN, NW, NC, and **S. tianshanica** (Central Asian montane), NE, S, NW, C, are choice slow growers — 6–12 in. annually, maturing at 10–15 ft. Berries Chinese red. Give these treelets ideal shade garden soil (*see* p. 28). *S. scopulina* grows multitrunked, *S. tianshanica* with a single trunk.

Sorbus Harrowiana. C. Leaves with leaflets more ample, longer, and heavier in aspect than those of other *Sorbus* species. Berries pink. Easy to grow in well-drained soil.

Stewartia. NE, S, NW, C. From Japan and other parts of Asia. Consultants in Georgia, New Jersey, Ohio, and Oregon named the stewartias among the choicest small trees for their garden regions. There are several species in cultivation, of two distinctive growth habits, spreading or almost fastigiate. *S. Pseudocamellia* is a tree of a few spreading branches. It has white summer flowers like single *Camellia Sasanqua* and elliptical leaves of turkey egg size, turning violet to purple before falling. *S. monadelpha* has upright branches, nearly fastigiate. Leaves and white flowers are small, the leaves turning dark red in autumn. In my garden, 23-year-old trees of both of the above *Stewartia* species stand 20 ft. tall; *S. Pseudocamellia* is 15 ft. wide, *S. monadelpha* 6 ft. wide.

Styrax japonicus (Styrax, Japanese Snowdrop Tree). NE, S, NW, C. Smallish or quite small: Grows about 9–15 in. a year, to 30 ft. in a partly shady location; half that in sun Takes on its best form — a graceful openness of branch — in the company of taller, shade-giving trees. Give it porous, well-drained ideal shade garden soil (*see* p. 28). Styrax has slender branches and a laciness composed of fine twigs, small leaves, and little fragrant white bells (early summer). A tree of gentilesse, permitting plantings closely beneath.

Styrax Obassia (Fragrant Snowbell). Another Japanese native, for the same garden climates as *S. japonicus*. To 20–30 ft. tall, with a few heavy, outstretched branch-arms. Big roundish leaves; little white flowers in summer. Likes a place in woodsy half shade. Horizontal branch habit gives this one special use as a nestler in the high shade of forest trees.

Taxodium distichum (Bald Cypress). Southeastern U.S. native, adaptable to all garden regions except GN. Deciduous conifer; needles in spring a pale spring-green, darkening in summer, and in autumn a light rust color. A pyramidal tree, to 120 ft. in about 60 years. The Bald Cypress and the equally handsome, less hardy Mexican *T. mucronatum* (Montezuma Cypress) are rare among conifers for their native ability to grow in wet soil, in swamps, and in sheltered lake coves in water up to several feet deep. In gardens, they are perfectly at home in well-drained soil with ordinary watering.

Taxus (yew). Conifers of solid character and stolid personality. The tree-form yews are typically dark evergreen and always dark at the heart of the branch, though some forms are variegated at branch tips, or goldish in new growth. With, perhaps, the sole exception of *Cocculus laurifolius,* no other trees in North American cultivation will get along on as little light as the yews: These needle bearers grow strong and full-foliaged in total shade. The dark blocky forms of yew show up strikingly against a light-colored high wall.

Taxus baccata (English Yew). NE, S, NW, C, T. The wild yew, a forest tree, is little known in gardens. Nurseries offer cultivated varieties, such as the narrowly pyramidal *T. baccata,* 'Fastigiata', to 30 ft. in 40 years, dark in hue; *T. baccata* 'Fastigiata aurea', yellow-green when growing in shade; and the broad and flattish-crowned *T. baccata* 'Repandens', black-ish green. A 35-year-old 'Repandens' planted in the shade of a north wall in my garden stands 14 ft. tall by 22 ft. wide, with a trunk cleared 6 ft. high by pruning. The roots are a dense mesh. A few years ago, I chopped holes (ax work) in the roots and soil several yards out from the wall and the tree trunk and planted tough rhododendron hybrids (Cunningham's Pink for one) in part shade cast by the yew boughs; the rhododendrons grow and flower handsomely, better than I would have thought possible, considering the root power of the yew. (*See* page 26 for a related experiment.)

Taxus ✕ ***media.*** NE, S, NW, C, T. *T. media* 'Hatfieldii', an irregular, informal column to 15 ft. in about 25 years, and *T. media* 'Hicksii', a short-branched tree growing (at same rate) as a slim formal column, are generally planted architecturally — that is, as trees in a line. They could be equally effective planted sculpturally, as trees in a grove varying in height — a piece of living sculpture well displayed against a shaded wall.

〇 ***Tsuga canadensis*** (Canadian Hemlock). The mature tree will shade out and starve all underplanting, even moss. But the young tree is amenable to underlings.

● ***Ulmus pumila*** (Siberian Elm). Weak of branch, gross at the root, a rampant self-sower.

To close on the pejorative notes of hemlock and elm would be out of keeping with the spirit of trees in gardens. Most trees are mostly good. And even the worst (which may come to the gardener who moves into an old garden property) hold shade gardening possibilities, as we have seen in this chapter.

10

Shrubs

The shoulders of the garden.

All the shrubs described below will prosper in ideal shade garden soil, with its inherent mild acidity. A good many are stout-hearted individuals that will grow healthily enough, if somewhat restrainedly, in poor ground — even a poor, dry location; these shrubs will be pointed out as survivors.

Note: See p. 87 in chapter 9 for explanation of the region codes NE, S, GN, NW, C, NC, SC, SW, and T, which are used below to indicate where each shrub will grow well. Page 28 in chapter 2 gives a recipe for ideal shade garden soil, to which you will find frequent references in this chapter.

The first plant is a nonpareil; there is nothing else like it in shade gardening. And come to think of it, the others are equal wonders, unique in leaf, flower, and garden value.

Abeliophyllum distichum. NE, S, NW, C. One of the daintiest of small woodland shrubs; of slow, wispy growth, to 4 ft. Little white flowers on bare stems in earliest spring. This tyke fits easily into a woodsy planting, and nearly anywhere else in part shade. Unshowy, but appealing.

Abutilon (flowering maple). C, SW, T. Generous plants, 10 ft. tall from cuttings, in a couple of seasons. Grown for their bell flowers, produced throughout the year. Branches slender, limber, and arching or laxly leaning — not the comeliest of plants. Wants to be thin and, for shade garden purposes, looks its best when thin; removing side limbs improves the plant. If cut to the ground in spring, comes back fast and fresh. Or grow it as a mural plant (a casually pruned quasi espalier of no set pattern) against a shady wall. The bell flowers of *A. megapotanicum* have red calyxes and yellow petals, with a prominent red bell tongue (the bunched stamens and pistil). In its native Brazil, this flower brings dozens of species of hummingbirds; our North American rufous and rubythroat will come to the garden plant. Many *Abutilon* hybrids are available; their flowers have green calyxes and petals in shades of yellow, red, and cantaloupe.

Acacia myrtifolia. c, t. A spreading shrub, useful as a pillowy ground cover, especially valuable for its tolerance of dry shade. Leaves slim, needlelike. Late-winter flowers, pale yellow and fragrant.

Aucuba japonica (Japanese Laurel). ne (hardy as far north as Cape Cod), s, nw, c, sw, t. This broad-leaf evergreen is one of the best plants for our purposes: an easy grower, of moderate habits; shapely, bright, and lively, even in heavy shade. *Aucuba* will grow in denser shade than almost any other shrub (*Cocculus laurifolius,* grown as a shrub, is its equal in tolerating dim conditions). Fertile, woodsy soil is best for *Aucuba,* but even poor, rocky soil that is dry in summer will sustain it. Easily shaped: Pruning the shrub from the side will make it conform to a narrow side yard, with room left for a pathway — or prune it from the top to hunker it down. Can be grown under trees that have cruel roots. Its handsome, glossy, boat-shaped leaves harmonize with those of other woodland plants, especially large ferns; a green background for azaleas, if you employ one of the green forms of *Aucuba.*

Aucubas are male or female. Plant one male to each group of female shrubs for assured production of the red winter berries; the females alone, without male help, will bear a fair crop. Commonest of aucubas, the old-fashioned Gold-Dust Plant (*A. japonica* 'Variegata'), with yellow-spotted leaves, is usually a gentleman, but lady Gold-Dust Plants are also known. The following forms are all females: *A. japonica* 'Picturata', leaves yellow with green margins and with yellow sprinkled in the green; 'Crotonifolia', leaves drip-painted with splotches and spots of white and gold; 'Fructu Albo', leaves white-marked, berries creamy ivory. Ask the nursery for a green-leaved male plant to go along with any of these. There are, as well, green-leaved selections of female aucubas, such as *A. japonica* 'Longifolia', a heavy bearer of berries (and my own favorite of the many varieties).

Azaleas. Listed under *Rhododendron,* where botany insists they belong.

Bamboo. s, nw, c, sw (sheltered from drying wind), t. Most low-growing bamboos are highly shade-tolerant; some are forest dwellers by nature. The foresters include Arrow Bamboo (*Pseudosasa japonica*), *Arundinaria viridistriata, A. pygmaea,* and *Shibataea Kumasaca.* These revel in a woodsy bed warmed by periodic shafts of sun between tree boughs overhead. *A. pygmaea* spreads widely and rapidly; useful cover for a large piece of secondary garden ground that would otherwise be a den of weeds. But a dangerously invasive plant near anything daintier than horsetail or Bracken. The other low growers in the list are moderate in growth, reasonably controllable. Hardy nearly to 0°F in a sheltered setting.

Buxus (boxwood). Three commonly planted boxwoods, the tall English (ne, s, nw, nc), the 4–6-ft. Japanese (c, sw, t), and the low-growing Korean

(NE, S, NW, C, SW, T), will venture into shade as far as rhododendrons and, in fact, will make an effective fine-leaved contrast to the crasser leaves among that genus. We usually see English and Japanese Boxwood used as formal hedges. Unpruned, the plants grow fluffy and graceful. Use either kind as a solo specimen in shade; thin the branches for still more airiness. Boxwood succeeds in nearly any soil, even with less than soil — in the poverty pickings of a subsoil friable enough for its roots to penetrate.

Calycanthus floridus (Carolina Allspice). For all garden climates. Deciduous shrub, a 10-footer with raggedy-petaled, reddish-brown flowers, followed by conspicuous fig-shaped fruit. Flowers and fruit eye-catching in floral arrangements. The wood of this plant when cut, the fruit when bruised, and the flowers when approached within five feet, give off a pungent sweet-and-sour, musk-and-pineapple fragrance. Carolina Allspice is easy to grow and performs well in part or full shade.

Camellia japonica (Common Camellia). S, NW, C, T. An oriental shrub fussed over for at least 300 years by hybridizers; by now there are nearly 4000 named garden varieties. The plant thrives on our West Coast and in the southern states; a densely foliaged, glossy evergreen bush for light shade or, at most, half shade. In a frosty climate, grow it out of the sun (morning sun or frozen flowers will brown them); in warmer regions grow it against an east wall or a fence side that's in sun all morning; in any climate, as a free-standing specimen, or as a hedge that will flower unhampered if pruned lightly, or even semiformally. As greenery, this heavy plant has only somewhat more life than the plastic shrubbery at the gas station, and its double flowering forms exude the warmth of porcelain roses.

Camellia Sasanqua (Sasanqua Camellia). S and NW in warm shade; C, T. Less hardy than *C. japonica,* a thinner grower, in some forms willowy or almost vinelike. I find established shrubs of this species to be amazingly tolerant of dryness. In my Auckland garden (climate like that of southern California), Sasanquas left unwatered for two dry summer months during my absence remain green and plucky. The flowers of *C. Sasanqua* are fugitive — here today, dropping petals tomorrow — but they keep coming on and on for a good six weeks. A shrub readily shaped by pruning. Cut from the side to hedgify it, form the top to keep it low, from the bottom to make a little tree of it. A favorite landscape treatment is to prune it into a formal or informal espalier or a solid wall cover. The naturalistic single-flowered forms of *C. Sasanqua* are agreeable even to the cantankerously opinionated gardener of fernshaw and wildflower glen who wants nothing to do with *C. japonica.*

Grafted camellias are sometimes sold barely healed at graft juncture; a couple of years' growth in the garden may be needed before the top of the shrub and its understock are soundly united. Examine the graft of a newly purchased shrub: If it appears flimsy, stake the shrub on two or three sides to save it from a windstorm and from being knocked about accidentally by gardener or children.

Camellia sinensis (Tea). The very same: The leaves, fermented just so and then dried, are the makings of the pale amber beverage of genteel tearooms, the same that Eskimos brew and then chew like tobacco, the same that boils down to brown ink in the billy beneath the gum tree in Australia. A hardy plant (s, NW, C, T): For about twenty Seattle winters I've grown and pruned a Tea plant as a leafy mural against a wall in half shade. Small white flowers, recognizably those of a camellia.

Carpenteria californica (Tree Anemone). NW, C, T. To 6 ft. tall in about 10 years. Evergreen strap leaves; the summer flowers, round and white, are ampler than those of Oleander, which this shrub vaguely resembles. Best in dappled shade, afternoon shade, or sun. Makes a distinguished hedge.

Cestrum nocturnum (Queen of the Night). C, T. Lankly upright, a shrub that likes to weasel its way up through tall shrubbery in a half-shaded planting. On its own, it is a lounger unless pruned repeatedly to compact the branches. Small white flowers exhale heavy perfume in the summer night. Tolerates poor, dry soil.

Chamaecyparis obtusa (Hinoki Cypress). s, NW, C, SW, T. Dwarf forms are fully hardy conifers for rock gardening and container gardening in shade that is light to nearly full.

Coprosma spathulata, C. areolata, and *C. virescens* make fine-leaved, ziggy-twigged, light and open shrubs. At age 7, the first and second of these stand upright, 7 ft. tall; *C. virescens* at 7 rises tortuously to a yard tall. *C. spathulata* has dark green spoon leaves an inch or so long, blade and stem. *C. areolata* has an even smaller tennis racket of a leaf, mottled pale yellow and lightest green, with an interlocking complex of coppery and bronzy veins that partition the leaf, like leading in some modern stained-glass window. *C. virescens,* with its arching, cascading, zigzag branches, seems a shrub out of a Chinese scroll painting; smooth tan-green bark and leaves the size, shape, and color of canned petit pois.

These three New Zealanders (growable C, SW, T) impart an effervescent lightness when used as mural plants or free-standers in full or part shade. Plants are the vocabulary of the garden, and in American shade gardening we have heretofore not had species that express just what these plants have to say. To remedy their absence and our lack, I've imported them (along with many other Antipodean species, in the 1980s) and have given them to nurseries in California. By means of cuttings, clever propagators (as I know my colleagues to be) can increase one small imported shrub into thousands in about four years' time. If all goes well, these newcomers will soon be available in rare-plant nurseries.

Correa. C, SW, T. Demure shrubs and shrublets, never fear their turning into leafy moose; they don't have it in them. Leaves small; flowers are bells, of pink, scarlet, banana, or white in the several species. Correas are of huge value in shade gardening because of their rare ability to tolerate drought in shade. These plants will prosper in the bright shade of lightly leaved trees or in part shade, in ideal shade garden soil or in unimproved mineral soil, but the ground must be fast-draining.

Corylopsis pauciflora. s, nw, nc. Six-foot shrub related to witch hazel. Soft-yellow bells linked in a short chain, March and April. At its best in patterned sun/shade beneath trees, or at the edge of a grove.

Cycas revoluta (Sago Palm). c, t. This will put you in touch with paleo-botany. Ancient palmlike plant, quite fascinating in a container. Part shade or bright full shade. Very slow growth — several inches yearly — to 10 ft. Give it "ideal" soil or a rich loam, sandy and fast-draining.

Daboecia. s, nw, c, t. Heath family member, native to Ireland and Spain. A low, dense mound, richly green, finely branched and finely leaved. Leaves are pointed ovals, $\frac{1}{4}$–$\frac{1}{2}$ in. long, covered with long skid-row whiskers. Rosy purple flowers all summer, small and egg-shaped, in racemes held above the foliage; pink or white flowers in named forms. In early autumn, shear the plant, reducing the branch mass by as much as half. For a choice moist bed in half shade, with gentians, polystichums, and primulas as companions.

Daphne. Add these to the *Daboecia* bed. *Daphne collina* and *D. retusa* are darkish, slow-growing shrublets; flowers rosy lavender, delicately fragrant. Planted 15 in. back from the edge of the bed (or sidewalk), they will not spill in the way of pedestrians very quickly. Placement is important, for daphnes don't prune well or transplant easily. *D. Blagayana*, half-ever-green, requires shade during the heat of the day. Where happy (usually in soil beneath young trees with roots that are still amiable), this plant makes a light, 6-ft.-wide, 1-ft.-tall ground cover in a few years. Flowers white, fragrant. All of the above are hardy in a sheltered garden down to about 0° F.

Daphne Laureola (Spurge-Laurel). All climates except gn; shelter, ne. The commonest daphne in and out of gardens. Birds eat the black berries (reputedly poisonous to humans), and the plant springs up in shady places from dropped seed, even in dense shade otherwise habit-able only by ivy, aucuba, and few others. Spurge-Laurel resembles a rangy, small-leaved rhododendron as much as it does a spurge or a laurel; a 3-footer with green-yellow flowers. Drought-tolerant and easy to grow.

Daphne odora (Winter Daphne). s and nw, with shelter; c, t. A waist-high shrub, usually a bit nude and gawky, but saved by its habit of pouring out one of the great scent baths of the garden world. This won't take frost below about 15°F. In the North, it is a shrub on the garden's protected list, to be planted in warm shade and covered with burlap before the storm comes.

Enkianthus. ne, s, nw, c. Japanese, elegant; a deciduous member of the rhododendron family. Best in open woods in shifting shade and sun, or in half shade near walls. *E. campanulatus* grows a foot a year and in time becomes more than a shrub — one of the most graceful small trees in the garden repertoire. It is usually a mistake for the gardener (both as artist and plant psychologist) to practice repressive pruning on this plant. Carve it from below rather than from the top. *E. campanulatus* carries small candy-striped, red-and-white bells in clusters; the azalealike leaves turn red in autumn. Quite a plant. *E. perulatus* is a slow one — 6 in. a year is usually flat out for this species. Habit upright and slim, even fastigiate. White bells, not showy. Its best features are refinement and the reddest of autumn leaves. *E. cernuus*, with dull red flowers, is another gentle shrub, growing even more slowly than *E. perulatus*.

Epigaea repens (Trailing Arbutus). NE, S, NW. Leaves oval, flowers pale-pink stars, innocently sweet-looking and sweetly perfumed. It is a flat-growing shrublet, its branches lengthening about 3 in. a year; the choicest of ground covers, although perhaps no gardener has enough of it to use as such. Plant in ideal shade garden soil in cool, moist half shade or full shade. For fifty years or more this beloved eastern American wildflower has been distributed nationally by one or two mail-order nurseries located in the southern mountains; they collect on their own land or buy from other landowners. Collected sods of Trailing Arbutus are best planted in early autumn. Nursery-grown pot plants are also available occasionally and are plantable almost anytime.

Eranthemum pulchellum (Blue Sage). SC, T. Winter flowers of a dark gentian-blue, on a somewhat sloppy shrub that needs whacking back from time to time. Native to cool, dripping ravines in India, it will not stand dryness in the garden. Shade should be three-quarters or half.

Eurya emarginata. S, NW, C, T. Slow-growing, with fine pinnate leaves and a fern clump habit of branch. Especially appealing when planted in a shady rock wall.

Fatsia japonica (Japanese Fatsia). S, NW, C, T. Good old shade garden evergreen, standby of professional landscapers and home gardeners. In a warm climate or in a sheltered northern courtyard, 15 ft. tall by 15 ft. wide in as many years — or potentially so if not pruned. In the Northwest, winter knocks fatsia back every few years and it seldom attains a height of more than 9 ft. Grown for its big, palmate, ivy-green leaves. The shrub is too ballooning to be in place against a bungalow house. Let it puff up and out in front of a tall north wall or fence; or plant in a woodland garden 20 ft. or more away from the path and well in back of choicer shrubs. Prune off side branches of fatsia if its natural hemispherical shape outdoes the place you've planted it.

Fothergilla. NE, S, NW, C. Native to southeastern U.S. Choice slow-growing shrubs related to witch hazel. In keeping with a planting in open woods (alternating sun and shade), or against an east wall or fence. Flowers, appearing on bare branches in spring, are little white tassels rather like those on a stocking cap. Autumn leaves are soft orange and rose.

Fuchsia (lady's-eardrops). The many hybrids are among the easiest and most satisfactory flowering shrubs for half-shady gardens in warm-winter climates; in colder areas, they are grown as annuals or as summer plants, to be wintered in a greenhouse or a cool room. Provide them filtered sun beneath the branches of fine-leaved trees or shrubs — hang the fuchsia on a limb or plant it in the open ground. Fuchsias are also good against an east wall or fence side. You can grow your own plants easily from cuttings 4–7 in. long, best taken in midsummer. Insert the cuttings in sand, in a half-shady place, and keep them moist. By fall you will have nicely rooted propagules, probably already in flower.

Some of the hybrid fuchsias make thin, whippy branches. To densen the plant, snip the branch tips from time to time throughout summer. In spring, cut back any scraggly fuchsia about halfway to its base.

Fuchsia magellanica (Hardy Fuchsia). s, nw, c, sw, t. Peruvian, native as far south as Tierra del Fuego. The hardiest of the hundred species in the genus, the longest known, the Lady's Eardrops of Victorian gardens. More than twenty named varieties of *F. magellanica* are in the trade. The strongest, such as *F. magellanica* 'Gracilis' and *F. magellanica* 'Riccartonii', both 6–10 ft. tall, are completely drought-tolerant when established — game to spend a northwestern or a western Californian summer without being watered, but this only in open ground, for no fuchsia withstands dryness in a container. 'Gracilis' and 'Riccartonii', and usually one other variety, 'Alba', are sufficiently hardy to be grown as perennials in winters down to 0°F. Mound sawdust or compost at the base of the plants, to be on the safe side. In a mild climate, where protected from strong wind, white-flowered 'Alba' will grow into a small, thinly attractive tree.

Gardenia jasminoides (Common Gardenia). c, sw, t. Easy to grow in rhododendron conditions of soil and shade — that is, in dappled shade and in ideal shade garden soil, kept moist. There are several upright forms and a spreading, ground-covering variety, *G. jasminoides* 'Radicans'. Planted 2 ft. apart and mulched, radicans makes a solid cover in about two summers; bears small gardenias of classic fragrance.

Gaultheria Shallon (Salal). s, nw, c, t. Native along the West Coast, Alaska to mid-California. The dominant forest undergrowth in the Pacific Northwest, it grows as a thicket 4–8 ft. tall in moist woods. The denser the shade, the sprawlier the growth. Cut back, the plant returns in tidier form; you can even stump it to the ground, with full expectation of its reappearance. No shade plant in western gardening is more willing. Certainly none is more valuable than this, with its round leathery leaves, glossy fresh green in all seasons, its little roundish floral jars in white, and its black-purple edible berries. Use the plant as background for shady beds of smaller shrubbery, as leafy footing for the walls of the house, or as a cover shrub on a shady bank. In places where you can legally dig Salal in the field — as, for example, along many power line access roads — select for digging compact plants growing in the sun; plants in shade usually have rangy, unmanageable roots. Early autumn is the best digging time.

Gaultheria sinensis and **G. trichophylla** are tenderish shrublets (NW, C) with startlingly blue berries — in *G. trichophylla,* a cobalt like that of deep water in the tropics.

Hebe speciosa and its hybrids. C, SW, T. A garden group of low evergreen shrubs, typically 5 ft. wide, 2 ft. tall. On a medium-size plant, medium-size leaves that are hart tongue–shaped (no garden writer would ever dare say "cow tongue–shaped"), glossy ivy-green. Flowers in spikes, beet-red, purple, or pink. These shrubs are first-rate in shade gardening, for they will flower unfailingly with as little as three hours of sun a day. Use as cover plants beneath trees or as edging in shady beds of mixed shrubbery.

Helichrysum 'Limelight'. C, SW, T. The popular name suits the plant, but what the heck is it, binomially speaking? The nursery practice of dropping the Latin names of lately wild plants in the course of supplying more salable sobriquets is maddening to the gardener who seeks the romance of plants through their proper names, without which one cannot learn in books their place of origin, how they grow in nature, or any of the other vital or pleasantly pedantic data to be found in the plant's dossier. This orphan showed up in Auckland, New Zealand, nurseries in the early eighties. "Limelight" will soon enough find its way into American supermarket garden stores, for it is a plant with an irresistible . . . something. Not its habit of growth: it is a low, sprangly bush, with branches thin and limber as spaghetti al dente, growing to 2 ft. tall, 5 ft. wide in a few years, always in need of an improving snip or two. But the leaves are the thing: the size of a twenty-five- or fifty-cent piece, heart-shaped, felty and soft, pale lime-green, the rarest shade of green in gardening — and an easy grower in light shade or shade most of the day. Needs fast-draining soil.

Hibbertia (button flower). C, T. Australian shrubs of great use as fillers and ground-cover plants in dry shade. Cheery yellow flowers in spring, like those of the sun rose. Soil and shade as for *Correa.*

Hibiscus syriacus (Rose of Sharon). For all climates. An old-fashioned plant about due for a revival of honor and interest. Available in flower colors ranging from white through all hues of rose down to black-purple. Takes much shade. If you are custodian of an old, tall specimen of this, consider radically thinning its trunks as detailed in the section "Arborizing a Shrub" in chapter 4.

Hydrangea macrophylla (Garden Hydrangea, Hortensia). Nearly the all-American, all-Canadian summer-flowering shrub, good for all climates except GN. Kindly forget the boresome institutional wall beds and obese park parkings of the shrub you may have seen. This summer dumpling of a flower can be next to graceful if planted sparingly (three or five) in part shade near the north edge of a tree grove, or in an open space within the grove, where the Hydrangea will flower satisfactorily in scant sun. It probably needs a backing of trees or tall evergreen shrubs. In a wall bed by itself, Hydrangea usually seems Brobdingnagian in summer and a spiky nothing in winter (except for its susurrant dead beige blooms, which, when picked, last practically forever in a dry arrangement). Grows in any soil, better in rich soil. Needs much pruning. The Lace Cap forms of Garden Hydrangea are decidedly graceful, with their well-named, spaced flower ensembles. Garden needs, same as for the dumpling forms of the plant.

Hydrangea quercifolia (Oakleaf Hydrangea). Eastern American native, growable in all climates, a shade shrub of first importance. Likes woodland shade, full or part shade near the house. A 4–6-footer with raggedy-toothed green leaves a bit like oak. Summer flower heads are loose congregations of showy white sterile flowers and quiet little working flowers. Leaves turn bronze before they fall. Easy to grow.

Ilex crenata (Japanese Holly). NE, S, NW, C, T. There are several forms, solid and stoical evergreen furnishings. Small leaves, rather like those of huckleberry or boxwood. Richest leaf color develops in full shade or afternoon shade. Dark green *I. crenata* 'Convexa' has a passing liveliness imparted by droves of bees that come for the rich honey of its tiny flowers. (Are they whitish? For all the years I've watched the bees working the plant, I've registered no distinct impression of the flowers.) Little black berries follow. *I. crenata* 'Helleri' is a 15-in.-tall, neatly spreading variety useful as a fill-the-bed shrub. Beneath trees, near sidewalks, in ground too poor or climate too cold for evergreen azaleas, this is a plant that will somewhat fill the azaleas' function as greenery. *I. crenata* 'Mariesii' is a swarthy dwarf with stiff vertical branches; usually 2 ft. tall at age 20. Nice little monster for the shady rock garden.

Kalmia latifolia (Mountain Laurel). NE, S, NW. Eastern North American, a rhododendronlike shrub, spare of branch. Planted in a garden, it is a slow grower. When 20 to 25 years old, it's about as tall as an adult human. Yet the plant is faster-growing where it occurs naturally. Soil, shade, and water requirements in gardens within the natural range of the shrub are as for the larger-leaved rhododendrons. In city and suburban gardens along its native Atlantic seaboard, it is one of the choicest tall shade plants. In country properties where it is spontaneous, it is a shrub that gardeners often handle as we of the Northwest do Salal *(Gaultheria Shallon)* — as a plant to be lopped and sawed away until it forms a background for the garden one plants in the soil gained by this clearing. But in the Northwest, Mountain Laurel is not so eager; to grow at all well, it needs a woodsy moist place near a body of water or in the mountains.

In the foreground, *Ilex crenata* 'Convexa', an old friend (see chapter 1), glistens in the wan winter sun and imparts welcome warmth to this frozen terrace on Beacon Hill. The ilexes along the fence afford privacy from the street. (GEORGE TALOUMIS)

Flower party in a half-shade border. Even sunlovers like roses and Sweet William will accept shade up to half the day. Garden of Michael Darlow.

Colt's Foot *(Petasites speciosus)*. Garden of Gerda Isenberg, Yerba Buena Nursery.

Dwarf hybrid impatiens with a young tree fern.

Rhododendron yakushimanum and a line of yellow *Trillium luteum* in a surf of double white *Anemone nemorosa*. Garden of Cecil Smith.

Cornus Kousa. Garden of Maxime Williams.

Adiantum pedatum, a hardy maidenhair fern.
Garden of Mr. and Mrs. George Drake.

In the shade of an oak are fuschia, Deer Fern, and *Saxifraga stolonifera*. Garden of Margedant Hayakawa.

Hosta decorata. Garden of Roy Davidson.

I mow my lawn of carpeting perennials once or twice a summer. Two and a half hours of crucial full sun lighten this mostly shaded corner.

Lamium maculatum 'Beacon Silver' lights up dark ground. Garden of Lester Hawkins and Marshall Olbrich (Western Hills Nursery).

Candelabra primroses and callas burst from wet ground. Garden of John and Claire Skupen.

Geranium lancastriense keeps this flower show going from spring until late summer. Garden of Roy Davidson.

Rhododendron 'Vulcan' in full shade. *Oxalis oregana* as a ground cover. Garden of Michael Darlow.

Mountain Laurel (*Kalmia latifolia*) in full shade. (DON NORMARK)

Kalmiopsis Leachiana. NW, NC. Dwarf alpine shrub. Needs ideal shade garden soil, moisture, and drainage. In a garden where the air is moist, this sometimes thrives in half shade; but filtered shade is safer for it on most properties. In habit it is a thicket of little dark green huckleberry leaves and rosy cups. To a foot tall and 18 in. wide in about a decade. There is something remarkable about this plant. It is clearly related to *Kalmia,* yet is clearly not that; it also vaguely resembles a miniature rhododendron. It is, in fact, botanically between the two — not a bigeneric hybrid, but some sort of link. Native to the Siskiyous, the plant lived undiscovered until 1935, I think it was: A Mrs. Leach went hiking and found something wonderful. (Mrs. Leach, forgive me — your full name, which I read in a garden article ages ago, has slipped my mind. Anyway, you've achieved immortality through your discovery, one of the final finds in North America of a plant species of garden importance.)

Kerria japonica. Native to woods in Japan. Growable in all climates, this is a slender-stemmed, deciduous shrub of the rose family. Leaves and branches bright green. Spring flowers orange-yellow, like a wild-rose in form (in the wildflower version of the plant); but the pompon-flowered double form is the popular one. Easy to grow in part shade or full.

Leucothoe Davisiae (Sierra Laurel). NE, S, GN, NW, NC. Native to the Siskiyou Mountains. A foot-high stoloniferous shrublet forming a rugged patch like a bearskin coat lying on the ground; in another form, a low

Kerria japonica, the single form — so much lighter than double kerria, that floral meatball. (DON NORMARK)

shrub hesitantly stoloniferous. Leaves small, leathery, dull green; little white barrel flowers in upright racemes top the plant in early summer. Place in part shade. The established plant will survive long dry spells.

Leucothoe Fontanesiana (usually sold as *L. Catesbaei*). NE, S, GN (shelter), NW, NC. Eastern American. An evergreen shrub of the rhododendron clan, a furnishing plant par excellence. Elliptical leaves, dark and lustrous; little barrel-shaped white flowers clustered on racemes in the spring. Has the arching branch habit of Solomon's Seal. In the leucothoe, canelike woody stems form a thicket to about 5 ft. high and 7 ft. across in moist, shaded soil; grows lower in dryish soil (will survive a couple of summer months without water, once established). Part or filtered shade. Rooted branches, grubbed up from the margins of a well-grown leucothoe, transplant well, slowly begin to stroll at the root and send up new stems.

Leucothoe Keiskei 'Minor.' NW, NC. From Japan. Tufted shrublet worthy of the choicest square foot or two of the shade garden — all the ground it will ever take, if the gardener is lucky. The few radial branches lean way low or lie quite flat on the ground. The leaves that line the plant are long-pointed, a polished dark green. White flowers larger than those of the *L. Fontanesiana* or *L. Davisiae,* in pendant racemes. *L. Keiskei* requires cool, woodsy shade and ideal shade garden soil. The plant won't survive dryness or weevils.

Mahonia Aquifolium (Oregon Grape). For all climates. Lacquered, hollylike leaves. The typical plant is a rangy 5–8-footer, improved by being pruned back. Effective against shady walls (here it needs at least a little sun). Form *M. aquifolium* 'Compacta' is an edging shrublet — a landscaper's finishing plant — to 30 in. tall. Any well-drained soil; drought-tolerant.

Mahonia Bealei. NW, C, SW, T. Needs a place out of the wind and in filtered or north-wall shade. A shrub of a few clustered, slim, and upright stem-staffs; at their tops, great horizontal wheels of gray-green ferny foliage, but leathery-firm and prickly. Dramatic against walls. Requires a goodly depth of ideal shade garden soil and abundant water. If the plant goes thirsty or receives too much sun, its leaves turn yellow. In warm climates, a 12-footer at age 20; usually half that height in the Northwest.

Mahonia lomariifolia. C, SW, T. Growth form is that of *M. Bealei.* In this species, the leaf wheels are dark green and tropically bold — to 4 ft. across. *M. lomariifolia* stands 14 ft. tall at maturity. Half shade; ideal shade garden soil or fertile clayey loam. Water requirements are moderate.

Mahonia nervosa (Low Oregon Grape). NE, S, NW, C. Woodland shrublet of tufted, fernlike habit; pinnate leaves, shiny dark green. Spreads very slowly by stolons into a colony 1–2 yd. wide. The vertical growth of each ferny-leaved stem is exceedingly slow: A 3-ft.-tall stem is perhaps 40 years old. Full or part shade; any soil, as long as reasonably well drained. When established, needs no summer watering.

Murraya paniculata (*M. exotica;* Orange Jessamine). SC, T. Graceful evergreen, upright to 10 ft. tall; in leaf and in raining branches, rather like Benjamina Fig. Star-form white flowers, jasmine-scented. Full shade or afternoon shade.

Myrtus. NW (some winter damage every few years), C, SW, T. The various forms of myrtle, taller or shorter, are useful as hedges of various heights, in shade up to three-fourths of the day. They are small-leaved — like boxwood in texture — but are livelier plants, with their sweet white flowers and deliciously fragrant foliage. When pruning *Myrtus,* one becomes agreeably spifflicated with its scent.

Nandina domestica (Heavenly Bamboo). One of the great shrubs for shade, S, NW, C, SW, T; a houseplant everywhere. Not a bamboo at all — a barberry relative, but in general appearance nothing like that plant, either.

Mahonia Bealei in berry (it will provide a superb tart jam). At the back, *Nandina domestica*. (DON NORMARK)

A clump of slender-stemmed (yet very tough-wooded) upright canes; from these uprights, narrow leaves radiate at a low, almost horizontal, angle. The plant is vigorous in pattern, gentle in the airiness of its slim foliage. Ideal shade garden soil or sandy loam; half shade or full. The typical nandina stands 6 ft., 12 ft. with age. Easily compacted by pruning, but interesting grown tall and spare. A good plant for a narrow passageway with light coming from overhead — an inducement for the nandina to make upright growth. The typical shrub is not suited to north-wall planting beneath eaves, where it would lean out to catch better daylight. *N. domestica* 'Nana' is a 2–3-ft.-tall clone with long, narrow leaves that turn dark bronze in winter when the plant is grown in shade (the winter leaf is brighter in sun). This plant doesn't lean noticeably in a north-wall bed and makes up in width what it lacks in height: a stoloniferous grower, to 6 ft. wide in a few years. Beautiful with large rocks in an entry garden or atrium. *N. domestica* 'Pygmaea', a densely compact 1–2 ft. tall, is an outstanding shrublet for edging or container planting. In a container, it stays healthy even if it becomes dry from time to time.

Osmanthus. NE, S, NW, C, T. Garden worthies, they cover the shady wall and fill the shady bed. They have a lively fragrance in their otherwise paltry white flowers. Tall *O. heterophyllus* (*O. ilicifolius*) makes an informal hedge.

Pentapterygium serpens. C, T. Himalayan. Odd member of the rhododendron family, a small, slow shrub with downward-growing branches and little waxy, pointed leaves, usually in two ranks. Under each branch in late winter and spring, bottle flowers dangle in a line, tomato-red, with fascinating darker red veins (that look as if they could bleed). Grow it high in a shady rock wall or in a hanging container. Half shade; ideal shade garden soil.

Pieris. Rhododendron cousins. They have the family need of a soil finely worked to accommodate their thread-fine feeder roots. Flowering in early spring.

Pieris floribunda (Fetterbush). NE, S, GN (with shelter), NW, NC. Southern mountain plant. Smallish elliptical leaves, matte gray-green. Atop the rounded mass of foliage, upright clusters of little poke-shaped white flowers. Easier to grow than a rhododendron. Content in a lean, too sandy soil; unhurt by two months of summer drought in unwatered soil. In such conditions I've grown the plant for thirty years; mine stands only 6 ft. (by 8 ft. wide) and would probably be bigger in a better place. Half shade.

Pieris Forrestii. NW (with shelter), NC. Burmese. Tall shrub, upright and broad; of moderate growth — about a foot a year. Long leaves that, when newly formed, are blood-red (in selected, cutting-grown plants) turning dark green and glossy bright when mature. Small white flowers open with the new leaves, but are the lesser show. Provide shelter from drying wind, keep in filtered shade and use ideal shade garden soil kept moist. *P. Forrestii* responds to pruning and can be narrowed into a leafy mural or a more definite espalier. *Pieris* 'Flame of the Forest', a hybrid of *P. Forrestii* and *P. japonica,* picks up some of the compactness and hardiness of the latter species and retains the brilliance of spring foliage found in the showiest forms of *P. Forrestii.* Depending on the heartiness of the rooted cutting, 'Flame' will grow to a 5–9-ft. shrub in about 15 years. Usually safe in warm shade in the "Inland Empire" of the Pacific Northwest.

Pieris japonica (Lily-of-the-Valley Shrub). NE, S, NW, NC. Has had the bad luck to become institutionalized. This was a favorite of landscape architects in the Pacific Northwest from about 1920 to the early fifties. Today masses of the shrub greet us outside many a menacing old public building, and thus a great plant has gone out of fashion, largely, I think, because of its association with bygone styles of architecture. A shrub easy to grow in a garden that has moist soil and air, but well-nigh impossible to keep in one that tends to dryness in summer. Give it ideal shade garden soil; afternoon shade, patterned shade and sun, or north-wall shade that is undeepened by trees in the vicinity. Growth is slow, about 6–9 in. annually. It is open-branched and upright in north-wall shade, compact and rounded in an east-wall planting. Leaves are rich glossy green, narrow, and distinctively down-curved. Lily-of-the-Valley flowers, in racemes, are pretty poison. In the mountains of Japan, signs warn picnickers not to sit beneath the shrub when it is shedding its blossoms. The flower corollas are virulently toxic if ingested, the berry-like green seed capsules even more so.

Pittosporum Tobira (Mock Orange). NW, C, SW, T. China and Japan. An evergreen shrub rather like a denser rhododendron — and a darker one, in its black-green leafage — but not related. Small cream-colored flowers in spring and summer, with perfume like that of orange blossom. Seed pods in autumn split to display bright orange seeds. Any fertile soil; half or full shade. Growth is upright, a foot or more a year, to tree height. Once the shrub grows to the perfect size, control it by pruning new twigs at their juncture with older branches. A container plant or entry plant of strong, clean lines, it is probably more effective as outdoor sculpture than most hard pieces.

Prunus Laurocerasus (English Laurel). S, NW, C, T. In its garden range, this is a common hedge plant. But the planting of an English Laurel hedge is an act of aggression against one's neighbor — against oneself as well. It is the fightingest of hedges, pushing outward and upward as soon as you turn your back. English Laurel is one of the greatest goads to giving up on the yard and moving into an apartment — in a very real sense, this shrub is a real estate agent. However, where it is validly planted, it makes a superb shade garden citizen. We have here a big, bold, fast-growing shrub with large, heavy, polished leaves of bottle-green. Plant it as a specimen in high shade, or in the north-wall shade of a tall building, or as a background shrub for a rhododendron planting within woods — the somewhat rhododendronlike laurel will nicely blend those lesser shrubs in with the trees. In time the laurel forms a broad canopy-head and would itself be a tree. Help it along by pruning away its lower limbs progressively as the shrub grows taller.

Prunus Laurocerasus 'Zabeliana'. NE (shelter), S, NW, C, T. To 6 ft. tall, 12 ft. wide, in about 20 years (with pruning it can be held to half size). Much planted by landscape architects on shady banks and along shady walls. Leaves bright in all seasons. Good performance in rather poor ground.

Prunus Laurocerasus 'Mt. Vernon'. NE, S, NW, C, T. A flat plant for full or filtered shade. Actually, not quite flat — a foot tall by 4 ft. wide in 6 years, but hardly ever taller than a foot. The shiny oval leaves, 4 in. long, are held horizontally in an agreeable pig-pile crowd, the upper branches pressing on the lower — this is a weed beater of a shrub. Ideal soil, moderate moisture. Can be used as a ground cover, as an under-planting for tall deciduous shrubs, or as a woods companion to bleed-ing-hearts, ferns, meadow rue, and comparable plants that are taller and airier than the Laurel. A little-known shade plant of high value.

Pseudopanax. "Ontogeny recapitulates phylogeny" goes the jawbreaking theory of recapitulation, and these New Zealand shrubs make a good case for it. From seedling to adulthood they progress through a number of leaf changes thought to represent different manifestations of the plant as it existed over eons in the changing climates of the land. Grow in part or full shade in any productive loam. Water needs are average.

Pseudopanax crassifolius (Lancewood). C, T. This transmutationist be-gins by producing, on the seedling plant, small longish oval leaves that reflect a cold climate. The juvenile plant has desert-formed leaves up to 3 ft. long, snake-slim and dark slate-green, with a soft orange or red-brown garter snake stripe down the middle. The maturing Lancewood has the foliage of a rainy jungle plant, with leaves splayed into three to five fingers. Then, when quite mature, the plant goes back to producing simple leaves that are, in size, outline, and color, about like a young zucchini; these are the leaves of mild, moist contemporary New Zealand. Curio for a large pot or tub and striking when planted against a plain wall.

Pseudopanax ferox (C, T) has juvenile leaves long and slim, like those of *P. crassifolius,* but here they are tan and toothed, suggesting the nar-row, fierce head of a crocodile. The narrow-leaf phase continues for 15 years or more, during which the shrub lengthens its spear of a trunk about a foot each year. *P. ferox* is one of the few shrubs that will thrive in deep shade.

Pseudopanax Lessonii (C, T), with a broadish trifoliate leaf, has an ability (exceedingly rare in shade garden shrubbery) to keep foliage on its lower quarters for some years in a fully shady location. Leaf keeping is especially notable in cutting-grown plants of the several clones of *P. Lessonii.* Of these, *P. Lessonii* 'Purpureum', with shining purplish-bronze leaf-hands, is a compact, slow-growing shrub, compatible with ferns in a north-wall bed. Seedling plants of *P. Lessonii* can be kept compact by pruning from the top.

Rhododendron. What the rose is to sunny gardening, the rhododendron is to shade gardening — a whole blooming world to roam around in, a flower of specialists, societies, and shows, a big-business flower, a nursery industry humming along. There are about a thousand rhododendron species growing wild in all the green continents, ten times that many garden hybrids and more each year, ad infinitum.

Most garden rhododendrons descend from shrubs native to the high forests and the above-the-forest shrub belts of western China and the Himalayas. Our best garden climate for rhododendrons somewhat matches that of their ancestral country. The West Coast of North America, down to about the San Francisco Bay Area, supplies in reasonable measure the fogs, rains, moderate winters, and short dry season that the plants are used to in Asia. The South is capital country for azaleas, both evergreen and deciduous (azaleas are technically rhododendrons). The garden climates of the East and Midwest support the native eastern American rhododendrons, the toughest ones from Japan, and those of European parentage.

Consult your local nurseries about kinds that are good bets, but be aware that you may be consulting the horticultural cousin of a racetrack tout. Nursery people are often the wildest gamblers on plant hardiness — seems as if they've got to have tempting new plants each season to keep us coming in. Many northern nurseries import flighty rhododendrons from wholesalers in more southerly states, varieties reasonably safe in warm shade in the North, but quite likely to pack up and take off in a severe winter. (On Long Island, on Cape Cod, in the Boston area, and in Connecticut, many nurseries and game gardeners have lately gone into revolt against what garden books say about rhododendron hardiness. Varieties supposedly tender, including reds and yellows, are being shipped by the carloads from the West Coast, and these plants, hitherto thought to be impossible, have made it all right, through some seven winters to date — and some of the severest weather on record.)

Grow rhododendrons in lath shade, in the filtered shade or patterned shade/sun provided by trees, or in north-wall shade (if in the shade of a house, far enough out from the wall so that the plant does not stand in rainless desert beneath eaves).

Shade gardener Gordon Emerson of Ohio gives a concise analysis of the benefits of planting rhododendrons — and all cold-sensitive shade plants — in sheltered areas. Note that such gardening is, by definition, away from winter sun as well as out of the wind.

Along the protective north side of the house, cold hardiness of plants and of flower buds is increased as much as ten or fifteen degrees. Rhododendrons that would kill to the ground at zero in the open, may bloom normally after withstanding ten below. Plant hardiness is also increased in a woodland site, due to protection from wind and sun and to a more stable soil temperature: Soil thaws more slowly in the spring, helping to prevent precocious flowering and growth. During a recent terrible winter (one of the severest on record), Rhododendron 'Roseum Elegans', *the most winter-hardy variety yet developed, was defoliated in open sites where its branches protruded from the snow, and the supposedly iron-clad species,* Rhododendron catawbiense, *suffered even wood damage. Yet in the woodland and in other shaded areas, these same varieties, and many others much tenderer, sustained absolutely no leaf or wood damage; they merely lost some flower buds.*

The conglomerate genus of shrubs known as rhododendron is separable into the following divisions:

I. Rhododendron species — nature's own wildflowers. Most are not as showy as the man-made hybrids. They have, however, an individuality in their leaves and flowers that makes our best hybrids seem bland in comparison. Most of those I describe below are small growers that fit easily into a half-shady rock garden; or give them a close-up position in the shade garden's best bed.

II. Rhododendron hybrids. Leaves usually large and elliptical; flowers — as Madison Avenue would say — "new and improved." The hybrids are furnishing plants or background shrubs.

III. Evergreen azaleas. Generally low-growing, small-leaved shrubs, to be used as bed fillers, in rockeries, and alongside walks and paths.

IV. Deciduous azaleas. Medium shrubs, eventually tall. Spring flowers are brilliant or demure, depending on the species, and an autumn leaf show, orange and red, equals that of the brightest azalea flowers. Plant in moving shade-and-sun within open groves of trees, or in other half-shady locations. Azaleas are famous in woodland gardening. The part shade and companionship of trees induces the plants to grow gracefully upright and open, with branches ascending, then fanning horizontally so that their leaves catch light sifting through the trees.

In the plant descriptions that follow, rhododendrons are listed under the above headings. Altogether, the list includes some of the finest of rhododendrons, selected from the thousands chiefly for their beauty of foliage and flower, or, in some cases, for their hardiness. All of these plants are growable (apart from the regions ascribed to them) in California's southern half, in its Great Central Valley, and in the Southwest, in sheltered, comparatively cool gardens or in lath shade — but only by gardeners who are green, not only of thumb, but up to the elbow, and usually only in raised beds of prepared soil.

I: SPECIES

R. Augustinii. NW, NC. Chinese alpine. Upright and open; 3–5 ft. high, 30 in. wide in 10 years. Narrow, 3-in-long leaves. Flowers lavender-blue. Named seedlings have clear violet flowers.

R. caesium. NW, NC. A 2-footer in 15 years. Soft blue, coin-size leaves, rounded and fringed; soft-yellow flowers.

Rhododendron lepidotum, fifteen years old, and about the same number of inches tall. (DON NORMARK)

R. catawbiense (Catawba Rhododendron). NE, S, NW, NC. Eastern American mountain flower, lilac-purple. A portly shrub about man-tall at age 15, sprucely dressed with oblong leaves 3–6 in. long.

R. fastigiatum. NW, NC. Himalayan. Grows to 3 ft. tall in 15 years. Amethyst flowers over small blue-green leaves that are like the carapace of some tidy little beetle — rounded on the end, rolled down along the edges, with a seam down the middle. When handled, the foliage is aromatic with a volatile oil meant to ward off the same beetle. A twiggy, upright, bare-flanked plant best planted closely with others of its kind in a garden krummholz. (In nature, a krummholz is a mountainside phalanx of rhododendrons or other shrubbery that are associated to shed snow like a roof — a cause of avalanches.)

R. Hanceanum. NW, NC. Chinese. Waist-high shrub. Leaves brownish green and leathery, like old Morocco bookbinding. Flowers pale yellow.

R. Hanceanum nanum, tidy and clipped looking, grows a foot tall, 18 in. wide in 10 years. An extravagant bloomer that will literally flower its head off unless the gardener removes spent blossoms to prevent seed formation.

R. lepidotum elaeagnoides. NW, NC. Tibetan. An elfin shrub growing to 10 × 10 in. in 10 years. Tiny roundish leaves; flowers bright yellow or plum-colored, the corolla nickel-size, flat, and facelike, with a sassy tongue sticking out (the stamens). Needs plenty of water.

R. macrophyllum (California Rosebay). NW, NC. West Coast counterpart of the eastern *R. catawbiense.* The westerner is a tall, rangy plant when it grows in shady woods; at the margin of the woods, a middling plant with compact branches and dense foliage. Hard pruning will induce compactness in a lank plant. Flowers rosy or magenta. Wherever a wild specimen of this shrub stands in the way of bushwhacking (while opening up garden space), it is certainly worth saving and incorporating into the garden.

R. mucronulatum. NE, S, NW, C. Siberian. Leaves deciduous, yet somewhat leathery and clearly those of a rhododendron rather than an azalea. The foliage is sparse, even in summer. A crane of a plant, upright and skinny growing to 5 ft. in a few years. Treat the shrub to the Mollis azalea type of pruning (see below) to densen or rejuvenate the branches. All is forgiven when it flowers, bright magenta, in January and February in the West; later-flowering in the East. Our New Jersey consultant Elizabeth T. Capen writes, *"Rhododendron mucronulatum* creates a lavender haze over our hillside in Daffodil time, before the deciduous trees have burgeoned. We plant with this variety pale yellow, white, or chartreuse Daffodils."

R. pemakoense. NW, C. From Pemako, Tibet. Shrublet twice as wide as high (2 × 1 ft. in 15 years). Polished, dark green leaves an inch long. Cloaks itself with comparatively huge mauve-pink flowers in March. One of the very few rhododendrons to spread (slowly) by stolons. Encourage this habit by mulching and topdressing the plant with sawdust, screened compost, or peat moss.

R. radicans. NW, NC. Translated, *radicans* means "rooting stems." An ankle-high shrublet from stony moors three miles high, near Lhasa in Tibet. To 5 in. tall, 15 in. wide, in 10 years. Narrow dark green leaves slightly more than ½-in. long. Purple flowers, comically large for the plant, bloom in leaf-hiding abundance in late May. Topdress to encourage roots along the branches. An old, established *R. radicans* can be propagated as one would a perennial, by pulling the plant apart into divisions. And it is the easiest of rhododendrons to grow from cuttings.

Rhododendron mucronulatum in earliest spring. (DON NORMARK)

A favorite plant of rock garden specialists and a cause of disputations — people get the plant mixed up with *R. keleticum*, a close relative that grows a foot tall: "No, no — radicans is the taller one; *keleticum* is tiny." In a fairly long career, I remember entering several arguments along these lines, in which nobody gave an inch, of course. Both antagonists are in the right. *Keleticum is* tiny (in one of its forms).

R. sanguineum. NW, C. Tibetan. Somber shrublet, stout and slow in growth (about 14 in. tall by 16 in. across in 10 years). The small black-crimson flowers tucked beneath the leaves do not liven the plant until low sun strikes through them, then they glow ruby-red, like stained glass. To get the full effect of this glass fire, plant the shrub where both early and late sun will reach it. Needs shade during midday. Late flowering; June and July. *R. haemaleum* and *R. didymum*, shrubs very much like *R. sanguineum*, also have red flowers that light up in the sun.

R. Williamsianum. NW, NC. From western China. Heart-shaped leaves, bronze in spring, green the rest of the year; bell flowers of a tender pink. The shrub varies, in mature stature, from a dense, flattened, 1-ft.-high shrub to a rounded 4-footer. The smaller forms came from higher up in the mountains. Give *R. Williamsianum* full shade during the heat of midday, and early or late sun (or both). One of the thirstier plants in the garden, registering drought instantly by rolling up its leaves. *R. Williamsianum* is the parent of two especially worthy hybrids, 'Bow Bells' and 'Moonstone'. As with all wildflowers that have given rise to garden hybrids, the parent plant is the stronger piece of sculpture. The hybrids are relatively amorphous but comparatively easy to grow, having "sold their birthright for a mess of comfort in the garden," as Reginald Farrer put it.

R. yakushimanum. NE, S, NW, NC; hardy at −20°F. From the volcanic Isle of Yaku in Japan. A densely leaved low dome, to 3 × 4 ft. in 20 years. Grown as much for its new leaves — they are covered with a pale chamois-colored fur — as for its large blush-pink bells. An easy-natured species and deliciously lovely in spring flower and growth.

II: HYBRIDS

'Avalanche'. NW, NC. To 8 ft. or more, at 6 in. a year. Pure white flowers, huge and fragrant.

'Betty Wormald'. S (shelter), NW, NC. To 7 ft. at 6 in. a year. Large leaves; funnel-shaped flowers, red in bud, pink when open.

'Blue Peter'. NE (shelter), S, NW, NC. Branches upright and open; to 7 ft. Small leaves; flowers lavender-violet, in cone-shaped trusses (clusters). Mid-spring.

'Blue Tit'. NW, NC. Compact, 2–3-ft.-tall shrub with small dark green leaves, gray-violet flowers that deepen in hue as they age.

'Bow Bells'. NW, NC. *R. Williamsianum* hybrid, with the attractive leaves of the parent — smallish, rounded, bronzy when new, mid-green when mature. Flowers cerise in bud, opening to pink bells. Rounded shrub, 3 ft. in 10 years.

'Brittania'. S (shelter), NW, NC. Dense, compact bush (4 ft. or more) with dark leaves and red flowers that are blood-bright, or close to it. Best in three-fourths shade; does not prosper in a garden where the air goes dry in summer.

'Carita'. NW, NC. Roundish leaves, canary-yellow bells early in spring, on a fairly compact 6-ft. shrub. Shade and humidity needs as for 'Brittania'.

'Cunningham's Pink' and 'Cunningham's White'. NE, S, NW, C. Smallish-leaved, smallish-flowered plants, uncommonly hardy, tough, and trustworthy. They are capable of soldiering through a season of abandonment and submergence beneath overgrowing weeds even in soil that dries in summer. The Cunninghams are slow growers, usually less than 6 in. a year.

'Fragrantissimum'. Only hardy in tropical or subtropical winters. Grown in the North as a tub plant, to be moved indoors for the winter. I'm liable to be picketed, piked, and poleaxed by militants for saying so, but this seems to me an especially feminine plant, with its willowy flexible branches and exquisite flowers, white with a rose suffusion outside, green-tinted within. The flowers exhale a heavenly scent of sugar and spice and everything nice.

'Gomer Waterer'. NE, S, NW, C. Very old selection or hybrid of the eastern *R. catawbiense* and one of the hardiest rhododendrons ever introduced. Wine-tinted white; to 6 ft. tall.

'Loder's White'. NW, NC. Unexcelled among the big-bodied, big-flowered hybrids. A 6-footer in its late teens; branches compact and lushly leafy; flowers mauve in bud, opening white with a ruffled pink margin.

'Mars'. NE (shelter), S, NW, C. To 4 ft. in 10 years. Flowers are crimson flared bells with white stamens; May–June.

'Moonstone'. S (shelter), NW, NC. Compact plant with rounded leaves, the flowers cream-colored cups flecked with red. To 2 ft. tall in 10 years or so.

'Purple Splendor'. NE (shelter), S, NW, NC. A rangy 4–5-footer. Flowers after the others have gone — in June in the North. Wide-open blossom with frilly petals, deep royal purple with black markings. Fairly drought-tolerant.

'Unique'. NW, NC. A rounded, leafy shrub, to 6 ft. Early-flowering, the corolla funnel-shaped, cream-yellow with red spots inside.

'Vulcan'. s, nw, nc. A compact 3-footer (in about 12 years). Massed with bright red flowers in June. Easy, and satisfying to one's hunger for a true red.

III: EVERGREEN AZALEAS

Gable azaleas. ne, nw, c, t. Twiggy, small-leaved shrubs. In the East, pink-flowered 'Louise Gable' is a deservedly popular plant. Other Gables are purple or white.

Gumpo azaleas. s, nw, c, t. Flat-growing, to a foot tall with age. Our Virginia consultant writes, "The late-blooming Gumpos, white, pink, and fancy, are practical shrubs. They make a great ground cover, low-growing, dense, with large flowers. I use them as edging along stone steps."

Indicum azaleas. c, t. Named forms stand 2–5 ft. tall; flower is white, pink, rose, purple, or salmon. Foliage rich: dark, lustrous green leaves, broadly elliptical.

Kaempferi azaleas. ne, s, nw. Small-leaved, open-branched, nudish shrubs to 3 ft. tall. Look their best when closely grouped and when clipped, after flowering, to compact and densen the branches. White-flowered 'Palestrina' is much planted in the South.

Kurume azaleas. nw, c, t. Neat, almost sheared-looking plants, low growers — mostly 18–24 in. tall. Little leaves of lion-ear shape, dense on the plant; lost beneath its flowers in May. Perhaps the most popular of the fairly countless varieties is 'Hinodegiri', crepe paper–red.

Mucronatum azaleas. nw (shelter), c, t. Under this heading, a pair of shrubs usually sold as *Azalea ledifolia* 'Alba' (white) and *A. ledifolia* 'Rosea' (rose-suffused white). To 2 ft. tall and wide in 10 years; branches bare-flanked and spiky, tipped with grayish-green leaves and big blossoms that have a hothouse look about them. Only half evergreen in a cold winter.

IV: DECIDUOUS AZALEAS

R. calendulaceum (Flame Azalea). ne, s, nw, nc. Eastern American, a tall mass of flowers, fire hydrant-yellow or orangeade-colored, in late spring.

R. luteum (Pontic Azalea). From eastern Europe. ne, s, gn, nw, nc. In semishade, an open shrub 6 ft. tall in 10 years, on its way to being a tree-shrub. May flowers of ripe-lemon color, sweetly scented. For a good loud flower party, underplant the azalea with *Endymion hispanicus (Scilla campanulata)*.

Mollis azaleas. s, nw, c. One of the grander color explosions of May-time, orange, yellow, cream, saffron, and an earnest near red. Growth is slow — about 6 in. a year — to 4 or 5 ft. Pick off fading flowers to prevent seed formation (which saps the strength of the plant). An old specimen gone thin or sluggish in its growth can be rejuvenated by heavy pruning immediately after the flowering. Cut away large branches at their juncture with main trunks, or cut out whole trunks at soil level (saving at least one). Paint all wounds. After such pruning, quick new shoots grow forth from old wood — usually.

R. quinquefolium (Cork Azalea). NW, NC. Japanese forest plant, best in moist, mossy shade. Leaves, in whorls of five, a soft green rimmed in spring with cordovan color. A slow-growing shrub — inches a year — but eventually tall and open-branched. White flowers after about age 12.

R. Schlippenbachii (Royal Azalea). NE, S, NW, C. Baron von Schlippenbach's name encumbers this magnificent woodland azalea from Korea and Manchuria. Big soft-pink flowers and big whorled leaves open together in April. Plant in a sheltered, half-shady location and keep it moist in summer. To 3 × 3 ft. in 10 years; an 8-footer at age 25. May enter into a decline in its mid-twenties, and then its name lends itself to a wry pun gardeners can't resist making. After its demise, a few seedlings usually spring up within a 20-ft. radius of the old location.

R. Vaseyi (Pink-Shell Azalea). NE, S, GN (shelter), NW, NC. Eastern American. Slender grower, arising in sinuous branches, becoming tall with age. Flowers pale pink with red spots.

R. viscosum (Swamp Azalea). NE, S, GN (shelter), NW, NC. Another fine eastern wildflower. Fragrant white or pink blooms late in spring. An 8-footer when in its twenties or thirties.

Ribes alpinum (Alpine Currant). NE, S, GN, NW, C, SW. Hardy Scandinavian shrub, useful in shade as a deciduous hedge. It is a close grower, leafy, self-neatening, and requiring little pruning except for formal effect; lends itself to the making of a hedge 5–8 ft. tall. Three-lobed leaves, small and roundish, medium green in the typical plant. Flowers greenish; currants red, but not palatable. Leaves of the form *R. alpinum* 'Aureum' open bright yellow, then deepen to green for the summer. Any well-drained soil.

Rosa (rose). Hybrid Musk Roses and the climbing roses will flower in full summer shade *if* they receive sun in spring, the season when they set their flower buds. Other roses, though they prefer sun, will accept half shade.

Rubus parviflorus. (Thimble Berry). NE, S, GN, NW, C. Stoloniferous shrub, 6 ft. or more tall. The 2½-in.-wide white flowers are like wild roses. Dark red raspberries, flavorful when ripe to the point of falling from the plant. Deciduous maple-shaped leaves of a fresh light green. Graceful in open woods; companionable with tall azaleas in high shade. Average soil or wet ground.

Sarcococca humilis (lance leaves) at the edge of a shady bed. Rounded leaves: *Cyclamen* × *Atkinsii*. Lower right corner: *Vaccinium Vitis-idaea*. Lower left: a bit of grass lawn, and just off the edge of the grass, the shiny, divided leaves of gold thread (*Coptis*). (DON NORMARK)

Ruta graveolens (Common Rue). Evergreen shrub for all climates except GN; deciduous NE. About 30 in. tall, glaucous blue in selected forms, green in others. Leaves compound, finely pinnate; small yellow flowers in clusters. A sun plant that performs well in shade up to three-quarters of the day. Valuable in its blue phase — a rare color in shade gardening. Prune to encourage bushiness. Any well-drained soil.

Sarcococca humilis. NW, C, T. Evergreen shrublet. Creeps slowly underground and tufts up a foot tall in stems of little dark, leathery leaves of willow leaf shape. The fragrant white flowers, in early spring, are like little bunches of sea anemone fingers; berries round and blue-black. Modest ground cover, reliable in full shade. Provide ideal shade garden soil.

Sarcococca ruscifolia (Fragrant Sweet Box). NW, C, T. Rounded shrub, a slow grower to 5 ft. tall. Pointed leaf broader than that of *S. humilis;* same fragrant white flowers; showy red berries. Goes well with *Aucuba.*

Skimmia japonica. S, NW, C. Shade garden standby, a 4–5-foot evergreen of a somewhat waxen weightiness, grown for its shiny green oval leaves and bright red autumn berries. Growth is slow — about 6 in. annually — the shrub compact and flat-topped. There is a white-berried form, of even slower growth. With either, you'll get a better crop of berries with a male shrub nearby. Any soil. North-wall shade, filtered shade, or afternoon shade. (With the last, there is a risk of sun-scorched foliage.)

Skimmia Reevesiana. C, T. To 2 ft. tall, 4 ft. wide, in 12 or more years. Retains its red, autumn berries until spring. The shrub is self-fertile. Acclimatability is the same as for *S. japonica.* Best in ideal shade garden soil, kept moist.

Symphoricarpos (Snowberry). For all climates. A group of rampantly spreading deciduous shrubs with white berries fall and winter. Crowd plants that will accept poor, rocky soil in nearly full shade. To get Snowberry started in a poor place, plant it in a fertile pocket of ideal shade garden soil and water it until the shrub gets going on its own; thereafter, it will need little, if any, help. However, recent garden hybrids are less wild-natured, more in need of good soil: *S.* 'White Hedger' is a compact grower; planted as a hedge, it won't get away.

Taxus (yew). NE, S, NW, C, T. Coniferous evergreens. The shrubby forms will grow in shade fuller than most plants can endure. Typical yew color is black-green. There are brighter foliage varieties: *Taxus baccata* 'Adpressa Aurea' is a goldish shrub to 6 ft. tall. *T. baccata* 'Argentea' is silvery white in new leaf, changing to straw color. *T. baccata* 'Aurea' is a compact bush whose leaves, gold at first, turn green in their second year. Others are gold or silvery, upright or bun-shaped.

Trochodendron aralioides (Wheel Tree). NE, S, NW, C, T. Japanese and Formosan. Slow-growing shrub when grown from a cutting; from seed, a small tree growing moderately fast. Handsome, tannish, evergreen leaves arranged in a whorl, with something of the visual mesmerism of a pinwheel. Ideal shade garden soil; half or full shade.

Vaccinium. Relatives of rhododendron, with the family's fine roots and abhorrence of drought. Tasty berries.

Vaccinium corymbosum (Highbush Blueberry). NE, S, GN, NW, C (worthwhile fruit production even in warm-winter areas). Eastern American native. One of the most valuable shade garden shrubs. A sun plant that will accept half shade readily and give a good crop, it will also set some fruit in a location warmed by only two or three hours' sun. A 5-ft. shrub in 10–15 years, in soil rich and moist, or boggy (dryish soil will retard this plant). Attractive in a woodsy planting with rhododendrons and other evergreen shade shrubs, which complement the deciduous blueberry. An exciting plant, with its year-round performance in five acts: In winter it presents a vigorous profile of upright and angular branches whose young twigs are a fresh russet or pale yellow. In spring it produces little white barrel flowers in clusters. Early-summer foliage is a tenderish green, the ovate leaves thin to translucence and lively with internal light. In later summer there are berries, black beneath a blue bloom, that, if unpicked, cling to the plant until autumn, augmenting the drama of leaves now lava-red.

Vaccinium ovatum (Evergreen Huckleberry). S, NW, C. Denizen of West Coast forests. A finely branched, small-leaved evergreen suggesting a refined Japanese Holly. Leaves leathery black-green with a waterish gloss. Small white flowers; black buckshot berries. Slow-growing: In most gardens, the shrub stands gardener-tall when about 25 years old (grows faster and taller in moist woods). Supply ideal shade garden soil with fast drainage; half shade, woods' shade, or north-wall shade.

Vaccinium parvifolium (Red Huckleberry). NE, S, GN, NW, C. West Coast native. In shade, an upright grower — to 8 ft. in 15 or 20 years — and one of the airiest of shrubs. Tiered branches with an intricate, angular, deciduous twigginess, the bark bright *Kerria*-green. Leaves are little light green ovals, pointillistic on the plant. Berries hang on the branches all through summer, a suspended shower of translucent coral-red globules. A rarity in nurseries but common enough in the woods. Seedlings up to about 10 in. tall transplant easily. Give it a sheltered location in full shade; ideal shade garden soil, moist and fast-draining. Will also grow in rotted wood without soil.

Viburnum × *carlcephalum*. April-flowering. A shrub for all climates; a treelike 10-footer when pruned up, a bushy 4-footer if pruned down. Grayish-green deciduous leaves; small white tubular flowers in rounded clusters 5 in. across. Any well-drained soil; half shade or somewhat more.

Viburnum Davidii. NW (shelter), C, T. An evergreen shrub all too popular. During the second half of this century, landscapers have planted many a thousand *V. Davidii* in parks and other public places. In spite of its handsomeness, *V. Davidii* (like Periwinkle and the plain big ivy) has become a plant no longer easy to view without tedium. Oval leaves 6 in. long, dark green and lustrous; on their surface, an interesting pattern of three deeply incised lines that follow the length of the leaf. Whitish flowers in flat corymbs. Gemmy turquoise-blue berries (to assure a crop, group several plants that have been grown from seed). *V. Davidii* is a flattish grower at a moderate rate, to about 21 in. high and 40 in. wide in a decade. Use it as an edging shrub in a shady bed and disregard my caviling about it.

Viburnum rhytidophyllum. NE, S, NW, C, T. To 12 ft. or more at about 15 in. annually. An upright grower that is responsive to pruning; easily turned into a mural plant or, by removing suckers and superfluous trunks, into a handsome, free-standing tree. Leaves canoe-shaped, nearly a foot long; dark grayish green with a low gloss; inset venation gives the leaf surface the quality of a relief map. Throughout winter and early spring, the shrub carries attractive fawn-colored flower buds in broad, flattened clusters. The buds open in May, displaying petals the color of parchment. Berries, red at first, then black, complete this shrub's performance, but only where several seedling plants are grown in the same garden. But who has room for more than one?

Big fellows such as this should be fitted into the landscape early on, of course, before the planting of any little sweetheart shrub, such as the one at the beginning of the list.

11

Ground Covers and Vines

Not so long ago, our only extensive uses of ground covers were in shade too dark for grass and on soil too steep for mowing. Then came the postwar influence of the gardens of Japan, with their cover plantings of such native greenery as evergreen azaleas, mosses, dwarf bamboos, epimediums, and Mondo. More recently, naturalism — that ground swell in North American style — has furthered the use of ground covers in place of manicured lawns. Up to a point.

The national outdoor carpet is still the grass lawn — wall to wall in most properties, with few other plantings. But in a generous minority of contemporary gardens, ground covers have taken over as the fashion of the day, partly or completely supplanting grass. In extreme examples, the absence of lawn and the overall sprawl of leafy mats and cushions that are not to be stepped on leave us nowhere to stroll in the garden except on strict walkways. In the parts of the garden to be carpeted, there is a golden mean between ground covers and lawn, and I think that it amounts to planting about half one and half the other. With moderation, the modern use of ground covers is a boon to the human senses, always in need of diversion from the routines of grass lawns and concrete.

Vines, meantime, have declined in garden use, along with the decline in the fashion for pergolas and trellises (they may all have come back in force by the time you read this). There is, right now, an agreeably antique atmosphere blended into the shade cast by an overhead vine, and by that of a side one as well. In the descriptions of plants below, many vines are recommended for ground cover planting: Simply provide no support and let the vine trail over the ground.

Many garden writers champion ground covers as work savers. Not true right away, possibly true in the long run. Surveying my own experience as a specialist in these plants, I would say they are work alterants, all right, but they're not likely to make liniment obsolete. All ground covers need weeding, and almost all require weeding by hand rather than with chemicals. The shorter the cover plant, the more weeding it will need year after year (a thyme or other flat plant of fine foliage is the perfect moist incubator for weed seeds that lodge in the leafy carpet). The better weed fighters among cover plants are those with dense, broad leaves held well above ground (such as the taller epimediums and hostas and certain geraniums), but even these usually require industrious weedings each summer in their first and second years and some weeding in the years thereafter. The upkeep of a ground cover, which includes occasional trimming and sprucing, certainly requires more of an investment of time and energy early on than one would put into the same extent of grass lawn, and in later years the maintenance of a cover planting cannot be much less than that of grass. The reward of planting ground covers is more sensual — for the eyes, the touch, the scent — and less a saving of time and energy for some preferred devilment.

Before setting out a cover plant, weed the ground deeply, taking care to remove any runners of wild grasses and roots of other gross invaders. Chemical weeding with a swiftly biodegradable substance may be of help, especially if the ground is tilled to a looseness that aids penetration of the poison. After planting, mulch the bare ground between the new plants; any kind of mulch except a weedy compost will help keep down weeds. Some gardeners spread weed-blocking plastic sheeting over the soil before planting shrubby ground covers, piercing the plastic wherever they would insert a plant.

Note: See p. 87 in chapter 9 for explanation of the region codes NE, S, GN, NW, C, NC, SC, SW, and T, which are used below to indicate where each ground cover and vine will grow well. Page 28 in chapter 2 gives a recipe for ideal shade garden soil, to which you will find references in this chapter. Where shade preferences are not given, dappled shade, afternoon shade, or bright north-wall shade will be just fine. Soil not mentioned? Ideal shade garden soil, kept moist, will suit the plant. Except for those plants identified as shrubby or woody, or any called a shrub or shrublet, all the entries in this chapter are nonwoody perennials. Here, then, are the best ground covers and vines for shade.

Aegopodium Podograria (Bishop's Weed). For all climates; most often planted in the cold-winter interior of North America. A reliable, undemanding ground cover for any shady piece of ground; a foot or so tall, rapidly spreading and invading, but roots are shallow and they harmlessly overlie those of taller companion plants. Bishop's Weed has divided deciduous leaves, Box Elder–like in outline, typically of plain green; but white-variegated *A. Podograria* 'Variegatum' is the form usually planted. To

Perennial ground cover, *Galium odoratum* (Asperula or Sweet Woodruff) will, if closely planted in spring, grow into a solid leafy quilt by September. These husky young plants are being set out about ten inches apart. Note that the gardener (August Libao, without whose care for my garden there would be no garden to write about) plants all the asperulas so that their stems lean in the direction of fullest daylight.

Same planting of Sweet Woodruff in flower a year later.

Bishop's Weed (*Aegopodium Podagraria* 'Variegatum'), of kaleidoscopic pattern.
(DON NORMARK)

shorten and freshen Bishop's Weed, run a lawn mower over it once in the summer; it will come back ankle-high.

Ajuga reptans (Carpet Bugleweed). For all climates. Low ground cover and coordinator of shady plants, its foliage flows like a tide around the bases of azaleas, ferns, and all others in a shady bed, and they become as comradely as members of a swimming party. The ajuga stands 4 in. tall in leaf, 10 in. with its springtime spikes of violet flowers. There are leaf forms green, purpurescent, or variegated; the last tend to revert and require frequent roguing to prevent the takeover of pure green leaves. *A. reptans* 'Atropurpurea', the commonest ajuga and among the best, turns purply bronze in part shade, shiny spinach-green in heavy shade (which affords only shy flowering). For full cover in one summer, plant divisions 6 in. apart in early spring or fall.

Anemone nemorosa (Wood Anemone). All climates except T. Spring anemone from European woods, and one of the greater delights of shade gardening. Grows 6–9 in. tall, with soft-blue cups over dark green cleft leaves. Wood Anemones have little twig-like, brittle rhizomes that creep and multiply rapidly an inch or less beneath the surface of woodsy soil. A planting of a few rhizomes can give you a thousand-flowered carpet in several years. Though invasive, Wood Anemone is harmless to other, taller shade flowers and ferns in the same bed. There is also a double white form of Wood Anemone, rather slow to increase.

Arabis caucasica (*A. albida*, Wall Rock Cress); and *A. alpina* (Snow-on-the-Mountain). Grand old rockery plants for gardeners everywhere. Cushions of toothed gray leaves, massed with fragrant white flowers in spring. Sun-loving, but they give a good show on as little as three hours' sun a day.

Arabis Sturii. All climates. Close-growing ground cover mat for sun or shade. Little dark green shiny leaves, showy white flowers (midspring). For solid cover in one season, set out divisions the size of small broccoli heads, at 6-in. intervals.

Ardisia japonica (Marlberry). s (in coastal gardens), NW (warm shade), c. Forest-inhabiting shrublet from Japan. Creeps about and sends up a colony of equal branches, in the manner of *Sarcococca* — but ardisia is an even slower and choicer ground-covering shrub. Requires moist shade and makes a superb underling for tall azaleas, vacciniums, and other Ericaceae. A foot high, more or less. Leaves in tufts at the branch tips, willowish in shape but thick and glossy, reddish bronze when young, ripening to a deep evergreen color. Little white flowers in fall and showy red berries that overwinter. Slow growth makes this a costly plant when used en masse, and therefore it is seldom given large jobs of landscape work. To use as a ground cover, plant a foot or less apart; or space widely, and then interplant the ardisias with a low, quick cover that has roots that are easy to get along with: mossy saxifrages, *Pratia*, *Soleirolia*, Corsican Mint, sedums, Strawberry Geranium. This scheme — interplanting with low, harmless companion plants — will give immediate garden fullness to a sparse planting of any slow ground cover.

Arenaria verna (*Sagina subulata*). All climates. Comes in two forms: Irish Moss (a bright green) and Scotch Moss (yellow-green). If, on his or her plan, your landscape architect assigns these pretty mat makers to ground areas that receive more than light shade, send the rascal back to the drawing board. Don't know how many failing plantings of these I've seen in professionally designed shady gardens.

Asarum (wild ginger). *A. canadense*, of eastern North America, and *A. caudatum*, of the West, are neat, flat ground covers — deciduous East, evergreen West; in regions NE, s, NW, c. Leaves are dark and heart-shaped; flowers are earthy red urns hidden beneath the leaves. The ginger-flavored rhizomes are delicious when candied. In a city or suburban garden, apply snail/slug bait frequently to divert these pests from a plant they relish above most others. Wild Ginger is easy to keep, however — even without baiting — in a large wooded garden that fosters its own pest-controlling fauna. *A. Hartwegii* of California (NW, c) and *A. Thunbergii* of Japan (c, T) are ground covers with beautiful marbled leaves. These two demand especially mossy-moist woodsy conditions. Plant any of the Wild

Gingers about a foot apart for solid cover in two years. Growth is slow at first, moderate after the plant settles in.

Asparagus Sprengeri. sc, sw (shelter), T. Fluffy-appearing, with its arching, cascading branches densely set with fine bright green needles. A famous hanging basket plant. Equally good as a ground cover (pleasantly tousled) or draping down over a wall (as much as 6 ft.). Shade, half or nearly full. Attractive with large ferns, philodendrons, and begonias.

Bergenia. Leaves large, roundish, glabrous, and lustrous, like Ping-Pong paddles made of green patent leather. They are clustered in a low perennial tuft that creeps slowly and forms a weighty evergreen ground cover. One-inch-wide white, rose, or purple flowers in clusters, on plump stems a foot high; late winter and early spring. Plant beneath trees or lanky shrubs. The common bergenias are hybrids of two Siberian species, *B. cordifolia,* with heart-shaped leaves, and *B. crassifolia* (Siberian Tea), with oval leaves; the purebred parents are seldom seen in gardens. These bergenias are hardy well below 0°F even without snow and thrifty in all above zero climates. Equally hardy is *B. ciliata* (Winter Begonia), which has delightful dwarf forms for the shady alpine bed. *B. Stracheyi,* hardy NW and in warmer parts, offers both a pink and a pure white 'Alba' form; the leaves turn crabapple-purple in winter. Once planted, bergenias carry on for years and need little care beyond the pruning away of withering leaves. They can be long-suffering survivors of poor soil, drought, and every garden neglect but will repay better treatment with lusher growth and ampler flowers on taller stems.

Bolax glebaria. For all climates except GN. From the Straits of Magellan. Strangely attractive. A hard cushion 5 in. tall, 16 in. across in several years, with dark evergreen leaves that are feathered; studded in early summer with green umbellifer flowers. Likes a moist half-shady place. To propagate, tear a large clump to pieces in high summer and plant the divisions where they are to grow; keep them watered. Pieces set out at 6-in. intervals will soon unite into an even ground cover.

Campanula Poscharskyana. Yugoslavian. A strong grower in all garden climates. Small divisions planted a foot apart rapidly form a finely textured, dark evergreen ground cover. In early summer, the plant explodes into a huge mass of violet stars: It is, for a couple of weeks, the most beautiful thing in the world. Then the flower stems lengthen and flop, and the plant will need tolerance for a month or so until it clears itself of spent parts (pruning will help). But listen to this: Full-flowering in full shade (also in lighter shades and in sun), it is a tough, permanent cover that will take drought beneath trees or even beneath north-wall eaves, and a natural wall plant that will climb stonework or old, moist brick.

Cissus antarctica (Kangaroo Vine). c, T. Scrambling or cascading skein of birchlike evergreen leaves. An alternative to English Ivy, in full shade or sun. *C. rhombifolia,* the well-known Grape Ivy, offers the same outdoor uses as the Kangaroo Vine, in the same climates.

Campanula Poscharskyana flowering exuberantly in full north-wall shade. The plant has the habit, acquired in its wildflower existence on stormy cliffs in Dalmatia, of bracing its flower stems firmly against any handy surface. Star flowers measure an inch across. Garden of Bob Putnam.

Clivia miniata. C, T. The foliage suggests agapanthus: evergreen strap leaves, thick almost to succulence, in a clump 1 or 2 ft. tall. In early spring, gorgeous orange-apricot flowers in a cluster; red berries in late summer. At the base of a tree, in moderate shade and reasonable soil, the clump will slowly broaden to 6 ft. or more across and increase in handsomeness for decades. One of the few ground covers healthy in dry soil beneath pines. To gain new plants, divide an established clump in winter or early spring. Place divisions a foot apart for quick cover.

Clytostoma callistegioides. C, SW, T. Better known by an older name, *Bignonia violacea,* or by the common name, Trumpet Vine. Generous evergreen curtain for a high shady bank: Plant at bottom or top. Big lavender flowers, shaped like tubas.

Convallaria majalis (Lily-of-the-Valley). All climates except T. A spring flower and an easy-to-grow deciduous ground cover 8 in. tall, with a good deal of spreading power. It has a crowd of alert fox-ear leaves arising in pairs, and brief flower staffs carrying fragrant white bells, not large and not showy — yet the world is in love with this flower. There is a double form, ampler than the single, but with a consequent loss of flower character; a washy pink form ('Rosea'); a streaked-leaved form ('Striata'), slow-growing, with the usual single white flowers and dark leaves, except that the latter are decorated with fine gold-green vein lines of wonderfully sure draftsmanship.

Plant Lily-of-the-Valley in the fall, from pips (a pip is a crown bud with an attached section of rhizome). Set them out beneath half-shady trees and shrubs, in new soil or in freshly turned old soil. The plant likes humus in the ground and *on* the ground in the form of a shallow topdressing of compost or peat during its dormancy. Once planted, Lily-of-the-Valley can be left alone for twenty years or more, "to go from strength to strength," as the British say of plants that settle in to stay. Or it can be divided any fall from the second one onward, as soon as the leaves turn yellow; transplanting in spring growth is less convenient but can be done. Very tolerant of drought in shade.

Cornus canadensis (Bunchberry, Creeping Dogwood). For all garden climates, including SC (but perhaps excepting T). Found in woods across North America, as far south as Pennsylvania, Minnesota, and the Mendocino Coast of California. I once sent a quantity of nursery-grown *C. canadensis* to southern California, at the insistence of an adventuresome gardener in Beverly Hills. I had tried to to tell my customer that the plants were not built for his climate and had little chance of surviving. A year later he wrote back: *C. canadensis* was growing apace; he wanted more plants with which to extend his planting.

It is an underground vine with stems that shoot along in woodsy ground just below the moss, or follow fissures in rotted logs. It tufts up half a foot tall, in stems of little Dogwood tree leaves and white bract flowers an inch wide. The spring flowers ripen into orange-tinted clusters of beady scarlet

Cornus canadensis beneath a rhododendron. (DON NORMARK)

berries. Pot plants are sometimes available, but more often nurseries sell collected sods.

In the East, Bunchberry is a protected rare plant. In western states where it is abundant, the U.S. Forest Service sometimes issues permits to collect plants for home landscaping. September–October is the best time for harvesting. Select cornus plants from the sunniest location possible and dig 7–10-in.-wide sods.

Plant Bunchberry in part shade or dappled shade, in ideal shade garden soil mulched before planting with a 2-in. depth of sawdust, fresh or rotted. To plant each sod or pot plant, scoop away the sawdust, set the Bunchberry in bare ground, and draw the sawdust closely about the plant. *C. canadensis* is slow to establish, then a vigorous spreader. Keep it moist.

Crassula multicava (C, SW, T) is the novice shade gardener's friend indeed. It will grow quickly into an evergreen ground cover anywhere, in sun or shade — even in dense shade, even in impossibly poor ground — and will fill the space with pleasant greenery, perhaps while choicer plants are growing on to take its place. Then, when or if the time comes, it is an easy plant to dissuade: Rake it from the ground and add it to the compost heap for still further service. When I recommended it to impossible ground, I was thinking of a straight up and down soil cut, dry, hard, and fully shaded, in which I planted rootless branches of this a year ago, using a large screwdriver to pick planting holes in the crude ground, then sticking in the crassula and plastering it in place with mud. Result, a year later: a solid foliage cover over an ugly soil cut. The leaves are racket-shaped, 1½ in. long, pea-green, with oddly human pores on the leaf surface. Flowers are pink stars in open sprays on slim stems, late winter and throughout spring.

Cymbalaria. Two mat-forming perennials and one scrambler. All are dainty in leaf and flower (quarter-inch snapdragons) and are evergreen in a warm winter. Use as small-area ground covers, edging plants, rock wall climbers, and hanging container plants, in shade light to full.

Cymbalaria aequitriloba. NW, C, SW, T. Sardinian. A 1-in.-high mat, leaves of lima bean shape and size (with a bit of a heartpoint at the leaf tip); flowers are little purple dragon heads.

Cymbalaria hepaticifolia. NW, C, SW, T. Corsican native. A soil-covering sheet of green, kidney-heart leaves with an attractive pattern of pale green veins; the flowers are tiny mock-fierce dragons, lilac-purple. In half shade, the leaves press tightly against the soil, and there the plant will tolerate being walked on; in full shade, the leaves and stems stand all of an inch tall and are too tender for foot traffic. The plant spreads about a 1½ ft. a year, on spaghettinilike thin white runners that lie just under the soil surface, harmless to taller shade plants. The fast-growing *Cymbalaria* will unite a new planting of ferns or evergreen azaleas and make a garden of it while the other plants are filling out. (Compare with *Soleirolia Soleirolii*, below.)

Cymbalaria muralis (Kenilworth Ivy). All climates except GN. European native naturalized in North American cities, in alley cat haunts. In appearance an elfin ivy (though not related), it is a downward or upward scrambler on thread-slim branches. The leaves are little scalloped hearts; tiny lilac or (rarely) white flowers hover over the foliage on nearly invisible stems. Kenilworth Ivy is a perennial that often behaves like an annual in the North. If frost takes it, seedlings will carry on year after year. Common in nineteenth-century gardens, the plant still grows in cracked retaining walls and in the dark shade cast by high old houses.

Like the true ivy (above), Kenilworth Ivy, *Cymbalaria muralis* (below), twines its way up a grapestake fence. (DON NORMARK)

Seed of Kenilworth Ivy is sold (as an annual) by at least one seed company, but if you find the plant growing somewhere, pinch a few pods of seed and scatter them in the darker corners of your garden. I believe you'll enjoy the vagrant self-sufficiency of this sprite.

Dichondra repens. c, sw, t. Little green gerbil-ear leaves in a carpet, useful as a lawn in shade or sun. If possible, prepare for the dichondra lawn, before you set out other plants in the vicinity, by treating the soil with a quickly biodegradable fumigant to get rid of weeds. Sow dichondra thickly in warm spring weather or in summer and sprinkle it daily to keep it moist; in six weeks your lawn should be thick and serviceable. Dichondra equals grass in resistance to foot traffic and stays green with less water when the weather gets hot and dry. In shade it requires mowing to keep it compact. (Compare this plant with *Soleirolia Soleirolii,* below.)

Duchesnea indica (Indian Strawberry). India and Japan. Hardy everywhere. Strawberry leaves, yellow flowers, and attractive but tasteless red strawberries held point upward above the foliage; an evergreen mat 5–9

Indian Strawberry *(Duchesnea indica)* in fruit beneath a philadelphus (branches at upper right): an early summer picture. (DON NORMARK)

in. tall. An easy cover plant, drought-tolerant and rampant (faster than ivy). Suited to rather wild ground in light-to-full shade, or to a shady passageway between buildings, with ferns and Solomon's Seal rising through the strawberry carpet.

Epimedium. Several in this genus are stoloniferous foliage plants of the highest value as covers for shady ground. Other epimediums are clump makers grown for the elegance of their leaves and small flowers. Leaves in threes at the tops of slim, firm stems, the leaflets in the shape of a Vandyke beard. Above the leaves hover flowers of grapnel form. In general, epimediums enjoy moist soil and all shades of shade except the dark or dense. Two of the plants are drought-tolerant.

Epimedium grandiflorum. For all climates. A Japanese wildflower with hybrid offspring. Available in violet and yellow, and in the descriptively named varieties Rose Queen and White Queen. All grow as slowly widening clumps of half-evergreen foliage. Propagate in early spring, using a butcher knife to cut the tough basal part of the plant into wedges.

Epimedium Perralderianum. For all climates. Algerian. Vigorous ground cover 2 ft. tall. Leaves bronzy evergreen. This, the only showy epimedium, has bright yellow spring flowers up to an inch across, one or two dozen together in a raceme. Divisions that are set out 9–12 in. apart (September and October) and topdressed with ground bark or sawdust will appear gardeny at once and will spread into a uniform, weed-beating ground cover in two years. When established, this plant is as tough and drought-tolerant as ivy. In botanical gardens and nurseries, *E. Perralderianum* has been confused with *E. pinnatum colchicum,* a subspecies with small bright yellow flowers.

Epimedium × *rubrum.* For all climates. A broadish clump: in ten years, 3 ft. wide by 2 ft. tall. The plant has considerable value as furnishing, and very possibly, as a ground cover: Divisions set out closely will form an even cover soon enough. New foliage is red-bronze with darkish markings; with maturity the leaves turn green. Small red-and-white flowers.

Epimedium × *versicolor* 'Sulphureum'. All climates. Grows 2 ft. tall, is strongly stoloniferous, and as a tough, drought-tolerant evergreen ground cover, is as valuable as *E. perralderianum.* Light yellow flowers, small and dainty, a few to a stem.

Epimedium Warleyense. All climates. Tangerine-colored flowers, evergreen leaves. The plant stands more or less a foot tall and spreads slowly — to 2 ft. wide in about five years. The plant was something of a bambino to its first owner. It appeared spontaneously (as a bee-ministered hybrid, no doubt) in England's Warley Garden. The lady of that estate would never give anyone a start of *Epimedium Warleyense,* but guarded it closely throughout her life, throughout decades of visiting

Shield-shaped leaves of *Epimedium* × *Youngianum* overflow the bricks. Alongside it, plants of impatiens, stippled in for summer color. (GEORGE TALOUMIS)

garden clubs. But a good plant, once entered into the trade, finds its way around the world with alacrity, as this one has. Seek it in rare-plant nurseries.

***Epimedium* × *Youngianum*.** For all climates. To 9 in. tall, and after 6 years or so, a foot wide. Deciduous. *E. Youngianum* 'Niveum' has snowy flowers, as the name claims; in the variety 'Roseum' (synonym 'Lilacinum'), the flowers are a pale lilac color; both are as light and fresh as a Mayfly. Plant in a moist, sheltered bed. This isn't much of a ground cover, though it could be a limited one if divided and replanted industriously. Accept its inclusion in this chapter, if you will, as an effort on my part to keep a good family together.

Episcia cupreata (Flame Violet). T. Colombian gesneriad with small scarlet flowers and elliptical leaves; many colorful named leaf forms. Plant in ideal shade garden soil or loamy soil, in moderate tree shade. The plant romps about, makes a choice ground cover.

Euonymus Fortunei (Winter Creeper). For all climates. This somewhat woody trailing plant of many garden forms is widely available. Easy to grow in good or poor soil, in light intensities varying from bright north-wall shade to dappled shade beneath trees to full sun. Green-leaved *E. Fortunei radicans*, a common old-timer, remains one of the best: a rough ground cover or wall screen, with 1¼-in.-long, dark-hued oval leaves. *E. Fortunei* 'Colorata' has similar foliage, except that it turns purple in winter; in growth and landscape uses, like radicans. *E. Fortunei* 'Vegeta', has larger leaves than the others, is a looser grower less able to support itself on walls or fences. *E. Fortunei* 'Kewensis', a delightful miniature with slender close branches and ¼-in. leaves, grows perhaps 6 in. a year. Plant in a shady rock garden, against the column of a birdbath, or at the top or bottom of a low wall. *E. Fortunei* is also available in several gold- or silver-variegated leaf forms, visual spice in the shady garden.

Ferns. Several kinds of ferns, described in chapter 12, make feathery ground covers. They are *Adiantum venustum, Dennstaedtia punctilobula, Gymnocarpium Dryopteris, Nephrolepis cordifolia, Polypodium, Thelypteris,* and *Woodwardia.*

Ficus pumila (Creeping Fig). NW (in warm shade), C, SW, T. Curtain for a north or east wall; affixes itself tightly to any surface, even glass. Its small leaf conveys a deceiving daintiness. With age, Creeping Fig grows woody and muscular; the vine is quite capable of covering a 40-ft.-high wall in 10 years or so (in the tropics at least — slower in more northerly climates). With maturity, coarse-leaved fruiting branches (analogous to those of a fruiting ivy) erupt from the smooth vine surface. Prune them off when they appear. As an occasional lesson in no nonsense, cut the entire vine to the ground; it will come again. This plant is the friend not only of the gardener but of the architect and builder, a leafy eraser of walls that are better unseen. *F. pumila* 'Minima', with smaller leaves and a less eager habit, is the one to use on low walls and smallish surfaces.

Fragaria chiloensis (Beach Strawberry). NE (in coastal gardens), S, NW, C, SW, T. Native to beaches along the Pacific Coast of North and South America but fits easily into settings worlds away from the beach, such as wooded gardens and in house shade (north or east wall). A dark evergreen mat made of shiny and leathery strawberry leaves zipping about on reddish runners; some of the leaves age to a bright red and keep the color over winter. Spring flowers are like white wild roses and grow an inch across, or half again as large in the selected form, *F. chiloensis* 'Green Pastures'. Fruit is not forthcoming in inland shade gardens. A spirited ground cover well worth a broadish ribbon of ground, as beside a half-shaded drive, along with small maples and mahonias. I would like to see Beach Strawberry — a natural sand plant — used as carpeting around the edges of a children's sand garden and, tufting here and there from the sand, nandina or phormium or other plants that are reasonably proof against tot and Tasmanian Devil.

Fragaria vesca (Alpine Strawberry). For all climates. By now, perhaps, better known as fraise des bois: Through brilliant advertising by an eastern American mail-order nursery, the French appellation has become common coin among gardeners all over the country.

In habit, Alpine Strawberries are tufted, rather than running, about 10 in. tall, with typical strawberry leaves. The white flowers and small tangy fruits appear sporadically through the summer and autumn. In a moist, semishaded garden, the plants will seed about in a most satisfying way into a permanent evergreen ground cover, a strawberry field forever. Alpine Strawberries are available in several named red-fruited forms, which are much alike, and in *F. vesca* albicarpa, whose white berry, fully ripened on the plant, is a luscious tidbit — the best of the lot. Incidentally, birds don't recognize white strawberries as ripe fruit; they leave them alone, waiting for the redness that signals sweetness.

Fragaria vesca. Naturalized Alpine Strawberries cover this north slope with a carpet self-made by a few original plants set out several years before. Japanese Maples, Vine Maples, and an azalea complete the woodland community. Garden of Sue Olsen. (DON NORMARK)

For ground-covering purposes as well as for berries, *F. vesca* 'Baron Solemacher' remains unexcelled among red-fruited varieties. Grow from seed, which is available from several seed houses. Soil for Alpine Strawberries needn't be particularly good; the plants will increase gladly in an unprepared clay or in gravel, as long as there is a little humus on top of the ground and the ground never goes dry.

Galax urceolata (*G. aphylla;* Wandflower). NE, S, GN, NW, C. Evergreen perennial native to woods in eastern North America. A beautiful foliage plant, with the appearance and habits of a creeping shrublet: It forms a low, dense clump of bronze-green roundish leaves 3 or 4 in. across, leathery and polished. The tiny white flowers in spikes are of minor interest. Rhizomes slowly extend the clump to a 1-yd. wide patch in perhaps 12 years. Requires moist soil and part or full shade. Choice ground cover beneath azaleas or small-growing trees.

Galium odoratum (*Asperula odorata;* Asperula, Sweet Woodruff). For all climates. An old-time flavoring herb. In shade gardening, a finely textured carpeting plant, about 6 in. deep and outward bound at a gratifying speed. A single rooted piece no bigger than your thumb can give you a Sweet Woodruff carpet the size of a living room rug in three years, if you divide the plant each season. Rooted pieces, planted in April or early May, 7 in. or so apart in ideal shade garden soil — or even in hard ground scantily topdressed with humus — will cover completely by early September. The unit of the plant is a thin rooted stem dressed in whorls of narrow evergreen or semievergreen leaves and topped with sprays of tiny white, honey-and-horehound-scented flowers. Sweet Woodruff flowers all-over white in May. Grow it beneath trees or in north-wall or afternoon shade. You can have your plant and imbibe it too. Add a few flowering sprigs to a fruit compote and pour in a bottle of Chablis or other dry white wine.

Gardenia contains, among its garden varieties, a fragrant ground cover. *See* chapter 10.

Gaultheria. Evergreen shrublets and shrubs, country cousins of the rhododendron, to be grown in ideal shade garden soil.

Gaultheria cuneata. NW, NC. Himalayan. Slow ground-covering shrublet; leaves small, grayish green; showy white berries. *G. Miqueliana*, of Japan, is closely related; berries pink-flushed or clear white.

Gaultheria procumbens (Wintergreen). NE, S, NW, NC. Eastern American native. Original source of oil of wintergreen (now largely synthesized); when bruised, the dark green lustrous leaves and red berries release their unmistakable scent. Flat-growing ground cover for half shade or the filtered shade of young trees. Plant at intervals of about 1 ft. Spreads moderately.

Geranium Endressii. Adaptable to gardens in all climates. Native to the Pyrenees. Pink flowers held on stems 15 in. tall. Spreads by prostrate

Gaultheria Miqueliana at the edge of a raised bed (one log high). This stoloniferous shrublet comes up in eight-inch-tall tufts of small olive-green oval leaves that are deeply netted with a crackle pattern, like the glaze of old pottery. White or pinkish urns in April; white corrugated fruits in summer. (DON NORMARK)

branches that plow along through the leaf mold epidermis of the soil, half in, half out; also spreads by self-sown seed. All in all, rather too much of a spreader if planted in the community of more circumspect, clump-forming plants. But one of the best of all perennials for use as a ground cover in casually cultivated areas, where it will out-muscle many weeds and survive drought. After the main summer flowering, the plant can be mowed or sheared to bring on fresh foliage neatly close to the ground and a second major crop of flowers. Half-evergreen, north; fully evergreen in warm-winter areas.

Geranium macrorrhizum. Growable everywhere. A Mediterranean native. A deep and dense spread of maplelike leaves, sweetly musky — oil of geranium is distilled from this plant. Flowers of available forms are magenta, clear pink, or bluish white (*F. macrorrhizum* 'Album'). One of the best of all ground covers, shrubby or perennial, macrorrhizum grows 10 in. tall and widens its territory about 9 in. annually. The plant is drought-tolerant and covers permanently in half shade or beneath deciduous trees without going threadbare in patches (the finale of many groundcovers). The dense, shingled leaves smother most weeds. Macrorrhizum is deciduous in the North, evergreen in warm-winter regions.

One plant from the nursery, grown on for about two summers, can give you stock sufficient to set out quite a sweep. To propagate, lift the geranium in mid-July, cut it into so many rooted branches, replant the branches in a half-shady nursery bed, and water them every day (or enough to keep the ground surface moist). By about mid-September the branches will have made additional roots and will be ready to function as separate plants. Plant them now in their permanent place, or wait until spring. With high success, I've used this same technique of summer propagating in the open ground (or in nursery flats kept in the open) for hundreds of kinds of shade plants that grow into divisible clumps — campanulas, astilbes, saxifrages, heucheras, epimediums, and many others.

Glechoma hederacea (*Nepeta hederacea;* Ground Ivy). This European native, brought over on some early Atlantic crossing, is now an escapee from old gardens in many parts of North America and a naturalized citizen in woodsy places. Two forms: the wild green one, which is hardy everywhere and permanent, and the white-variegated garden form, miffy in a northern winter. Either kind is a plant for grown-ups only, I would say — not for a garden frequented by children. I would say this because of something I recall: When I was a five-year-old habitué of the woods near our home, I loathed the plant. The pungent smell of the foliage was enough to make me instantly sick and dizzy; I had to hold my breath and dash over the part of the path where it grew. But by my young adulthood, the odor of Ground Ivy had faded to an agreeable sageiness, and now, in middle life, I find it almost without scent. A plant for the mature gardener, then, whose sense of smell has declined, as happens with the passing years. Leaves small, reniform, scallop-edged, dark green in the typical form; tiny blue flowers like discreet gems amidst the leafage. A durable plant for poor ground beneath trees, growing several yards wide in several years.

Hedera (ivy). In terms of square footage, the most important shade garden plant. The total dimensions of the all-American ivy blanket that covers ground, fences, walls, tree trunks, and lost tools and toys no doubt equal the acreage of Connecticut, add or subtract Rhode Island. More than 200 named garden forms of this woody vine are to be found in North America. As a project for this book, your intrepid author has grown and studied 130 ivies obtained from the American Ivy Society, an organization that supports itself by selling nicely rooted cuttings of the hederas in its comprehensive collection. I've kept the plants in pots for seven years now and have kept an open mind toward them. By now, I'm ready to say that many of the named ivies are as distinguishable one from another as a potful of collard greens. At the same time, I've come to recognize several dozen ivies as being special. In listing a selection of these I use, for the most part, nomenclature put forth by the American Ivy Society in its *Preliminary Checklist of Cultivated Hedera.*

Hedera canariensis (Algerian Ivy) and *H. colchica* (Colchis Ivy). NW (warm shade), C, SW, T. Two ivies as alike as Tweedledee and Tweedledum. Both dark, coarse climbers with three-to-five-lobed leaves as wide as salad plates; there are also variegated forms. Sensitive to frost, hot sun, and drought. Shear in spring to flatten the branch mass against a wall; snip wayward branches when they appear during summer. The coolly colored form *H. colchica* 'Aureomaculata Variegata', has achieved a place in art history, in photographs of its leaf by Edward Weston and others. The big leaf (on a stem of soft wine-red) is cream-margined around its three lobes; inside, it is dark green, marbled together with two shades of gray-green.

Hedera Helix (English Ivy). NE, S, NW, C, SW, T. Some forms are hardy in sheltered gardens in the western prairies. The big-leaved parent plant is a yard-a-year ground cover; as a climber it will ascend or descend to cover a 30-ft.-high wall in a couple of decades, and a tall dead tree even faster. A tree had best be dead before ivy is turned loose on it; ivy's taking over of a living tree is a botanical horror on a par with *The Invasion of the Body Snatchers.* Please *do* mind that ivy when it first starts up the tree trunk.

English Ivy — the parent plant or its offspring — will prosper in denser shade and in poorer ground (including gravelly subsoil) than almost any other plant. If you have a hardship location to plant, ivy will survive, even thrive, if anything will. Plant in fall or spring. If the ground is hard and dry, irrigate deeply and cultivate. Dig in humus and add fertilizer if the ground is deficient (for though ivy would, as I claim, grow in rocks, it will cover faster and more lushly in a good soil). Plant starts of the parent ivy about 2 ft. apart, smaller kinds more closely.

To grow your own ivy from cuttings, take firm pieces mid-August to mid-October. Cuttings should be about 3–15 in. long (the longer the yearly vine growth of the ivy variety, the longer the cutting). Insert them closely together, in the greenhouse or in the open, into ideal shade garden soil. If the cuttings are to be rooted in the open, choose a temperate (not too chilly) location in filtered shade. Keep the cuttings and ground moist. By the following May or June, if all goes well, you'll have strongly rooted ivy plants ready to be regimented out as a ground cover. (Cuttings taken in summer, and planted again in the open, may not make it, but if they do, they'll root more vigorously than fall cuttings.)

Shear and edge established ivy in spring, and as needed during summer. In snail country, broadcast bait over the ivy patch several times a season.

When the typical ivy meets a climbable object and makes its way upward, a remarkable latent sense comes to the fore in the cells of its stems: Of a sudden, the plant develops in its higher reaches a mind to flower and set seed. Dense, short, shrubby branches grow from the vine and on them appear unlobed leaves, chartreuse flowers, and black berries. Cuttings of the fertile branches will grow into shrubby ivies rather than viny ones. Several of these shrubs are described below, along with some of the best of the medium-size and smaller vine-forming ivies with foliages and habits smaller than those of the old father/mother ivy, with its leaves big as bear paws.

Hedera colchica 'Aureomaculata variegata' guarded by a stone lion. The poor beast has shattered its jaw trying to pronounce the name.

English Ivy (*Hedera Helix*) greens this north wall completely. The plant, common large-leaved ivy, has climbed seventeen feet of masonry at about a foot a year. Shrubs are Portuguese Laurels, trees are London Plane.

Ivies, ivies. English Ivy (*Hedera Helix*) — like the common dog (*Canis familiaris*) — has ramified into an amazing number of breeds, dainty or jumbo, swift or mincing. More than two hundred different English Ivies grow in North American gardens. Here are portraits of some distinctive varieties: A. The parent plant, *Hedera Helix*. And its progeny: (B) 'Green Feather', (C) 'Carolina Crinkle', (D) 'Discolor', (E) 'Buttercup', (F) 'Ray Supreme', (G) 'Fluffy Ruffles', (H) 'Pedata', (I) 'Needlepoint', (J) 'Goldheart', (K) 'Trieste', (L) 'California Fan'. Scale: The small oval leaf (of Mountain Ash) located near the lower left of the composition measures an inch long.

And more ivies. (M) *Hedera Helix* 'Triton', (N) 'Deltoidea', (O) 'Silver Emblem',
(P) 'Pedata', fruiting branch, (Q) 'Baltica', (R) 'Ivalace', (S) 'Pittsburgh',
(T) 'Cockleshell', (U) 'Conglomerata' (ruffly leaves) and 'Erecta' (leaves in two
ranks) on one branch (a sporting branch from an old specimen of 'Conglomerata'
here gives rise to 'Erecta'), (V) 'Manda's Crested'. Scale: The small oval leaf (lower
left) measures one inch.

Pet ivy. Years of disciplinary pruning have gone into the training of this small-leaved English Ivy (*Hedera Helix* 'Shamrock'). The lively corner planting in full shade contains small-growing rhododendrons and the plumiest of ferns (*Polystichum setiferum* 'Plumoso-Divisilobum'). (GEORGE TALOUMIS)

Hedera Helix 'Baltica'. Discovered growing under pines in Latvia and sent to the Arnold Arboretum in 1907. Perhaps the hardiest of ivies — few, if any, equal it — and one of the best ground-covering ivies. Dense, flat grower; leaves smallish, dark green with pale veins. 'Big Deal' is slow and shrubby. This is the "geranium ivy," so called for its medium green rounded and puckered leaves, rather like those of garden geranium. For pot gardening or a choice shrub bed.

Hedera Helix 'California' is a stocky-branched, bushy ground cover, full of leaves and readily rooting along the stems. Moderate in growth, glossy medium green. 'California Fan' has fan-shaped leaves with five to nine short lobes, the spaces in between are goffered. Leaves the color of the hide of a smooth-skinned avocado. A handsome ivy with plenty of foliage and breadth of individual branch (formed by the many short side branches), even though this is not a pronouncedly self-branching variety. Widely available in the greenhouse-supermarket trade. Grow in a pot or open ground patch. 'Carolina Crinkle': rounded 3-in. leaf, crinkly-surfaced, deeply incised, glossy olive-green. Leaves openly spaced on the branches, imparting a tracery effect. Use as a pot plant placed high, branches pendant; or plant it so that it trails down over a stone. Henri K. E. Schaepman of the Ivy Society rates this "Possibly our most handsome ivy, becoming more beautiful with age."

'Cascade' is a vigorous miniature. A roundish patch of many branches that ascend, then arch and touch the ground and flow outward. Bright ivy-green with medium gloss. 'Cockleshell' (synonym 'Shell'): leaf cockle-shaped, bright pea-green with paler veining. Choice shrublet for pot gardening. 'Conglomerata' is a dense, slow, tortuous shrub, 18 in. high, 6 ft. wide at age 20. Small spearpoint leaves, dark matte green.

Hedera Helix 'Deltoidea' (synonyms 'Cordata', 'Sweetheart'): perfectly flat, soil-conforming blanket of deltoid leaves that resemble *Epimedium* leaflets somehow shingled on the ground. An interesting ivy, well worth the few feet of soil it would ask (not a rampageous grower). 'Scutifolia' (Heart-Leaf) is a similar, if not identical, plant.

Hedera Helix 'Erecta' has stiffly upright stems lined with two close and rigidly regular ranks of small scoop-bladed leaves. Grows only to about 16 in. high. Useful for screening out a raw concrete foundation or for greening a narrow side yard. I believe this form of ivy to have been derived from *H. Helix* 'Conglomerata'.

Hedera Helix 'Fan' is a slow shrublet that could be made into a bonsai. Broad, ivy-green leaves, highly variable in size, ranging from 1 to 4 in. across. Stems angularly upright, shaggy with adventitious roots. 'Ferny' is a finely textured ground cover and surely one of the best of ivies for pot culture: Branches rise briefly, then spill down all sides of the pot in a fountain effect. Smallish leaves, medium green with a low gloss, abundant on the slender stems. 'Fluffy Ruffles': slowly developing pot plant. The polished clear green leaves are roundish, wavy, and crested (like one of the mad ferns) along the edge.

Hedera Helix 'Glacier' is well known as a houseplant; in the open, not as hardy as most others. Brightly white-variegated little leaves in masses on a twiggy, full plant. 'Gladiator': light green of leaf — and amusing.

My plant is a resolute rope twelve feet long, with no side branches. Should be named Rapunzel and draped down over a high wall. 'Gold Heart' has green leaves that are bright gold at the center. An established plant of this in a friend's garden garlands an old multitrunked Vine Maple. But the ivy does not take over trees; it needs assistance to climb at all. My friend drapes the ivy branches over forks in the tree trunks. 'Green Feather' (synonym 'Meagheri': sometimes a hummocky shrublet, sometimes a slow mat maker to 6 ft. or more across. Many small green leaves, all alike in size and shape, give the plant a clothlike quality. A similar ivy bears the name 'Pin Oak'.

Hedera Helix 'Ivalace' has small dark leaves with margins curled upward, suggesting lace. One of the best ground-covering ivies, copiously self-branching, which results in a fullness of the leaves. 'Little Diamond': dwarf plant, a foot or so across, an uneven, animalistic hunch of leaves. Little diamond-shaped leaves, variegated light green and gray, with a white margin.

Hedera Helix 'Manda's Crested'. With its jade-green wavy-surfaced leaves, the plant gives the visual effect of wind-ruffled water. Best displayed in a sizable pot, say 10 in. across. 'Margaret': superior ground-covering ivy of the middleweight class, not sweeping in growth, not slow. Light green. 'Minima': twiggy little pot plant with tiny leaves. In the open ground, the foliage and branches become grander and the plant's considerable charm diminishes.

Hedera Helix 'Needlepoint': a troll with twisty thickety branches; in slow years, a foot tall and a yard across. Each square foot of the plant holds hundreds of little — $\frac{1}{4}$–1-in. — leaves, most of them ranked along two sides of the stems, like the leaves of Traveler's Palm.

Hedera Helix 'Pedata' (Bird's-foot Ivy): a famous one, grown for more than a century. Leaves small, cleft like a bird foot, black-green with whitish veining. The slim leaves give the vine an airiness (in contrast to the ballasty aspect of the heavier ivies). A strong and relentless grower, lengthening its branches at least 18 in. a year; a good climber on concrete walls. An established plant becomes a fervent parent of fruiting branches. Unlike most other ivies, Bird's-foot will fruit close to the ground if it has no tall surface to climb. 'Pittsburgh': better known under a newer name, "Hahn Selfbranching." Appears to be ordinary stout-hearted English Ivy scaled down to about half size in leaf and in branch power: nevertheless, a lot of ivy. Probably only Bird's-foot Ivy and the typical *H. Helix* equal 'Pittsburgh' in acreage of planting.

Hedera Helix 'Ripples': one of the best middleweight ground covers. A 2-in. leaf, shallowly lobed and triangular, the surface undulant; light green, changing in winter (when exposed to sun by winter-bare trees) to a marbled soft rose.

Hibbertia scandens (Snake Vine). c, t. Evergreen vine for a trellis against a north or east wall or as a quilt over shady ground. The foliage is tidy, the leaf egg-shaped, glossy green; branches woody. Two-inch-wide canary-yellow flowers all summer. They are like single roses and are scented, but not pleasantly. Give this plenty of water.

Hieracium aurantiacum. All climates. Little orange Hawkweed daisies, pretty as can be, over an evergreen carpet of small rabbit-ear leaves held almost flat on the ground. Spreads fast: One plant will soon give you many. Withstands drought. An evergreen ground cover that will survive the acid leaf rain of a short-needled pine such as *Pinus contorta.* Half shade is best.

Hosta (plantain lily). Sent to join the perennials in chapter 13, but might just as well have been kept here. Although hostas are not nature's cover plants of stoloniferous habits, they are often gardeners' ground covers by dint of division and replanting. As our Michigan consultant Kay Boyd-ston — one of North America's most industrious landscapers with ground-covering plants — says, almost any plant is usable as a ground cover if you have enough of it. Most kinds of hosta soon increase amply to the purpose. Buy a single division (crown bud and root) from a mail-order nursery, and in three years it will have increased enough for you to set out a plantation of the noblest foliage to be found among hardy perennials for shade. We who grow hostas are led almost irresistibly into covering ground with them and must remember not to go too far, since there will be only a blank area in winter in the place of these deciduous plants.

Hoya carnosa (Wax Plant). C, T. A shrubby vine of tropical forests in Queensland, Australia. Best known as a houseplant, it also does well in full shade in the garden, twining up over a stump, on a trellis, or on a low wall.

Hypericum calycinum (Creeping St.-John's-Wort). All climates except GN. A woody creeper, tan-green of leaf, a foot high; covered with blazing yellow saucer flowers in spring. Plant rooted pieces about 18 in. apart. Best use in shade gardening is as a ground cover beneath established trees (lay down a blanket of fresh soil to give St.-John's a clear field); the plant will completely absorb and hide the droppings of such litterers as California Pepper, Black Locust, and Western Red Cedar. A powerful spreader and not a suitable neighbor for choice shade plants.

Juniperus. Growable in all climates. Although they are sun shrubs in nature, the many junipers of low, spreading habit will cover the ground beneath trees handsomely with their scented branches, bright blue, gray, or somber dark green. Half shade is the most wholesome for the juniper planted in such locations, and three-quarters shade is tolerable: The shading tree should have its trunk cleared of branches high enough so that at least a couple of hours of undiluted sun warm the blood of the ground-covering conifer. Some of the best junipers for this use are *J. horizontalis* 'Bar Harbor', *J. horizontalis* 'Plumosa', *J. horizontalis* 'Wiltonii' (small carpet, so plant beneath a small tree), *J. communis* 'Pfitzeriana compacta', and "Tam" juniper (*J. Sabina* 'Tamariscifolia').

Lamium (dead nettle). All climates. Evergreen cover plants with small heart-shaped leaves and little flowers of a form rather like the pope's hand with fingers raised in blessing. Easy growers in moist or dry ground, fully or partly shaded. If planted in ground that goes dry, lamium will need full shade. For quick cover, plant rooted pieces a foot apart. *L. maculatum* "Variegatum" makes a 6-in.-high cushion that spreads widely at a moderate rate. Rough green leaves with a splash of white along the midrib; flowers purplish or, in *L. maculatum* 'Album', clear white. *L. maculatum* 'Beacon Silver' has leaves of an exquisite greenish silver with a narrow jade-green rim at the scalloped edge; soft-rose flowers. 'Beacon Silver', together in a ground cover combination with silvery green *Carex comans* 'Frosty Curls', needs no words.

Lapageria rosea. C, T. Slender evergreen vine that has large crimson-rose campanulate flowers pendant on the shrubby branches now and again through summer and autumn. Serenely beautiful; there is also a pure white form. Provide the lapagerias ideal shade garden soil and an arbor or trellis in part shade, or grow it indoors. I once saw a red lapageria twining and flowering upon the stand of a floor lamp in a day-lit living room.

Linnaea borealis (Twinflower). NE, S, GN, NW, C. North American woodlander of the honeysuckle family. A dainty prostrate vine, never ascending. Long wiry branches form a loosely woven mat that roots down at intervals in moss, leaf mold, or rotted wood. In garden use, a limited ground cover 6 in. tall in full shade, ground-hugging in half shade (where it is at its best). Leaves round, button-size, glossy evergreen. Closely above the foliage, pink bells, two on each thread-fine stem, appear in late spring. Bend closely over them to catch their scent of almond. Plant Twinflower according to the directions given for *Cornus canadensis*.

Liriope and ***Ophiopogon*** (both called "lilyturf"). Tussocklike, tufted plants similar in appearance and use, a step down in scale from the carexes (true tussocks) and two steps down from clivia. *Liriope* and *Ophiopogon* are Asian liliaceous plants with slender, recurving blade leaves, and modest flowers in little torch clusters. These perennials fit handily into many shady places: around tree trunks, on steep banks, as edging plants, and in compositions with sand or rocks. Tufted at first, the plants slowly stool out to form broad clumps. Divisions planted several inches apart in ideal shade garden soil will usually unite, with one summer's growth, into an attractive rough lawn. The following spring and every spring thereafter, before new growth begins, clip the old leaves or mow them with the mower blades set high, using care not to cut too low, into the plant's dormant crowns. To gain new plants, divide the clump in early spring.

Liriope Muscari (Big Blue Lilyturf). S, C, SW, T. In late summer, violet flowers much like grape hyacinth, over tufted foliage 1½ ft. tall (where the plant receives plenty of water). A single division will grow in several years into a 2-ft.-wide clump. Variegated forms are available.

Liriope spicata (Creeping Lilyturf). All climates except GN. Half the height of *L. Muscari;* flowers violet-purple in some forms, but more commonly washy violet or suspect white. Neither this plant nor any of the ophiopogons that follow is much in flower.

Note: In order to keep together the genera *Liriope* and *Ophiopogon,* closely associated in gardening, the descriptions of *Ophiopogon* species follow here, instead of being presented in alphabetical order.

Ophiopogon Jaburan (Jaburan Lilyturf). C, SW, T. A big clump, as tall and broad as *Liriope Muscari;* in various forms, ivy-green or variegated. Flowers white or wine-stained, in a curved raceme; berries steel-blue.

Ophiopogon japonicus (Mondo). S, NW (shelter), C, SW, T. Dark green, typically; to 8 in. tall. The dwarf form, *O. japonicus* 'Compactus' — winsome plant — stands a mere 1½ in. high. A pale yellow form is in the trade, and could be of use in a Burle-Marxian, sharp-edged, two-tone planting with a dark green Mondo. These plants will cover slowly in dry shade, moderately fast in the best soil, well-watered.

Ophiopogon planiscapus. Best known in its black-leaved form, *O. planiscapus* 'Arabicus', hardy in all climates. A slow clump former, 'Arabicus' is visually and physically well matched in a ground-cover contest with *Mahonia repens* — in other words, they look good together and grow well together. 'Arabicus' also makes a pot plant that is easy to grow, indoors or out; striking in beige or oyster-color pottery.

Lonicera (honeysuckle). All climates. As you probably know full well, this is a deliciously scented flower on an octopus of a vine. Its use in a shade garden is as a rampant cover plant on a high, half-shady bank. Any of the woody, twining honeysuckles are of service here and will help prevent erosion.

Lysimachia Nummularia (Creeping Jennie). For all climates, but miserable in a dry garden. A jolly cover for a wet or moist bank in semishade. Thumbnail-size roundish leaves, of a vivid green, apple-green in the form 'Aurea'. Round yellow flowers in summer, big and bright as twenty-dollar gold pieces. Fast-spreading — a sheet maker — but the stems are too flat and delicate and the roots too shallow to harm any taller plant it encounters.

Mahonia repens. Shrublet of forest margins in western mountains. Choice ground cover for gardeners east or west, in prairie regions, and in high deserts. Grows 1 or 2 ft. tall, spreading slowly at first, then heartily. Plant in part shade at intervals of about 18 in. I find the bluish-leaved form from California mountains to be more reliable in gardens than the bronzy green *M. repens* native to the Northwest interior.

Melissa and *Mentha* (lemon balm and mint). These well-known herbs will prosper in all climates. Vigorous spreaders for moist ground in part shade.

Melissa officinalis (Lemon Balm) grows 2–3 ft. tall in deep soil, but with occasional clipping can be kept low and compact. Untrimmed, the plant has a fluffy, woodsy aspect in the open arrangement of its triangular leaves. It is a moderate seeder, and within several years one plant will sow into a colony several yards across. A lush stand of Lemon Balm makes one of the best weed fighters among ground-covering plants.

I grow Lemon Balm, along with several mints, beneath a laundry carousel in an out-of-the-way garden nook. In hanging out the wash, one brushes the herbs, and they respond as a live potpourri, releasing a blended scent.

Mentha Requienii (Corsican Mint) forms a bright green mat of lentil-size leaves skin-tight on the ground, deliciously minty when stepped upon. One of the best places for it is at the side of the garden path, into which the plant will creep. Corsican Mint is annual in areas of cold winter, but seedlings carry on; half-hardy s and NW; soundly perennial in warmer climates. The plant is shallow-rooted and no trouble to taller plants that it may meet.

Mentha spicata (Spearmint) is an aggressive plant that is only safe in wildish ground; or grow it in a large container, lavishly watered. Slower and more controllable are *M.* ×*piperita* (Peppermint) and *M.* ×*gentilis* (Apple Mint). *M. Pulegium* (Pennyroyal) is a free seeder and makes a wonderful ingredient in a casual lawn, together with *Prunella vulgaris* (Self-Heal) and wild grasses. The plants will tolerate being mowed, but the delight is in letting the herbs come to flower unhindered.

Mitchella repens (Partridgeberry). NE, S, NW, NC. Woodland wildflower native to eastern North America. A low meshed mat of fine creeping branches, small roundish leaves; in foliage and habit, the plant greatly resembles *Euonymus Fortunei* 'Kewensis' but is usually even more modest and choice in growth. Small jasminelike flowers, long-tubed and scented, appear in spring. A slow-growing ground cover — plant 6 in. apart — for a small patch of moist, mossy soil in shade.

Mosses. Many gardeners fight it; a few love it and court it. The following notes are on the courtship and connoisseurship of moss, the most calmative ground cover. It comes of its own wherever lawn grass grows sparsely in the shade, for shade is not the native element of lawn grasses, which are meadow plants by nature. Where moss clearly wants the piece of ground and grass clearly does not, the lawn gardener may do well to change sympathies, pluck out the last of the weedy grass, and work to perfect a full and deep-piled carpet of moss. Consultant Gordon Emerson of Ohio tells us how.

I cultivate mosses and transplant them into special gardens. These plants are ideal for an area under large trees such as mature maples, where they provide year-around greenery with low maintenance. I use a variety of mosses for varied texture and pattern, adding some stepping-stones, a few rocks, a couple of patches of ferns. I have one moss area approximately fifty by fifty feet, and several other extensive patches. Moss makes excellent cover for fast-shriveling spring flowers such as clintonias.

But one must decide: moss or rodents. The squirrels and chipmunks won't leave moss alone. They dig it in search of fallen seeds. For years, I've box-trapped fifty or sixty chipmunks a season, and still I must repair their gougings (like divots on a golf course, the damages always look worse than they really are). Autumn leaves are no problem. Careful work with a wire rake gets them off. But the heavy seedfall from maples and ash requires hand-cleanup, tedious and time-consuming. One thorough early-summer weeding and degrassing is essential; after that, one or two light goings-over. Frequent watering promotes lush growth, and moss looks its best when wet. An elixir of manure is beneficial. Altogether, this amounts to really minor care for a considerable area of garden ground. The rest is moss viewing.

Ophiopogon. See *Liriope* and *Ophiopogon*, p. 170.

Oxalis magellanica. C and T; growable in sheltered places, S, NW, SW. Evergreen ground cover; a charmer, with its little shiny, dark clover leaves sprinkled over with white floral cups. A single plant makes a mat 4 in. high, 2 ft. wide in about 3 summers. Moist, humusy soil; half shade or more.

Oxalis oregana (Redwood Sorrel). NE (coastal gardens only), S (shelter), NW, C, T. A soft-green spread of shamrock leaves and white, pink, or rose flowers; 6 in high, advancing not too fast, but eventually as far and wide as you wish. Native to Pacific slope forests, and one of the most valuable shade plants for casual gardens along the West Coast, but it is not a plant to turn loose near miniature woodlanders. Set out divisions or pot plants about 8 in. apart in full or half shade. One of the few plants that will cover ground beneath conifers as well as under deciduous trees. Soothing in character, a companion for ferns and woodland flowers that stand at least a foot taller than the shamrock carpet.

Pachysandra terminalis (Japanese Spurge). NE, S, GN, NW, C. Among the cover plants employed in North American shade gardening, only common ivy and Periwinkle are as ubiquitous and boring and indispensable as this plant. Curiously, gardens in Japan — for all their dependence on ground covers — make no use of the plant, as far as I can see: In three months' study of gardens there, I never found a planting of Japanese Spurge. The plant is a spreading evergreen perennial, not woody but of shrubby quality. Spurge is at its best in full or dappled shade, beneath trees or shrubbery or in odd shady corners. Given too much sun, the plant turns an incriminating yellow. Provide a rich soil and keep it moist in times of drought. Growth is moderate: an easily curbed plant.

Phlox divaricata (Wild Sweet William). Will grow and flower in all climates but is a bit cautious about spreading out and covering ground anywhere except in its native East. Oval leaves flat on the ground; 1-ft. tall scapes topped with gray-violet, bright violet, rose, or white flowers. In the East, use it as a woodland ground cover in the dappled shade of deciduous trees, or in afternoon shade.

Plectranthus australis (Swedish Ivy). Withstands light frosts: C, SW, T. A spreading perennial with the landscape presence of a low shrub; to 16 in. tall (at once) and 6 ft. across in 5 summers, grown from a single branch that you might root in a glass of water. Burgeons in all shades of shade; in any soil — swampy, gardeny, or summer-dry; overpowers many weeds. Leaves are the shape and size of a child's toy top, shiny green with a purple tinge, grape-purple on the underside, or leaves at upper surface green with white variegation. Whitish flowers in leaf-top pagodas. One of the fast and easy covers for shady ground. And as is usually the case with the easy ones, rejoiced over for the first two summers, vaguely registered the third year, and afterward, whenever focused upon, lightly resented and shrewdly considered, with thoughts of rooting it out (easily done) and replacing it with "better" plants — but what else would grow in the poor place where it thrives? That gives pause.

Pratia angulata. NW, C, SW, T. Only a few inches high, but potent. It has trailing stems, wiry and thin, yet succulent, that root down; little round matte green leaves with bumpy edges; white flowers, ¾ in. wide (in selected forms), shaped like those of Common Lobelia (same family); roundish rose-purple berries. Vigorous cover for a few square feet or yards of moist soil in semishade or sun; grows well in full shade, but flowers there only sparingly. A natural waterside plant that will float its stems out over a garden pond a few inches, concealing concrete edges. Plant 1 ft. apart.

Primula. (Primrose). Often planted as a ground cover. *See* chapter 13.

Pulmonaria (lungwort). NE, S, GN, NW, C. Deciduous perennials. Of the several species, the most apt at covering ground is the old-time Spotted Dog or Blue Lungwort *(P. officinalis)*, with ample white-spotted green leaves in a loose, spreading clump and spring flowers that open reddish, then turn to mottled violet and muscat; to a foot high and 3 ft. across in several years. For quick cover, plant divisions a foot apart. The plain green variety, *P. officinalis immaculata,* should appeal more to the many gardeners who object to the Dalmatian pattern of the typical plant.

Other pulmonarias, such as the bright blue-violet *P. angustifolia* and the deep violet *P. longifolia,* form low, tight clumps that are readily converted into ground covers by dividing an established plant in early spring and setting out the divisions about 9 in. apart. Full shade to half shade for pulmonarias; beneath trees and shrubs, they make tough quilts of leaves and graceful stands of down-turned trumpet flowers. Pulmonarias accept soil of almost any composition but must have moisture in the ground.

Ranunculus repens 'Flora Pleno'. All climates. Creeping Buttercup in a double-flowered form. Flowers shiny yellow, most welcome in a wet place

Good old Spotted Dog *(Pulmonaria officinalis)*, faithful cover beneath trees and shrubbery. (DON NORMARK)

in spring woods. A rampant plant, a single start of which will cover yards of ground in a few summers. Another profligate, useful in the same setting, is the yellow-flowered form of *Ranunculus Ficaria* (Lesser Celandine).

Rubus calycinoides. s, nw, c, sw, t. Himalayan. Flat-growing shrubby vine conforming to the contours of soil, stone, and wall and descending or climbing a couple of yards on masonry or wood; stems lengthen about 18–36 in. each year. The plant is easily controlled by edging. Leaves dark, polished evergreen, lobed and rounded, the surface deeply channeled; as big as a circle formed by a thumb and index finger signaling OK. Little white raspberry flowers and salmon-colored raspberries (never enough for more than a nibble). Half shade; any soil.

Saxifraga (mossy kinds): *S. rosacea (S. decipiens), S. moschata, S. muscoides,* and their hybrids. For all climates, but in the desert they will probably need lath shelter or a shady spot in an atrium. Mossy saxifrages are long-

Saxifraga rosacea. Soft-rose flowers on rhubarb-colored stems. (DON NORMARK)

time favorite edging plants and rockery plants for shade. *S. rosacea* and its garden hybrids form bright green cushions of little pawlike leaves in mossy rosettes. Flowers usually have rounded faces, blankly pretty but not much for conversation, and usually of some shade of pink or burgundy, or occasionally white; on 5-in. — later 9-in. — stems arising in spring. The other two mossies *(S. moschata* and *S. muscoides)* are both family plants with numbers of hybrid progeny. Characteristically, they grow as loose, broad mats of large paw-leaves, with flowers starry and white (but there are pinks and pale yellows).

All three species of mossy saxifrages have interbred, blurring the garden specialties of the purer types. But you can foretell the growth potential of any particular plant that you may have your eye on at the nursery by sizing up the individual leaf rosette: If it is densely leaved and more or less an inch across, the plant will form a clump about 9–12 in. wide in one summer. If the rosette is loosely leaved and about 2 in. across, the plant will luxuriate into about an 18-in.-wide mat in a season. Give mossy saxifrages ideal shade garden soil. They are easy and permanent in a moist garden, but difficult in a garden that dries in summer. A well-grown mossy — a term in good standing among gardeners, by the way — will allow division into many sure little tufts of rosettes and roots, late summer to early fall, or in early spring.

Saxifraga stolonifera (Strawberry Geranium, Roving-Sailor, Mother-of-Thousands). s, nw, c, sw, t. Evergreen perennial from woodlands in Japan. A mat of round leaves, the size of a silver dollar, forest-green with silvery streaks along the leaf veins. The plant extends its territory by casting about like a dry-fly fisherman — with long reddish whips for pole and line; baby plants engender, root down and grow at the end of each line. Flowers are little white muscae volitantes fluttering over the plant on fine stems. Small-scale ground cover in shady corners and beneath shrubbery; a curtain cover for a shady rock wall, a hanging container plant, and even a houseplant. Hardy down to 0°F or below. Less hardy is *S. stolonifera* 'Tricolor', a form with leaves of marbled green, rose, and white.

Saxifraga umbrosa (London-Pride). ne, s, gn, nw, c. An old-timer, a folk plant: Folks give thinnings and edgings of this generous carpeter to young and needy gardeners, and so London-Pride has come to be grown in about a million places. Often planted along shady walks, about tree trunks, and beneath azaleas, lilacs, or forsythias — often with spring bulbs poking through its rosetted mat. The leaves are spatulate, pea-green, and glossy, in a flattened rosette the size of a medallion. Little pink starry flowers in open clusters on 1-ft.-high stems. The packed growth of the plant's rosettes keeps out many of the smaller weeds (after the plant fills in). With that in mind, I'd say a sizable swath of London-Pride — perhaps 5 × 15 ft. — would not be too much to take care of. Plant rooted rosettes at 6-in. intervals for full cover the first summer. Nurseries specializing in rock plants offer miniature forms that make pixie carpeting for a few feet of ground.

Sedum (stonecrop). Several quick carpeters for semishade number in this big group of plants, which can provide a most thrifty ground cover. One nursery plant broken apart into branches, with or without roots, will provide just that many slips: Sedums grow readily from branches stuck in the ground and kept watered.

Sedum spurium covers soil and flags at the base of an old apple tree. A clump of Alpine Strawberry and another of Forget-Me-Not hold their ground in the sedum carpet. What else? Much else: a fine antique watering can, and a four-tiered background planting in nearly full shade. Bottom to top: 'Good's Selfbranching' ivy, *Bergenia cordifolia,* yew (*Taxus ×media* 'Brownii'), Zabel Laurel. (GEORGE TALOUMIS)

Sedum mexicanum (usually sold as *S. sarmentosum*). Hardy NW, C, SW, T. A single branch in ideal shade garden soil will ramify in one season into a leafy garment about a yard across, pale green and flat on the ground, with soft-yellow flowers. If you want to plant something else in its place, you can get rid of the fabric by simply raking it away.

Sedum rupestre, hardy everywhere, forms a spread of fine-leaved, glaucous rosettes — a juniper-gray moss mat with yellow flowers. Set out pieces 6 in. apart.

Sedum spurium. Through generations of gardeners, this has remained one of North America's commonest shady-ground covers, especially in cool- or cold-winter climates, though it will also grow where winters are warm. Ease of propagation and the generosity of gardening neighbors who pass it on over the friendly fence probably have much to do with its abundance. Advertising by mail-order nurseries plays a part as well (the much-touted sedum, 'Dragon's Blood', is a form of this species). Spurium grows as a thick, flat tangle of wormsnakelike branches, a Medusan affair largely concealed by pretty scalloped leaves, green or bronzed, packed in rosettes. Summer flowers, rose-pink, pinkish white, or vivid crimson-magenta (dragon's blood). One branch will stool out in a summer's time into a plant the size of a large pancake. Grow it beneath deciduous trees in half shade (or somewhat more); spurium will curtain down to cover shady rocks or a knee-high retaining wall.

Selaginella Kraussiana (Trailing Selaginella). NE (shelter), S, NW, C, SW, T. A ferny carpet, 4–6 in. thick, of leaf sprays shaped like those of arborvitae, soft to touch, and spring-green in color. The plant will cascade over steep, shady streamside banks, rooting down as it travels. Goes with tall ferns or makes a cover plant for a trillium bed — its delicate roots run shallow and are easy to get along with. Keep it moist.

Sempervivum (Hen-and-Chicks, Houseleek). For all climates. Though better known as sun plants, often planted as ground covers in well-drained, half-shady places. With shade, the rosettes grow especially large and impressive, and their spring colors develop richer tones (some growers say).

Soleirolia Soleirolii (Baby's-Tears). C, SW, T; S and NW, when blackened by frost, it grows again the following summer from the scraps that survive. Bears the most melodious name in the entire binomial system, but the common name has always been to me a puzzle: *Baby's-Tears?* In habit, a soft-green ground fog, a mist of minute leaves on thread-fine stems, spreading over the ground at a rate of 1–3 ft. a year (a moist summer results in acceleration). In all parts of the plant, the thin enclosing cell walls are easily shattered or mashed, but when damaged, the plant is quick to repair itself as good as new. It will grow in all degrees of shade, dark to light. The darker the location, the looser the growth — to a lax ½ ft. high in a shade garden cavelike in depth. Two inches is its more usual height in full shade. In dryish soil and half sun, Baby's-Tears grows tight on the ground, to a condensed ¼ in. tall; here it will make a path plant somewhat resistant to foot traffic. Other shade garden uses: harmless interplanting for slower, taller ground covers, perennials, and ferns; blanketing for bulbs; and underplanting for shrubs. But think thrice before planting this mighty infant in a greenhouse or near beds of shade garden miniatures. It is ever the relentless crawler forth and invader. A chartreuse form of Baby's-Tears (*S. Soleirolii* 'Midas'), as attractive in its way as the common green one, grows for me much more slowly.

Tradescantia fluminensis (Wandering Jew). c, sw, t. Invaluable quick cover for heavily shaded ground that becomes droughty in summer, and perhaps the only plant that will thrive beneath a close stand of tree ferns. A ground vine that will climb no more than a couple of feet wherever it meets tree trunk or wall, but will easily flow across 6 ft. of ground in a season. A glossy plant, stems succulent and brittle, leaves translucent green and shiny; leaf shape and size like lush lips in a cosmetics ad; sparse display of white flowers. A shallow-rooting plant easily dispached by raking it away and then picking at the ground with a garden fork to get out its runners, which lie just under the surface. (This is in case you decide to listen to gardeners who scoff at you for cultivating a weed, for it is common in shady waste places in some of the warmer parts of the world.)

A dwarf relative of Wandering Jew, *Gibasis geniculata* — delightful in a hanging container or as a cover for small ground (sc, t) — has leaves reduced to one-tenth the size of those of Wandering Jew, extends its branches to about as long as your arm in a season, and blooms copiously all summer: a cloud of ¼-in. white flowers, three-petaled and like tiny trilliums, hovering above the foliage.

Vaccinium Vitis-idaea (Lingonberry). ne, s, nw, c. A 1-ft.-tall creeping shrublet, a close colony of equal vertical stems, and small evergreen leaves that are dark, shiny ovals; pale pink bells in racemes during spring; edible fruits, in autumn, are like small cranberries. In open half shade or under shrubs and small trees, Lingonberry makes a ground cover more enduring than most; full-leaved for about fifteen years before showing wear in the oldest part of its fabric (with dead patches pruned away and bare spots mulched, the plant will fill in). Plant container-grown Lingonberry about a foot apart, divisions more closely.

Vancouveria chrysantha. Californian perennial, growable s, nw, c. One of the choicest (that is, slowest) ground covers. The leathery, grayish evergreen foliage, divided into several leaflets, and the dainty yellow flowers are reminiscent of those of a relative, *Epimedium*. For an even cover, plant closely in sheltered shade and wait several years.

Vancouveria hexandra. Western. Deciduous cover plant for all climates. Hexandra grows below ground as a belligerent spread of wiry rootstocks; above ground, a 14-in. deep flock of elegantly segmented sylvan leaves and panicled white flowers. It grows almost as fast as ivy and is certainly as invasive, but it has its uses in rough, woodsy places. Hexandra will even cover dry ground under pines and other conifers, and that may be the best place for it.

Vancouveria planipetala (Inside-out Flower). From woods where rolls the Oregon. s, NW, C, SW. Something of both *V. chrysantha* and *V. hexandra* in this one (though it is not a hybrid). Trifoliate leaves, glossy, dark evergreen or, in another form of the plant, matte grayish leaves tending to deciduousness; white flowers. Either form is a ground cover of quality for a patch of your best shady ground. Moderately slow-growing.

Veronica filiformis. Growable everywhere — all too growable in the eyes of some gardeners. This is the veronica that gets into lawns and makes them so despisedly beautiful with that light blue sky of flowers hazing the grass over in April and May. Deeply appreciated by manufacturers of chemical weedicides (they should hang a portrait of this caviar-winner in their board rooms) but loved by those of us who know the garden uses of good weeds. A plant of flat sheeting habit and fine, shallow roots, the

Veronica prostrata flowers and flows among the arising spring leaves of Lily-of-the-Valley. (DON NORMARK)

veronica will serve as a first-rate bulb cover and as a living mulch beneath shrubbery, conserving moisture and regulating soil temperature. The name *filiformis* says the plant has threadlike branches, and so it has — a fine thread to add to a terrestrial tapestry, along with such other equally determined weavers as Lily-of-the-Valley, Ajuga, small ivies, Australian Violet, Indian Strawberry, Self-Heal, and Pennyroyal — all of them good weeds and, strength for strength, well matched with the veronica. Together, such plants make a fabric rich to see and somehow thrilling to tread upon (no harm if done sparingly).

Veronica prostrata. For all climates. A bunch of garden hybrids travel under this name — or under the aliases *V. latifolia (V. Teucrium)* or *V. rupestris.* Several of the more vigorous and more flat-growing among them make sturdy carpets in filtered tree shade. Rooted bits of the plant, set out 7 in. apart in ideal shade garden soil grow into a solid, tough, 1-in.-thick evergreen mat in one summer, a lawn that will take almost as much traffic as grass. The following spring, the green lawn will flower and transform itself into a bright blue lake. Mow it afterward — just once, during midsummer. But let me caution you not to give too much ground to *V. prostrata,* or to any other flat, fine-leaved ground cover that bears flowers: 10 × 10 ft. may be a reasonable maximum, since this much of the plant will require about a half day's hand-weeding in a season.

Veronica repens. All climates. Exceedingly flat and tight against the ground, a fast-widening sheet of little roundish evergreen leaves, brightest green and shiny; pale blue flowers in short racemes. A path plant and bulb cover in moist half shade.

Vinca minor (Common or Lesser Periwinkle, Myrtle). A perennial for all climates and all time. Among ground covers for shade, one of the big three, ivy and Japanese Spurge being the others. Some gardeners might say "the unholy three." Yet these plants do the hard work that few other ground covers will touch. Periwinkle makes a thick, subwoody mat of branches held out at fish pole angles or lying flat. Leaves are dark evergreen, thick, glossy, and shrublike, the shape and size of the space between thumb and index finger when held together to form an ellipse. Limpid blue-violet flowers in spring are five-petaled, an inch-wide, and rounded. If Periwinkle were difficult to grow, garden lyricists the like of Reginald Farrer would no doubt have devoted passionate pages, even chapters, to this love, whose only fault is in being around too much. Plant rooted branches 6 in. apart for cover the first summer. Periwinkle grows best in a half-shaded or fully shaded bed of good soil, but will take poor ground; when established, it will survive drought and competitive tree or shrub roots. Years ago I lined out a planting of Periwinkle in a two-inch-deep topdressing of new soil (all the site would allow) over darkly shaded, root-clogged ground beneath a vicious old English Laurel hedge; the Periwinkle is still there, spreading bravely. And the plant makes one of the better covers for Daffodils.

V. minor 'Gertrude Jekyll' is a petite white-flowered variety with branches and leaves much reduced. One plant takes years to grow a yard across. Good cover for miniature Daffodils. There are also variegated leaf forms of Periwinkle and single and double flower forms in purple, lavender, reddish copper, and white (on a full-size plant). *V. major* (Greater Periwinkle), a taller, looser-growing, larger-leaved relative, is useful as a bank cover or woodland filler to be viewed at some distance. It overgrows many weeds (*V. minor* does not) and opens blue-violet flowers 2 in. across, but is less drought-tolerant and less hardy (s, nw, c, sw, t).

Viola. Violets and "violas" — the latter name is the one that many people give to slim-flowered perennial forms of Pansies, plants mostly derived from the wildflower *V. cornuta*. Violets and violas have flowers of five irregular petals tucked around into a kind of mild face. All are at their best in moist, ideal shade garden soil. Grow violets in afternoon shade or bright north-wall shade, or in dappled shade throughout the day. Violas (and Pansies) flower best where they receive at least several hours of unfiltered sun. Except for the Australian Violet, the plants described below are hardy and floriferous in all garden climates. Plant violets and violas as rooted divisions (watered daily until they begin making new foliage, kept moist afterward) in late summer to early autumn, or in early spring after the main danger of frost heaving has passed.

Viola hederacea (Australian Violet). c, t; with shelter, s, nw, sw; hardy to about 20°F; in colder regions, this vigorous, long-lived perennial is planted as a summer-flowering annual in rockeries and hanging baskets. In moist, open ground, a trailing ground vine that spreads its light green kidney-shaped leaves a foot or more a year; flowers white at the outer part of the petals, purple toward the inside, in a sharp and natty contrast. Blooms throughout a long summer-fall season, and is at its best with at least two or three hours of pure sun.

Viola labradorica (Labrador Violet). For all climates. In ne and nw gardens, the plant seeds about majestically. A 20- × -20-ft. flawless carpet of the handsome, rounded, purplish-green leaves and dark violets is an expectable reward, in time, for the planting of a single start in open ground in the high shade of deciduous trees. Low-growing — almost flat — and harmless to taller growers, but bulky in beds of shade garden miniatures.

Viola odorata (Sweet Violet). Hardy in all garden climates. No other catalyst in human experience is quite like this scent in early spring. Compelled by it, swains buy violet corsages and make speeches in tremolo, gardeners (more down-to-earth types) get out rakes and trowels, and small children, for whom the suddenly appearing flower is simply and surely a divine manifestation, will nibble of a violet in communion — but only one: a thing that looks and smells heavenly should taste no less so, but as I recall, a fresh violet is as bitter as unsweetened chocolate.

Viola labradorica, a carpet maker when planted in open ground. (DON NORMARK)

Sweet Violet, the wildflower, has small, intensely fragrant, deep violet flowers and will sow itself into hundreds and thousands, filling a woodland floor. Plants of this wild type are not easily divisible. Named garden forms of Sweet Violet divide readily, have larger violet, rose, or white flowers of blander fragrance. Double forms of fragrant violets belong both to the species *V. odorata* and to the closely related *V. alba.* The doubles of this latter plant, called Parma Violets, are often difficult to establish in the garden. Best chances for them are in providing ideal shade garden soil, planting them in mid-spring, in afternoon shade or blocky sun/shade. The wild form of *V. alba* has a small, fragrant, single white flower. The plant seeds about freely and appears in the harshest places — as a Tennysonian flower in the crannied wall and in many an incredible corner, bursting forth with flowers of white samite, mystic, wonderful.

Viola rupestris (*V. arenaria*). For all garden climates. A benign weed that is a reckless seeder. Good for covering wildish ground between tall ferns and woodland plants; or use as a carpet beneath lilacs or tall viburnums. *V. rupestris* is a deciduous violet whose spring leaves and flowers open close to the ground. During the growing season, the plant heightens to about 8 in. and flowers sporadically until fall frost. The form *V. rupestris* 'Rosea', with soft-rose flowers, is better known in gardens than the typical lavender-lilac flower.

Viola septentrionalis (Northern Blue Violet). For all garden climates. Of New England and Newfoundland. The plant is a flat-topped pie of bright green leaves and has 1-in.-wide violet-purple or white flowers. Many good nurseries sell the white phase of the flower as a form of *V. odorata* — at many good nurseries, botany is not the strong point. You will know if you have *V. septentrionalis* in hand if the plant's rootstocks are little elongate tubers that pry apart easily; plant divisions ½ ft. apart in spring for an even ground cover by September. (*V. odorata* has stringy rootstocks that must be cut or torn apart.) Closely related to *V. septentrionalis* is *V. sororia* (*V. priceana;* Confederate Violet) of Kentucky, which has broad-faced flowers, white with a dilute blue center; its growth form and uses are identical to those of *V. septentrionalis.*

Waldsteinia fragarioides (Barren Strawberry). For all climates. Eastern American woodland ground cover belonging to the rose family. A flat and tidy creeper in half shade, looser and taller in full shade; medium green leaves (bronzy green where any sun touches the plant), divided like those of the strawberry, but somewhat leathery, firmly evergreen, and suggestive of shrub leaves in their substance. Flowers are yellow cups in spring. Plant 12–18 in. apart in any reasonably fertile soil mulched an inch deep with sawdust, compost, or peat moss. Draw the mulch closely around each plant as you set it out. Waldsteinia is a tough plant that will take drought and hold its ground when planted beneath trees.

This one will let you walk across it, if you don't do so too often. One crossing every day probably would not result in any noticeable wear or discouragement of the plant. All firm-leaved ground covers, come to think of it, will allow at least that much foot traffic. And right there is a goodly part of the fun of growing these plants. The leaf walker is manitou and master of this rare element. It is next to being a cloud walker, or a child splashing across a mud puddle.

12

Ferns

These are the plants that put wings on the garden. Nothing else in the vegetable kingdom affords us quite the visual buoyancy of ferns. They lighten the garden, and so they lighten the gardener.

There are ten thousand known species of ferns on the planet. Of these, about a thousand are in cultivation in North America and a hundred grow in my gardens. The numbers may seem suspect in their neatness, but they are pretty close to the mark. Actually, I've grown upward of twice as many kinds of ferns as I have right now. Slugs have taken some, and others have departed because of an indisposition to grow lower down than their native mountains, or simply out of dissatisfaction with me. Those that remain seem to celebrate the law of survival of the fittest for garden life.

For this chapter, I've examined the ferns that I grow or know with the eye of a beauty contest judge — that is, with a perception narrow and patently absurd: How dare I dictate that Miss Ostrich Fern is better-looking than Miss Deer Fern? Anyway, I dare, and I have paraded the whole lot in order to single out those that seem the best of ferns for North American gardens, the indispensable, irreducible few. I've settled on two score. Except where noted, these ferns are hardy and growable throughout North America,

Adiantum hispidulum (Rough Maidenhair). One-foot-tall plant of tropical and subtropical origin. Easy houseplant and equally easy in a shady garden where winters are frost-free or lightly frosty. Deciduous. The rounded leaflets of the fronds are extremely fine — a fabric of green sequins.

Adiantum pedatum (Maidenhair Fern). Found wild over most of North America, it is 3 ft. tall and tropically luscious on shady wet banks

Maidenhair (*Adiantum pedatum*) and polystichums (*P. setiferum* 'Acutilobum') grow at left and at right, respectively, on the margins of a dry stream bed — actually a dug and gravel-filled drain field thirty inches deep, a device that tames runoff after hard rains. (DON NORMARK)

in coastal forests; 6 in. tall and with imbricately compact fronds in the tundras of Alaska. Deciduous. Provide with full shade. The tundra-inhabiting dwarf (known in nurseries as *A. pedatum* var. *aleuticum,* and by other Latin names) needs cool sun morning and/or evening, and shade during the heat of the day.

Adiantum venustum. Himalayan. With snow cover, hardy at 0°F or below; without snow, hardy at 15°F in a sheltered garden shaded through the winter. An evergreen that strolls slowly by means of stolons:

Beside a slow woodland stream, tea-colored with the tannin of redwood needles, grow Lady Ferns (*Athyrium Felix-femina*), Colt's Foot (*Petasites speciosus*), at bottom, and a skunk cabbage (*Lysichiton americanum*) with its huge broad leaves. (DON NORMARK)

A single planted division forms a 1-yd. wide colony within several years. One-foot-tall ground cover of maidenhair delicacy, yet tough and permanent in full shade; but its soil must not become dry.

Asplenium bulbiferum (Hen-and-Chicks Fern). Australasia and India. If I were to confine the list to only ten, this would number among them.

Fairly well known in California, and hardy there down to the low twenties. A neat cluster of arching evergreen fronds finely cut into green lace; to 6 ft. wide, 3 ft. tall. The best exposure for it is about three-quarters shade, with a little cool sun morning and evening. But it is a stalwart plant that will grow in various exposures.

Asplenium Trichomanes (Maidenhair Spleenwort). A saxatile miniature that is native to shady cliffs in mountains all over the world. Well under a foot tall, a mere tassel of black leaf stems beaded along their length with tiny oval leaves. Give this little evergreen a position raised above the median of the garden — for example, between rocks in a shady wall.

Athyrium Filix-femina (Lady Fern). Circumpolar. The wild North American plant is upright in habit; to 6 ft. tall in marshy soil, half that in a dryish spot. Translucent light green fronds, delicately cut, that turn soft yellow before dying down in autumn. Prefers half shade. An adaptable, resourceful, opportunistic plant that will flourish even in dryish gardens where most other ferns would languish. As I say, opportunistic: If Lady Fern likes you and your digs, as it almost surely will, it will naturalize by spores and will spring up in surprising places, sun or shade. A good one for a rough wall or a wild patch. Many garden forms of European origin are fancifully embroidered or embellished ("crested") in the divisions of their fronds. These are much smaller growers than our native, North American Lady Fern, and are not apt to get about in the garden on their own.

Athyrium Goeringianum 'Pictum'. Japanese. Low-growing and choice. Small fronds, marbled silvery gray, in a clump that broadens slowly with the years. Full shade, constant moisture. Said to be sensitive to deep frost, yet this plant grows in sheltered East Coast gardens. Deciduous.

Blechnum Spicant (Deer Fern). Inhabits our more northerly coniferous forests. A dark evergreen rosette, big as a tricycle wheel, flat on the mossy ground. Spore-bearing fronds of a different cut rise straight up in the center of the plant. Full shade: It will grow in darker places than almost any other fern.

Cyrtomium falcatum (Japanese Holly Fern). Big, bold, leathery evergreen fronds with toothy serrations, the pinnae about the size and shape of the teeth of *Tyrannosaurus rex*. Hardy to 15 or 20°F; in colder climates, a favorite greenhouse fern.

Dennstaedtia punctilobula (Hay-scented Fern). Grows 18 in. tall and several yards wide, spreading moderately fast. This common easterner is an excellent ground cover for summer-dry ground, in half shade or sun. When established, this tough deciduous plant will even thrive in ground close to pine trees, in sun/shade — but not too dark a spot. Best set out in the form of sods, for small divisions usually fail.

Dryopteris austriaca (Fancy Fern). Woods in North America; widely distributed and common. A 3-ft.-tall evergreen with particularly fine leaf partition: The green delta of the frond is mazy, with spaces that run like rivers and rivulets. Likes a cool, woody spot.

Dryopteris erythrosora (Japanese Shield Fern). Asia. Hardy nearly to 0°F. Slenderish, upright evergreen to 2 ft. tall. New growth rose-bronze; mature fronds polished light green. Shade three-fourths or full. A favorite with fern specialists.

Dryopteris Filix-mas (Hard Male Fern). The common name aptly contrasts the plant with the light green, lacy Lady Fern. This one is dark evergreen (or semievergreen) and has firm fronds; in a decade it forms

Ferns and flagstones. Left-side plantation: *Athyrium Goeringianum* 'Pictum'. To the right of the flags, near to far, an athyrium, a dryopteris, and a Christmas Fern. The hedge at the back is chamaecyparis, harmonious with ferns. (GEORGE TALOUMIS)

a substantial clump, like a shuttlecock in outline, to a yard tall and equally wide. Tolerates drought. The Hard Male Fern is of circumboreal range, but is best known as one of the "British ferns." Hundreds of fancy forms of this species — now mostly lost — were cultivated in Victorian and Edwardian England. The wild form remains one of the best furnishings for the shady garden, a plant on the order of our Christmas Fern or Western Sword Fern, but finer in the cut of its fronds. It is as sizable as these American ferns and goes well with them. *D. Borreri*, another Britisher, resembles *D. Filix-mas* and is equally valuable.

Dryopteris marginalis (Marginal Shield Fern). A 2-footer with fronds of broadsword outline. One of a trio of eastern American woodlanders common in the wild and commonly available through mail-order nurseries. The others are *D. cristata* (Crested Wood Fern) and *D. Goldiana* (Goldie's Wood Fern), both 2–3 ft. tall, the former with narrow evergreen fronds, the latter deciduous and with broad fronds.

Gymnocarpium Dryopteris (Oak Fern). An abundant North American forester. Makes a deciduous ground cover that is frothy light, a green spume advancing swiftly. Too low — 10–14 in. tall — and too airy to damage taller shade garden plants that it may surround.

Matteuccia Struthiopteris (Ostrich Fern). Grows wild in eastern American bogs and there a 5-footer. Deciduous, it forms a narrow, erect clump of dark glossy green fronds. Best in wet soil and part shade. In ordinary upland shade garden conditions, a smaller plant by half.

Nephrolepis cordifolia (Sword Fern — one of several so called, but not the western American plant of the name). The common fern of tropical and subtropical gardens all over the world; an old-timer in California's gardens. Fronds sword-shaped, simply cut, to 3 ft. tall. A colonizing fern that widens its patch slowly but inexorably. There are old plantings of this as much as 30 ft. across (very possibly from a single original division). Yet because the plant is predominantly upright in habit, it is well-suited to planting in narrow side yards. To keep it in bounds, edge the colony from time to time with a sharp spade, as if it were a spread of grass. For full or lighter shade. It is drought-tolerant, and there is none tougher.

Onoclea sensibilis (Sensitive Fern — the fronds die down with the first touch of fall frost). Eastern American bog fern that demands wet soil, or at least a place that is constantly moist. Its 2-ft. frond is unfernlike in its divisions and rather like a palm leaf.

Osmunda (flowering fern). Big, coarsely cut, deciduous ferns of upright impressiveness and a certain saurian fascination that fixes the fern hunter's eye while their native swamp grabs the ankle. Collected osmundas (commonly offered by eastern mail-order nurseries) crave bog conditions but will make do with heavy watering; half shade suits them best. Eventually they spread, but may take years to get going. *O. cinnamomea* (Cinnamon

Sword Fern (*Nephrolepis cordifolia*) and maranta intergrow beneath bamboo.

Fern) has young leaves densely downy with red-brown tomenta. *O. Claytoniana* (Interrupted Fern) has fruiting fronds peculiarly differentiated along their length, with some areas devoted to spore masses, others to green leaflets. But when given a cursory look, it seems ordinarily fernlike, with leaves feathered in the general manner. *O. regalis* (Royal Fern), however, has leaves cut like those of the locust tree, yet with larger leaflets; in the fall, before going down, they develop the yellow of the autumn locust leaf.

Polypodium vulgare, P. virginianum, P. glycyrrhiza, and **P. polypodioides** are closely related North American representatives of an odious crowd of ferns — an 1100-member worldly genus. By common name (not really in common usage), the first three are known as Licorice Ferns, the last as Resurrection Fern. Licorice Ferns have rhizomes that taste vaguely like their namesake (your taste buds will perhaps tell you you've gone too far if you investigate the resemblance). Resurrection Fern — apt name — dries up crisp and brown in summer, greens again with autumn rains. These plants grow as epiphytes on mossy tree trunks, logs, and rocks. To transplant them to the garden, use a knife blade to jimmy the fern from its native place, as you would an oyster from a rock; take with it all the moss and leaf mold that clings. Once home, press the mossy base of the fern firmly into a shady bed and water well. A small piece will ramify slowly and make of itself a ground cover patch the size of a welcome mat in three years or so. In my breezy hilltop garden near Seattle, with air that is prairie-dry for a couple of months in summer, all the Licorice Ferns emulate their resurrecting relative, drying off in summer, shedding their leaves, and going to sleep. Fall rains bring up new foliage that lasts through winter and spring.

Polystichum (shield fern). Dark evergreen ferns, clump-forming, very long-lived for perennial plants (some in my garden approach forty years in great vigor). In their general outline and different sizes, the various polystichums are like the fanned tail feathers of turkeys or of peacocks.

Polystichum acrostichoides (Christmas Fern), of our East, and *P. munitum* (Sword Fern) of our West Coast, are similar plants, 2–3 ft. tall, artistically strong and simple in the cut of their dark evergreen fronds. Both make excellent bedding plants or specimen plants in the shady garden.

Polystichum Andersonii (Anderson's Holly Fern) and *P. californicum* (California Holly Fern), a closely related duo, have finer fronds than the more boldly cut Christmas and Sword Ferns. *P. Andersonii* produces roly-poly baby ferns along its leaf midribs; *P. californicum* reproduces only by spores. No other differences are discernible in the two plants. Both are natives of West Coast mountain woods. *P. Braunii*, of the Great Lakes states and of mountains to the east, is botanically close to *P. californicum*. All three polystichums are choice as specimens or if you can acquire enough of them, as furnishings. I find *P. Braunii* uneasy to grow; the others very willing.

Polystichum setiferum acutilobum (or, less validly yet in general usage, *P. setiferum* 'Proliferum' or *P. viviparum*). Darkly evergreen, but fluffy in the intricacy of its leaf division. Baby ferns pop up along the leaf midrib. Peg the gravid frond flat on the ground in late summer; the babies will usually take root and grow into detachable, plantable youngsters by late the following spring. This British plant is often sold as "Iceland Fern" or "Alaska Fern"; the next species also bears these nursery monikers.

Polystichum setiferum 'Plumoso-Divisilobum' (also known as *P. plumosum*). Plumiest of ferns, its evergreen leaves are finely divided and thickly piled, like a brocade woven of moss. As strong and sure of life as it is delicate of aspect, but quickly damaged if the ground ever dries out.

Pteris cretica (Cretan Brake). For areas of light frost or none. Grows 16 in. tall, with evergreen fronds that have ribbonlike leaflets not particularly ferny. But the structure is apparently greatly attractive, for in Europe and North America this plant has become the most popular of small ferns for the house. A white-variegated form, *P. cretica* 'Albo-lineata', looks its best in full shade; the green parent plant (and the several green-leaved varieties) will take shade or half sun.

Thelypteris. Sudden spreaders suited to a rather wild stretch of ground. Deciduous, they turn from green to soft yellow before dying down. Hardly anyone will care to use their formidable Latin names, but even so, I'd better introduce the plants formally. *T. hexagonoptera* (Broad Beech Fern) and *T. Phegopteris* (Long Beech Fern), with broad and deltoid fronds, prefer upland soil; *T. noveboracensis* (New York Fern) and *T. palustris* (Marsh Fern) are narrower, attenuate ferns for wet ground. Marsh Fern is perhaps the strongest of these strong growers: Where moisture is unfailing, this one will extend its patch a yard a year.

Tree ferns. Tropical and subtropical plants of the genera *Cibotium, Cyathea,* and *Dicksonia.* Tolerant of light frosts in West Coast gardens. Cyathea, the tallest of the tree ferns, is rather like the Coconut Palm: trunk slender, clear, and upright (or leaning toward available light) and at the top, a broad, recurved umbrella of leaves. To make handsome growth, tree ferns need constant moisture and protection from drying winds, requirements best met in a sheltered garden, especially within a wooded canyon (that is not a wind tunnel). Provide *Cigotium* and *Dicksonia* filtered shade beneath trees or the afternoon shade of buildings; *Cyathea* grows best in part shade or full sun. Within a few years the young tree fern will stand tall enough to plant a garden community of small shade plants beneath it. Before planting, spread fresh shade garden soil at least 6 in. deep at the base of the tree fern — but no closer than a foot from the trunk, for fear of smothering the great fern.

Woodwardia (chain fern). *W. areolata* (Narrow-leaved Chain Fern), with fronds a foot long, and the somewhat larger *W. virginica* (Virginia Chain Fern) are rampant swamp plants native to eastern America from Canada to the Gulf. The western *W. fimbriata* is the grandest of American ferns, with arching evergreen fronds 7 ft. long. It is best known in the wild as an understory plant in the Redwood groves of Oregon and California. The plant is a clump maker (not a spreader) that requires percolating water in the ground — fresh moistness and a shady position so removed from the wind that you could read a newspaper there while a stiff breeze is blowing all around.

For that matter, all the ferns in the list will grow to perfection in a wind-sheltered part of the garden. The shade of lath, north wall, fence, or tree suits most; sometime exceptions are the bog ferns and the tree ferns. Provide ferns with a 6-in. depth or more of ideal shade garden soil (*see* p. 28), tree ferns with twice that depth. A rooting medium made up entirely of well-rotted humus, or of humus and sand, will also support ferns, if you add fertilizer in solution once in early spring, before fronds unfurl, and once more in high summer. Animal manures are perfectly usable on ferns.

Polystichum munitum, unrolling its new fronds in spring. Last year's foliage can be seen at bottom and at back.

Most literature advises against them, but any kind of decayed manure forked into the soil before planting produces whopping big fern plants.

Ferns appreciate moist soil, abhor drought. Try to give them enough water all summer to keep the surface of the ground damp. In winter, water those beneath eaves.

Propagating Ferns

Few kinds of ferns are today available in nurseries. So the best means of acquiring a fernery of unusual varieties is to grow them from spores. Packets of spores of about a thousand different ferns are available from the American Fern Society. Join up, and the spores are yours for a coin or two per packet. Large libraries subscribe to the society's journal, in which you'll find information on becoming a member. I must forewarn you — this journal is a formidably scientific publication. The articles in it dispense

Common Bracken *(Pteridium aquilinum)*, lower right and upper left, is usually considered a weed, yet there could not be a better plant in this setting. The owner edges the fern colonies by pulling out wandering stems. Garden of John W. Pitman. (DON NORMARK)

Latin polysyllables with the jarring relentlessness of a jackhammer. But I hope to put down here in plain English the essentials of spore culture. It is quite a rigamarole, but with experience it gets to be easier, and finally it will be routine.

Start with purchased spores in packets or collect your own from friends' gardens, or from nature. If you're collecting, late summer–early fall is the high season. Brown when ripe, the powder-fine spores will waft away when you tap the frond. A creased sheet of paper held beneath the frond while you tap it will catch some of the millions of escaping spores.

Spores germinate readily in a cold frame or indoors. With a cold frame, sow the spores as soon as you gather them, into a container that is to be kept inside the cold frame. Or fold them in a piece of paper and store them dry in a sealed container, to be kept in the refrigerator (spores, paper, and container must be perfectly dry). Spores that are to be germinated indoors are best sown in late winter.

Sowing medium: sphagnum moss rubbed through ¼-in. screen, moistened, and then squeezed as dry as possible. Fill flowerpots, clear plastic refrigerator boxes, glass casseroles, or nursery flats with the sphagnum. Tamp the peat moss, to level it, and put in a plant label. Dust the spores over the peat moss. Don't cover them, but do cover the container tightly with a transparent lid (or bag). Place the covered container on a windowsill that receives no direct sunlight, or near the window. But if you're using a cold frame, the container goes *uncovered* in a tightly sashed frame.

Most kinds of spores germinate within weeks into scalloped green growths, called prothallia, that look uncannily like liverworts. Next, tiny true fronds appear. When these grow half as long as your little finger, the sporeling ferns are ready to be separated, as you would seedlings, into nursery flats or flowerpots. Here they should remain, in order to batten before they go into the open ground. Mid-spring is the best time to plant them into the garden.

Ferns that bear live young along the fronds can be propagated by detaching the babies, together with a piece of the bearing frond, planting them, and caring for them over the winter in nursery flats as if they were shrub cuttings.

Ferns that stroll or romp in the garden by means of rhizomes are propagated by cutting a well-grown plant into pieces about as broad as the palm of your hand. Do this in early autumn or very early spring, before new fronds begin to unfurl (into wings, green wings).

13

Perennials

The late touches in landscaping, fillip plants that have leaves more tender and flowers spritelier than others, flowering collectibles and arrangeables — all of these are decor to be added after the trees, shrubs, ground covers, and ferns that are the floor, frame, and roof of the garden.

Nearly all the shade-craving or shade-tolerant plants in this chapter (indeed, in the book) are at their best in half-and-half shade and sun throughout the day, such shade as is provided beneath a tree whose open leaves sieve the light, or by the ribbed pattern within a lathhouse. Most shade plants will also grow to lushness in part shade — that is, in a blocky pattern of shade and sun alternating during the day: one to three hours of sun at a time and equal shade time. Wherever the perennials and other plants in this chapter vary in their needs or tolerances from these generally acceptable shades of shade, I'll specify the conditions that they prefer.

Where I say nothing about soil, assume a preference for ideal shade garden soil and a tolerance for soils more sandy or humusy than the ideal.

Note: See p. 87 in chapter 9 for explanation of the region codes NE, S, GN, NW, C, NC, SC, SW, and T, which are used below to indicate where each perennial, biennial, and bulb will grow well. Page 28 in chapter 2 gives a recipe for ideal shade garden soil, to which you will find frequent references in this chapter.

Except where otherwise described, all the plants to follow are perennials. We begin with a shade leaf celebrated in ancient architecture.

Acanthus mollis (Artist's Acanthus). S, NW, C, SW, T. Native to Mediterranean countries. A dark, polished evergreen clump about half the height of the gardener — after a couple of years, when the plant has gotten its

Woodside planting. Clockwise: 7:30 on the clock face, *Vancouveria planipetala;* at 8:30, *Viola odorata;* 10:00, *Meconopsis cambrica* (poppy flowers); 10:30, *Saxifraga muscoides* (small white flower at path edge); 11:00, choice little ferns and alpine tufts along the path; 11:30 to 1:00, tall rhododendrons and conifers; 2:30, clumps of big-leaved hostas: 3:00, montia, fine and lacy; 4:00, Lady Fern; 4:00 to 5:00, *Helleborus orientalis,* with palmy leaves and inverted, bowl-shaped flowers. Path surfaced with pea gravel. Garden of Ellen Martorano. (DON NORMARK)

roots down and its leaves up. The leaf is a brutal frond, a 2-ft.-long heart, ragged with slashes. The summer flowering produces 5-ft. spires of beak-like lilac, rose, or dull white flowers. In fertile, moist soil the plant spreads into a community, a rich cloak beneath trees or anywhere in light-to-full shade. The leaf is the one stylized on Corinthian columns. Today, Acanthus grows as a weed and a moral among those columns fallen in ruins.

Acorus gramineus (Grassy-leaved Sweet Flag). Any climate. From Japan; immemorial in Japanese gardens as a poolside plant. A grassy tuft half-a-yard tall, dark green or white-variegated. Will grow in full shade (in ordinary garden soil) or in full sun (in shallow water or in soil surely moist); also an indoor plant. A miniature form, *A. gramineus* 'Pusillus' grows 2 in. tall, a grassy imp for a choice shady bed or a terrarium.

Agapanthus. South African. Big clumps of strap leaves and showy blue, violet, or white flowers in summer. Any soil. Lighting should be three-quarters shade to full sun. At their best in warm and moderate climates.

Agapanthus campanulatus ("*A. Mooreanus minor*" in Reginald Farrer's *The English Rock Garden*). NW, C, SW, T. The hardiest: With a mulch, it will take below-zero temperatures, even those of most Northeastern winters. Irislike deciduous leaves and starry soft-violet flowers held 2–3 ft. tall on staff stems.

Agapanthus inapertus. NW, C, SW, T. Deep, yet glowing, violet-purple flowers in the form of long bells, on 4-ft. staffs. Deciduous foliage (in the NW, at least). Withstands short-term freezes down to 10 or 15°F.

Agapanthus orientalis. NW, C, SW, T. In warm climates of the world, one of the most planted garden perennials. Employed as stand-in shrub or hedge, as container specimen, or as ground cover. Forms a broad clump of evergreen leaves, fleshy and recurving; in summer, big umbels of starry flowers, white, porcelain-blue, or violet, on 3–5-ft. stems. Survivor enough to suffer the indignities of highway planting and castaway landscaping (dug out of the garden as too much of a good thing and tossed down a bank with grass trimmings and whatnot, it takes root and flowers uninsulted). Loves moisture, revels in a wet stream bank, but endures drought. Related to this species is the popular *Agapanthus* 'Peter Pan', a dwarf tuft about a foot tall, with blue flowers held a few inches above the foliage. Grown as far Northwest as Vancouver (in sheltered gardens).

Agave attenuata. C, SW, T. A Mexican succulent that won't take much frost. Softly grayish leaves in a rosette of wagon wheel girth when mature; a live sculpture for filtered shade. Plant in a container, or in a bed topped with sand or shared with *Ajuga reptans* 'Atropurpurea'.

Alchemilla vulgaris (Lady's-Mantle). Also sold as *Alchemilla mollis*. All climates. Ankle-high in spring flower, knee-high in summer flower, over a mound of yellow-green leaves, rounded, fluted, and serrate; frothy sprays of little chartreuse flowers. Lady's-Mantle planted with Daffodils will conceal their yellowing foliage. Or plant it along a wooded path, which the alchemilla — a free-seeder — will soon invade. However, mown once or twice a season, the plant forms flat growth that will take all foot traffic and provide a mudguard of tough foliage. When grown near smaller, less boisterous shade plants, Lady's-Mantle becomes a weed. Semishade; in any soil.

Alocasia (Elephant's-Ear). Alocasias are calla relatives and have the family's hooded flowers, amongst huge shield leaves.

Alocasia macrorrhiza (Giant Alocasia). sc, t. Forms a gardener-tall clump in rich, moist or wet soil; waist-high in a dryish spot; the clump spreads — not too rapidly — and will in time develop into a jungly ground cover. Full or part shade.

Alocasia odora (sc, t) has delightfully fragrant flowers within yellow-green hoods, stands 1 or 2 ft. taller than *A. macrorrhiza*, and forms a dignified, narrow clump — a slow giant. An old-fashioned flower of the raj, a favorite of British settlers in tropical Asia and the Pacific. Best in half shade, in wet or moist soil. Alocasias go well with shade-loving palms and bamboos.

Anemone japonica (*A.* ×*hybrida* var.). The Japanese Anemone; for all climates. Autumn-flowering perennial about 4 ft. tall, a plant that possesses wildflower character and fits easily into many semishady locations: near the bases of trees, in front of tall shrubbery, in flower borders, and against shady walls and fences. Large leaves divided into several leaflets that are maplelike in their shape and jaggy edges; sizable flowers, formed like saucers, in wine colors, white, or pink, with yellow stamens a pleasant contrast. A strong, long-lived clump that widens about 2 ft. a year. Propagate by digging deeply about the edges of the plant, prizing away some of the long, ropy roots, and replanting them at once in new places. Ideal shade garden soil or heavy loam.

Angelica Archangelica (Angelica). All garden climates. A 3–6-ft. biennial with a big compound frond of a leaf, coarsely pinnate and yellow-green; over the foliage, a spread of umbellate greenish flowers. Handsome plant for rich, moist soil, in half shade or filtered shade. Try the spicy leaf stalks candied or cooked with rhubarb.

Angelica pachycarpa. s, nw, c, sw, t. Tall biennial whose dark green frond leaves glisten with one of the brightest hard wax polishes in the plant world. Cooperative with any vegetation in the shady garden; a superb cut foliage.

Anthurium (tailflower). t. A major plant in tropical shade gardening. Large shield leaves; shiny bract flowers (also of shield form) that are red, pink, or white, with a rude caterpillarlike appendage at the center. Moist ideal shade gardening soil, nearly full shade.

Aquilegia (columbine). Growable everywhere. Centuries old in gardens. Renaissance paintings show Columbine attending lawn parties in castle gardens, along with daisies and Dandelions, courtiers and courtesans: Flowers and floridly garbed people stand together on the casual lawns of the time. Columbine is shown with dark violet or white flowers and is clearly *A. vulgaris* (European Crowfoot or Garden Columbine), a 2-ft.-tall perennial with upright stems, lacy leaves, and nodding flowers that are in form somewhat like a crown. The species is easily naturalized in open soil in a half-shady garden, from broadcast seed or from carefully planted seedlings (Columbine transplants uneasily). This same plant, crossed with several American species, has produced the many-colored border columbines. Give these light shade.

Two other columbines play significant roles in North American shade gardening, the red-and-yellow *A. canadensis,* of eastern woods, and the softly red-flowered *A. formosa,* native to half-shady glades in the West. The plants are not difficult to establish (technique as for *A. vulgaris*) in a moist, woodsy garden, but low humidity is their enemy.

Arthropodium cirrhatum (New Zealand Rock Lily). NW (shelter), C, SW, T. About 2 ft. wide and tall, a clump of grassy green leaves, strap-shaped and recurved; starry white flowers in airy sprays, in spring. A most accommodating evergreen landscape plant, good with stones, beneath trees, with ferns, on cliffs, and against walls that are partly or mostly shady. Guard from snails.

Arum maculatum (Lords-and-Ladies). All climates except GN. Tuberous perennial that will increase and eventually form a broad colony beneath trees — in places darker and in soil more root-clogged than most flowering plants will accept. Leaves in the shape of arrowheads pierce upward from the ground in spring, the blades green with purple markings. The foliage stands less than a foot tall at first, but later arises twice as tall on stalks. The spring flowers are hooded candles, the hood creamy or greenish, sometimes with deep purple spots. The yellow candle ripens in autumn into a conical cluster of bright red, shiny, bead-seeds. Needs moist or wet soil in spring; withstands summer dryness. A related species, *A. italicum,* (Italian Arum), differs in sending up its leaves in the fall. It has the same needs and virtues.

Aspidistra lurida. NW (shelter), C, SW, T. An old favorite among houseplants and the Aspidistra of Gracie Fields's theme song. Big dark evergreen leaves of lance-blade shape, clustered in a 30-in.-tall clump of sturdy character. Valuable in shade gardening for the rare ability to prosper in dense shade and famous for never (or hardly ever) saying die. With a sometime nickname of Cast-Iron Plant, Aspidistra is celebrated as a survivor of all bad gardening, including poor soil, no water, and total neglect. Naturally, it will look better with better treatment.

Astilbe. Plumy flowers on firm vertical stems, above leaves airily divided. Early-summer flowering; fall seed stems effective in dry arrangement. The numerous border hybrids stand 18–36 in. tall; the flower is white, salmon, rose-pink, raspberry, or pomegranate. Grow in moist soil and half shade

Astilbe against an east wall. The variety is 'Ceres', one of the many garden hybrids.
(DON NORMARK)

or wet soil in full sun. With constant moisture, the plants are easy to grow. Where the soil dries at any time, astilbe weakens and usually dies out within several years. The following species offer special values.

Astilbe chinensis var. *Davidii.* For all climates. Foliage low, flower stem a reedy 6 ft. tall, topped with a big display of blue-anthered lavender flowers. Unlike other astilbes, davidii does well in moist or dryish soil and will flower in full shade, though part shade is more to its liking. The plant's strange, splayed homunculus of a rootstock does not take to being divided. Grow this one from seed (which is so eager that the plant will even self-sow). All the other astilbes described below are easily divided by cutting the carrot-textured crown of the plant into wedges with a butcher knife — anytime, even when it is in plume.

Astilbe glaberrima 'Saxatilis.' For all climates. Pink-flowered dwarf (5 in.) for the semishady rock garden.

Astilbe simplicifolia. For all climates. Japanese woodlander, to 18 in. tall. In its fine leaves and gossamer white flowers, an Ariel of a plant. Give it a foreground spot in a choice, moss-covered bed, in shade filtered or nearly full.

Astilbe chinensis 'Pumila.' For all climates. Grows 1 ft. tall and is stoloniferous; to 18 in. or more wide. In flower, it is a grove of little fir tree towers of shocking pink — trees in a Fauve painting, with branches all puffs and spaces, as if cloud-pruned by a Japanese gardener. Half shade.

Begonia. Absent from here (and to be found with the shade garden annuals in chapter 14) are the fibrous bedding begonias and the tuberous begonias. There remain two perennial species of shade garden importance and a prodigious bunch of hybrids (rhizomatous begonias, Rex begonias) with beautiful leaves and small perky flowers, generally pink, that are grown as outdoor-indoor plants in cold areas but that can be left in the open in filtered shade year-round in warm climates (sc, t).

Begonias have their devotees, enough of them to sustain begonia societies and specializing nurseries. Many of our cities contain nursery greenhouses filled with begonias in dazzling array. Nearly all are hybrids that carry on their pot labels such names as hybrid plants are usually saddled with: 'Tiny Gem', 'Neon Lady', 'Raspberry Ripple'. Arriving home with plants of such christening, I manage to lose the labels quickly enough, or they lose themselves. I never directly throw them away, but somehow they slink out of sight, separating the plants and me from names not to be lived with.

Among the hardiest and easiest of hybrid begonias are those of the strain known as 'Cleopatra' (a name I've cared to remember). The leaves are maple-lobed, new ones claret-colored on the under surface, greenish on top: Light glowing through the young leaves fires them with October maple colors. Later, the plant's foliage ripens to an opaque Granny apple–green streaked with reddish brown.

'Cleopatra' is but one of a populous group of hybrids scooped up in the grab-bag term *rhizomatous begonias*, which term, however, conveys considerable garden information. Plants of this group broaden their clumps slowly by means of nubbly short rhizomes. In two or three years, the begonia grows broad enough that rooted pieces can be detached and potted separately. Pot gardening, with its heightened drainage, is the usual means of keeping these begonias outdoors, since their succulent rhizomes dislike water-retentive soil. But the plants are trusty in a fast-draining raised bed of ideal shade garden soil; when planting, bury the roots but let the rhizomes rest on the ground uncovered. The garden climate must be virtually frost-free. Temperature below about 28°F is a worry, below 24°F, fatal.

I don't know whether I'll ever work up the courage to remove my Rex begonias from their pots and plant them in the open ground, no matter how raised, and even altarlike, that spot may be. These plants simply seem too unearthly for a place in plain dirt. Mere leaves, with flowers not there or not remembered, if they were ever present — but *what* leaves: marbled, ocellated, silvered, gilded, alchemically suffused with essences of amethyst, emerald, topaz, and ruby, leaves star-form, or like angel wings, or like lily pads, with satiny or brocaded surfaces — the most resplendent of shade garden foliages.

Propagation of the Rexes is by division (very slow work) or by leaf cuttings: Cut off a mature leaf, stem and all, and insert the stem in peat or in ideal shade garden soil up to within slightly less than an inch of the leaf blade. New plants will sprout at the juncture of stem and blade.

Begonia foliosa var. **miniata** (*B. fuchsioides;* Fuchsia Begonia). C, SW, T. Mexican. Probably belongs in the shrub chapter: It has some wood at its base and certainly has the presence of a lightweight shrub. A cane-stemmed plant to 6 ft. tall (or long), it grows upright in part shade; in full shade, it leans low and becomes a ground cover. A fresh, rather dainty entity, with small shiny leaves and bright pink 1-in.-long flowers pendant in clusters of a few, like cherries. The foliage is pea-green in part shade, ivy-green in full shade (where the plant is shy about flowering). *Miniata* responds to pruning and can be shaped into a hedge or kept flat against a house foundation or a fence. Drought-tolerant.

Begonia grandis (*B. Evansiana;* Hardy Begonia). NE, S, NW, C, SW, T. Graceful Chinese and Japanese wildflower, 1–2 ft. high. Small pink flowers on furry stems, above leaves shaped like angel wings; leaf blades about 4 in. long, soft green in a shady place, with a grayish cast imparted by the play of light on the transparent down that covers the leaf surface. The plant grows from a small tuber that is safe in open, semishady ground. *B. grandis* is known to be hardy outdoors as far north as New York.

Billbergia (vase plant). S, C, T. Epiphytic bromeliads (tree-perching pineapple relatives), among the easiest to grow of the huge bromeliad clan. Collectors cultivate the many billbergia species and hybrids beneath moderately shady trees, or in the trees themselves, either hanging in pots of orchid mix or with their roots spider-packaged in sphagnum and twine, the plant then tied to the tree limbs (with natural-looking brown string — not, I hope, with pink plastic stuff, as I once saw it done). Beneath trees, billbergia will succeed in a spread of fresh, fluffy ideal shade garden soil, or in a raised bed filled with coarse bark chips, into which potted plants are plunged. *B. nutans* (Queen's-Tears), the hardiest of all, will take ten degrees of frost; narrow tan-green leaves; flowers nodding, vaguely lily-like, the petals green with blue rims. *B. zebrina* has deep green, gray-banded leaves; greenish flowers with apricot-colored bracts, in a dense spike, curved and weird. There's much entertainment in these plants and no foreseeable end to it, with new hybrids coming out yearly.

Bletilla striata. S, NW, C, SW, T. Terrestrial orchid from Japan. Up from bare ground in spring, 1–2 ft. tall, with narrow plaited leaves and slender amethyst-purple blooms. Grows from a crocuslike pseudobulb that is hardy nearly to 0°F when mulched or snow-covered (there is a white-flowered form, less hardy). Half shade or filtered shade. Can be plunged

Narcissus at the edge of the woods. Young Dogwoods in the middle ground, old maples and clumps of polystichum at the back. (DON NORMARK)

in a pot during the growing season, the pot lifted and the plant stored for the winter in a cold garage (the modern root cellar for many of us).

Brunnera macrophylla (Siberian Bugloss). All climates. A 2-ft.-tall forget-me-not, soundly perennial. Large, heart-shaped evergreen leaves; in spring, little azure flowers in sprays. Moist soil; semishade.

Bulbs. With one exception, noted below, those to be discussed are grow-able in all fifty states (in Hawaii probably only at cooling elevations) and throughout Canada. Most spring-flowering bulbs offer good prospects for flowers in tree shade, as long as the trees are deciduous ones that take kindly to underplanting. Certain bulbs, such as *Scilla campanulata* (Endymion hispanicus), *Galanthus* (snowdrops), and *Leucojum* (snowflakes), are in their native element in woodland shade; many others, though natural meadow plants, adapt to woodland gardening unexpectedly well. Planted beneath deciduous trees, these bulbs are well able to complete their work (food storage in the bulb and all) *in the sun,* before the tree leaves have grown full and shady. Among meadow bulbs, the whole tribe of Daffodils, including the miniatures, are capable of flowering and propagating superbly in woods, even in moderately heavy summer shade. They require no special care other than occasional feeding, and replanting whenever bulbs have overmultiplied. Many other bulbs flower well in deciduous shade: *Muscari,* camassias, *Eranthis,* and anemones (though it's hard to get bulbs of these last two that are fresh enough to grow), *Triteleia laxa (Brodiaea laxa), Chionodoxa,* certain native alliums, *Crocus* — especially *Crocus Tomasinianus.*

The most shade-tolerant plant mentioned above is probably *Scilla campanulata,* now known to botanists as *Endymion hispanicus* or *Hyacinthoides hispanica.* (Do wish they'd stop juggling this bulb, perfectly well known to millions of us as Scilla.) Scilla will often seed and naturalize in woods under high-branched deciduous trees; great sweeps of the campanulate violet flowers are to be seen in May in certain long-established woodland gardens.

Allium, the onion genus, several hundred in all, is represented in the shade garden first by *A. Moly* (Lily Leek), a bright and shiny yellow flower — a lot of flowers — over gray-green tuliplike leaves; the small edible bulbs taste like shallot. Performs well in shade that is light to nearly full. *A. triquetrum,* a foot tall, has broadish grass-blade foliage; white scillalike flowers early to mid-spring. Small pearly white bulb with a delicate onion

Spring again. Snowdrops bravely up, through a litter of last fall's Japanese Maple leaves. Prickly evergreen leaf at lower left is Mahonia nervosa. (DON NORMARK)

flavor; good raw or pickled. This plant is widely naturalized in England, New Zealand, and parts of North America. Competes successfully with rough grasses and can be mowed. A pretty flower and leaf for shady way-places. The odorless foliage dies down by the end of spring, and the plant completely disappears. *Tradescantia fluminensis* (Wandering Jew) or *Duchesnea indica* (Indian Strawberry) will carry on as evergreen cover plants in the same ground.

Erythronium. Dogtooth violets and trout lilies hold nodding flowers 1 ft. or less above the ground and are magnetically attractive to slugs and snails. Only diligent spreading of bait will save these bulbs. *E. Dens-canis* (Dogtooth Violet), from Europe, is the strongest-growing; white, pink, and violet-purple in its named forms. California's buttery yellow *E. tuolumnense* is virtually as strong, but lacks elegance. *E. revolutum* of California is a reasonably stalwart garden plant, available in white, pink, lavender, or rose. The Oregonian *E. Hendersonii* will seed about readily and colonize its lilac flowers. These four are perhaps the surest to establish themselves in the shady garden. But quite often the corms of any *Erythronium,* even when supplied by our best nurseries and properly set out early in the autumn bulb-planting season, fail to overwinter and to show up as leaves and flowers next spring. Either the corms were too dry when purchased, or underground pests (mice or weevils, or slugs, rooting like swine) got to them.

Fritillaria imperialis (Crown-Imperial) is growable across our continent, but is at its best in GN — the cold-winter, dry-summer interior of North America (the plant enjoys "a good baking"). A magnificent spring bulb: at the top of a 4-ft. staff, a cluster of large orange or yellow bells and, crowning the flowers, a jaunty tuft of leaves. Grow in high, filtered shade or in the open on a north-facing hillside. Where Crown-Imperial is especially happy with its situation, it will naturalize from seed. *Fritillaria Meleagris* (Checkered Lily) is a strange and interesting nodding purple flower with white checkers, or a white flower with faint checker marks; on a 15-in. stem. For checkered shade.

Lilies are late about ripening their foliage, and so location in cool dappled shade doesn't suit them; a blocky sun/shade pattern is acceptable, as long as shade doesn't fall more than half the day.

Good old **Montbretia** *(Crocosmia ×crocosmiiflora),* with its orange-scarlet summer flowers, will naturalize in half-shady places S, NW, C, SW, and T.

See also the genus *Cyclamen,* a group of tuberous plants for semishade, described below.

Cacti. C, SW, T. The tropical perching cacti *Epiphyllum, Hylocereus, Selenicereus,* and *Schlumbergera* (which contains the Christmas Cactus) require filtered shade when they are grown as outdoor plants. Give them well-drained, ideal shade garden soil and water them plentifully in summer, hardly at all in winter. In the desert Southwest, many of the cacti of such terrestrial genera as *Echinocereus, Echinopsis, Lobivia, Mammillaria, Parodia,*

Erythronium Hendersonii — best planted early. (DON NORMARK)

Rebutia, and *Trichocereus* grow best in light shade, as beneath mesquites or palos verdes. In all, there are enough shade-loving cacti to make of them a complete shade gardening hobby. Consult growers' catalogs (advertised in garden magazines).

Caladium (Mother-in-Law Plant). C, SW, T. With a mulch, these calla relatives from tropical America are hardy wherever the soil freezes no more than skin deep. Grown for their large arrowhead leaves, gaily decorated in shades of rose, white, silver, or green. They are nurtured from dormant tubers by the same method used for tuberous begonias. In cold-winter climates, caladiums are pot plants summered outdoors in shade. In the tropics and subtropics, use them as bedding plants. Their broad, colorful leaves are a perfect foil for lacy green ferns.

Calathea and **Maranta**. T. The two genera are closely related. Tufted foliage plants, the leaves with patterns like those of African shields, with lines and patches of variant green, white, and coppery rose. Effective in a forest garden.

Calceolaria polyrrhiza 'John Innes'. Chilean plant hardy at −20°F; growable everywhere except GN. Loose green mat less than a foot tall, slowly creeping and rooting down. Summer flowers, on wiry stems, are buttery yellow with purple spots. Give the plant semishade, ideal shade garden soil, and plenty of water.

Caltha palustris (Marsh Marigold). For all climates. Spring wildflower native to eastern North America. Large buttercups over shiny heart-shaped leaves. A nursery form has fully double flowers. Marsh Marigold needs wet or damp soil in semishade.

Campanula (bellflower). The many species flower cheerfully in shade up to half the day. The ones described below are hardy and growable everywhere.

Campanula cephallenica. Related to *C. Poscharskyana* (see chapter 11), but smaller and tidier. In the wild, an inhabitant of shady cliffs. A climber, even of brick. Planted in my garden at the base of an old brick wall whose mortar has become mellow and fertile, the plant has reached the top by pressing its stems against the wall face, rooting, and hoisting itself (by its own bootstraps, almost).

Campanula lactiflora. A 6-footer with milky-blue summer flowers; in keeping with a wild garden. This species and *C. persicifolia* are tough, long-lived plants that prefer rich, moist soil; yet they will also thrive in rather poor, dry places. Both are among the best of flowers for dry shade — shade up to three-quarters full.

Campanula persicifolia (Willow Bellflower). Narrow leaves in a hearty clump. In late spring, the plant sends up stems 2–3 ft. tall on which demitasse-size cups, china-blue or white, open abundantly. Thirty years ago I sent off to Burpee for a packet of seed of this campanula. A few seedlings sprouted for me, and over the years these have reseeded themselves into thousands. They take up more of the garden than I would wish, but give a bonanza of color with no care — a free flower.

Campanula Portenschlagiana (formerly *C. muralis*). In the North, a green clump; in a subtropical climate, a generous mat; everywhere a plant covered in its spring season with dark violet urn flowers. Light shade (or full sun) in the North; afternoon shade or part shade in southerly climates.

Campanula rapunculoides (Rover Bellflower). Planting this in a kempt garden would be something like selling one's soul to the devil. It is a seasonal glory, no denying that, yet one that would collect its dues forever in weeding time; given a place near politer garden citizens, it is a tireless invader by way of white radishlike roots. But in a shady wild garden or in an open woods, it is a safe and stately plant; flower stems

3–5 ft. tall, lined with violet funnel-shaped flowers all summer. Moderately drought-tolerant.

Carex (sedge). Grasslike clumps for moist shade. Refreshing evergreen foliages, easily grown in pots or in the open ground. All are readily converted into ground covers by pulling a hefty clump apart into many divisions and planting these closely enough that the leaf ends touch.

Carex comans 'Frosty Curls'. s, nw, c, t. New Zealander. Silvery green tussock 10 in. tall; leaves arching and trailing, to 2 ft. long. Once I saw this flourishing as a ground cover between the hogback roots of an old Moreton Bay Fig Tree — where no plant will grow, but there it was.

Carex conica 'Variegata'. All climates except gn. Japanese. In time, a tuft 10 in. tall and somewhat wider, the curving leaves green with a white midrib.

Carex Morrowii 'Variegata'. Japanese. Hardy up to central New York. Well known as an edging plant both in conservatories and in water gardening. To 16 in. tall, the white-margined leaf blades stiffly vertical. A foil for the big green foliages of the arum family.

Carex Morrowii 'Variegata Aurea'. Hardy nw (with shelter), c, sw, t. Slow grower. Curved 10-in.-long leaves with a wide, pale yellow midstripe bordered narrowly with dark green. Will grow in full shade, even double-shaded by taller plants. An easy houseplant.

Ceratostigma plumbaginoides. All climates except gn. Creeping perennial with bright violet phloxlike flowers in late summer. Good performance in moist soil with half shade or dappled shade. Eventually spreads to ground cover proportions.

Chlorophytum elatum var. *variegatum* (Spider Plant). c, t. In appearance, a decorative Bunchgrass (though in fact a relative of the lilies). A big clump of broadish white-striped grass blades, so well known in indoor gardening. Outdoors it is easy to grow — and generously increasing — beneath trees, even in rather darkly shaded, dryish soil. The grassy clump sends out little replicas of itself on spider-line stolons; the growth of these young ones and of *their* offspring will turn a single clump into a 2-yd.-wide ground cover in several years.

Chrysogonum virginianum. Eastern American woods plant. A pleasant little 3-in.-tall mat, growable everywhere; a single division spreads to 15 in. wide in a couple of years. Dense and tight on the ground with its fresh green spoon leaves, and it stays fresh through the winter; in spring, yellow daisies faceup on the foliage. Dislikes summer dryness.

Cimicifuga (bugbane). Will take the coldest North American winters and all other winters except those of sc and t. Late-summer wildflowers, slender spikes of white held several feet above an airy bushel of compound leaves. Graceful plants for cool, constantly moist ground, partly shaded.

WOVEN GARDENS

Plantings of woodland perennials look their best when the different foliages meet and mix somewhat. Several of the perennials shown in these photos are listed in the book under ground covers.

Asarum caudatum (lower right), *Oxalis oregana* (shamrock leaves), *Fragaria virginiana* (strawberry foliage), *Polypodium glycyrrhiza* (small fern fronds), *Petasites speciosus* (top of picture), *Dryopteris arguta* (fern at lower left). (DON NORMARK)

Fine foliage, white flowers: *Dicentra formosa* 'Sweetheart'. Palmate leaves: *Helleborus orientalis*. Big heart-shaped leaves: *Hosta plantaginea*. Lance-leaved clumps: *Hosta lanceolata* hybrids. Garden of Frances McBride. (DON NORMARK)

Plectranthus australis (lower left with rounded leaves, pagoda flowers), *Cymbidium* (center, with curved strap leaves), ferns in variety, *Monstera deliciosa* (the well-known Split-Leaf Philodendron). Author's garden in Auckland, New Zealand.

Corydalis. Any climate except GN. Small, cheery spring flowers, usually yellow. The foliage is ferny and a tender green, the flowers are little steeple assemblies. Plants for moist semishade, where they will self-sow.

Crassula lactea (Flowering Crassula, Tailor's-Patch). C, SW, T. Stout, shrublike succulent, to 2 ft. tall, of great help for its extreme tolerance of shade: Will prosper in as dark a place as can any plant higher in life's hierarchy than the mosses. If this won't take it, nothing will. Dark green leaves approximately the size and hollow, ovalish shape of spoon-bowls; starry white flowers in loose clusters at the branch ends. In foliage, the plant is rather a dark presence to place in dark shade, but it is an excellent container plant, and a container will give it definition.

Cyclamen. NE, S, NW, C, SW, T. The region codes apply to the small European wildflowers of the genus. These are available, American-grown, from bulb suppliers and from rock garden nurseries. They are sold soilless or potted up; if soilless, they come as small bun-shaped tubers, rounded at the bottom, dented on top. Plant the dented end upward, in ideal shade garden soil; cover the tuber only ¾ in. deep.

The hardiest and easiest is *C. hederifolium* (*C. neapolitanum;* Baby Cyclamen), autumn-flowering, with small shooting-star flowers, rose or white, held ½ ft. high over 3-in. marbled leaves that are rather like those of a minor ivy. With smaller leaves and flowers, and slightly less hardy, are *C. coum,* flowers carmine or white in late winter and spring, leaves dark green and rounded; *C. europeum,* carmine or white in autumn and spring, leaves heart-shaped, green with a silver zone; *C. × Atkinsii,* a hybrid involving *C. coum,* foliage of coum shape, but with silvery markings, the early-spring flowers pale rose or white; and *C. repandum,* heart-leaves marbled or not, the spring flower, carmine to white, with a darker part at stem end.

In California and warmer places, all these plants are surely hardy and are likely to naturalize from seed if planted in well-drained ideal shade garden soil, in part shade. The northwestern winter of rain and freeze and thaw is about the nastiest these plants can take (snowy winters in colder regions are actually easier for cyclamen). Yet they will survive the Northwest handily in warm shade or in the shady shelter of evergreen conifers (those whose roots and shade are not too dense).

Cymbidium. C, T. Easy-going orchids. With insouciance they face the average gardener's alternating wild enthusiasm and total absence from the path of duty. They have become hobbyists' plants, with the result that there are now enough of them to make a hobby of unending exploration (the only worthwhile kind). Thousands of cymbidiums are available, hybrids largely derived from six wildflower ancestors native to highland forests in Burma, Annam, and Sikkim. Their garden progeny have inherited an ability to withstand a few degrees of frost.

Cymbidiums are at least as valuable for their foliage as for their flowers. The plant is an evergreen clump of leathery strap leaves, 2–3 ft. long and arching — a blendable leaf (as narrow, curving leaves usually are) that goes well with ferns and begonias and practically all others in the shade garden

Flowers exceptionally long-lasting, in soft shades of terra cotta, chartreuse, yellow, and grapes (of all kinds), and in white.

The plants are long-lived in containers or in the open ground, without being divided. Many gardeners say that leaving cymbidiums undisturbed for years (to grow, if in a container, crammed at root and crown) stimulates heavier flowering. Fertilize cymbidiums frequently — at least once a month from midwinter until the following autumn (some gardeners fertilize the plants with each watering; that is, at about ten-day intervals). In early winter, water cymbidiums sparingly and hold off fertilizer.

The ideal shade garden soil recipe is right for cymbidiums; they also do well in a chunky orchid mix (recipe in chapter 2). In any case, drainage must be superlative, as in a pot or in a sloping or raised bed. Cymbidiums often produce a greater number of flowers in light shade, but here the foliage takes on a detracting yellowishness. Lath shade or moderate tree shade (with its constantly shifting speckles of sunlight) is the best exposure, producing deep green, lustrous leaves and a goodly number of flowers.

Cymophyllus Fraseri (*Carex Fraseri;* Fraser's Sedge). All climates. Eastern American. A grassy starfish flat against the ground, the many rays (leaves), strap-shaped. Likes wet soil and full shade or semishade.

Cyperus (umbrella sedge). Two of these somewhat grasslike perennials are considerable blessings to the shade gardener. They will perform handsomely in full shade or in lighter shades, in soil soggy or summer-dry. With their stems and leaves of bamboolike lightness, the cyperuses blend easily with other shade garden foliages.

Cyperus albostriatus '**Elegans**' (*C. diffusus*). C, SW, T. A sedge 2 ft. tall. In summer-dry ground, it is a rather slow clump, but in a swampy area, off to the races. Leaf fingers at the tops of the stems are like broad grass-blades. In summer the stems lean under the weight of the grassy heads of leaves combined with that of sprays of pale green grasslike flowers at the top, lending the plant a graceful ease. Good with plants in general, especially with mahonias and ferns.

Cyperus alternifolius (Umbrella Plant). C, SW, T. A reed 3 ft. tall in open garden soil, where it is moderate in growth — a yard wide in about 5 years; in water or in waterside mud, the plant goes ahead much more quickly. Stems of glossy rich green; at the top, a palmetto hand of many slim leaf fingers arranged in a circle. The brittle stems are vulnerable to children roughhousing in the garden.

Cypripedium (Lady-slipper). NE, S, GN, NW, C. The North American species linger in the mail-order trade, and are likely, in every case, to be plants collected from the wild. Eastern cypripediums are woodlanders. In the garden they require ideal shade garden soil and a dapple-shaded, sheltered spot where the air and soil surface remain moist in summer, but the ground must be airy and fast-draining. None of our cypripediums is especially easy to grow. The least intractable are the eastern *Cypripedium Calceolus* var. *pubescens* (*C. pubescens*) — petals yellow-brown, slipper yellow

— and *C. reginae* (queenly indeed, with its large flowers, the petals white or blush, the slipper soft rose). *C. californicum* (sepals yellowish tan, slipper white) grows in seacoast bogs and on the mossy banks of snow-water freshets in the Siskiyous. The plant can be established in a half-shaded garden, in sloping soil constantly wet with spring water. Take care that the orchid, a fastidiously slow grower, never becomes pressed against by the usual crowd of water-loving weeds. The dignified western *C. montanum* (Mountain Lady-Slipper), with its brown-petaled, white-slippered flowers (and its roots that attempt to defend the plant by giving off a strong smell of horse at the moment it is dug and kidnapped from the wild), usually can only be grown in gardens in the inland mountain regions, in a half-shady bed or woodland planting that is allowed to "bake" (an old garden term, meaning don't water after the Fourth of July; let the ground go dry so that plants will aestivate in a dormant condition).

Dianella tasmanica. c, sw, t. With its staunch bladed leaves, this is like a great iris or a middle-size phormium. Good landscaper's foliage, but the plant is grown more for its sprays of turquoise-blue berries. Smaller-growing by half — to 18 in. tall — is New Zealand's *D. nigra*, with berries turquoise or milky blue. Grow these liliads beneath friendly trees, in half shade or dappled shade.

Dicentra (bleeding-heart). Spring herbs, up early and quickly dressed with their delicately lacy leaves and heart-shaped flowers drooping on arching stems. Flowers stay fresh on the plants for a couple of months. In a moist garden (the best for bleeding-hearts), the tender foliage remains until fall and then turns soft yellow or violet before dying away:

Dicentra eximia (Turkey Corn, Wild Bleeding-Heart). NE, S, NW, C. Eastern North American wildflower native to half shade. A narrow, 12-in.-tall clump with heart flowers slender and rosy. This plant has a short and glorious flowering life and will leave plenty of seed. It may self-sow — and if any of the forms of *D. formosa* grow in the vicinity, the seedlings will come up hybrids. An outstanding hybrid of *D. eximia* and *D. formosa*, *Dicentra* 'Bountiful', has plump rosy red flowers over a long season, lives for several years, and can be maintained permanently by starting new plants from divisions. Even more vigorous than 'Bountiful' is the rosy pink *D. eximia* hybrid 'Luxuriant'. Less easy to keep is the albino, *D. eximia* 'Alba'.

Dicentra formosa (Western Bleeding-Heart). NE, S, NW, C. Western North American. Stoloniferous and permanent: Makes itself into a light green, ferny carpet overarched by many stems of cool lilac or rosy hearts. *D. formosa* 'Bacchanal' is a bright burgundy-red seedling named and introduced by your author (1960). *D. formosa* 'Sweetheart', white over pale green leaves, is a perfectly gardenable albino, a blithe spirit of a shade flower. Blooms throughout spring and again in early fall. Grow any of the Formosas in moderate tree shade, afternoon shade, or bright north-wall shade.

Dicentra spectabilis. NE, S, NW, C. Japanese. A great big ferny clump, 3 ft. high, 4 ft. across — a fern mimic startlingly decorated with large, crimson-rose hearts hanging in neat rows on horizontal stems (later in spring than the flowers of other bleeding-hearts). Needs a sheltered, half-shady place; ideal shade garden soil or a fat loam, with constant moisture. There is, as well, a good strong white-flowered form of the plant.

Digitalis purpurea (Foxglove). For all garden climates, but uneasy in a dry region. A tall European biennial with purple or white floral towers in early summer. Abundantly naturalized in the Pacific Northwest in woods' margins and on road cuts, in part shade, light shade, or sun. Plant by broadcasting seed in moist, open soil where you want the flowers to stand.

Doronicum. For all climates, but weakened by even the briefest dryness. Big bright yellow spring daisies over a widening clump — finally a mat — of heart leaves. Foliage a glabrous tender green, quite salady-looking (slugs are most appreciative of it). In rich, moist soil, in the part shade of trees, doronicum will take care of itself for years before having to be divided and reset. The 12–18-in.-tall plants sold under the names *D. cordatum* and *D. Clusii* are usually hybrids (of considerable wildflower character). *D.* 'Miss Mason', an especially vigorous grower, has a grandness of flower more suited to a shady border than to casual planting under trees.

Echeveria elegans (Pearl Echeveria). C, SW, T. Mexican succulent, generous with offsets. In sun, the plant is gray-white, the rosettes shaped like artichokes, 4 in. across when mature. Filtered shade turns it greenish white — a soft soapstone color — and the rosette enlarges and opens so that the leaves lie nearly flat; as shade-grown plants will, the echeveria takes on a visual gentleness. Wedge a few rosettes in the seams of shady stonework and let them increase into a leafy trim for the rocks. Or plant in a tallish container and place it, perhaps, in a shady bed of bronzy ajuga. Other gray-leaved echeverias work equally well as foliage plants in shade, but their flowers are usually not forthcoming here.

Epipactis gigantea (Giant Helleborine). For all climates. Western American terrestrial orchid, easy and permanent in moist soil or in springwater-soaked ground, in part shade. Small greenish orchids that also have rose and brown parts.

Equisetum hyemale (Scouring Rush). All climates. Evergreen canes with natty bands of ash and charcoal colors. Stands about 42 in. tall and spreads like one of the dynamite bamboos, if given the chance. A dramatic container plant in shade; or plant in watery ground with *Hosta, Alocasia,* or *Lysichiton;* or in the poorest dry ground (poverty will slow it down, but will by no means halt its explosion).

Euphorbia rigida. NW, C, SW, T. A bushy 2-ft.-tall Grecian plant, with the look of a drylander in its stocky stems, grayish semisucculent leaves, and

Equisetum hyemale (banded rush stems) intergrowing with hostas and *Iris Douglasiana* in my garden near Seattle — I don't mind plants in active mixtures.

yellow-green flowers in broad umbels. Of special value in California and the Southwest for its willingness in droughty shade.

Francoa ramosa (Bridal-Wreath). c, sw, т. Chilean relative of the saxifrages. A lushness of evergreen leaves that are rather acanthuslike (only smaller and of a lighter green); yard-tall spikes of pink or white four-petal flowers in summer. An easy grower in moist semishade and a burgeoner, at a moderate pace, from a planted piece into an eventual patch. Landscaper's plant, good for many an invention — as, for example, francoa in a dichondra lawn, or francoa with thalictrum.

Gentiana (Gentian). Plants for ideal shade garden soil or a lushly caloric loam, the garden equal of a rummy fruitcake. Gentians grow as wildflowers in soil never dry, in regions where clouds, dews, and abundant vegetation temper the sun. These plants *need* sun, but sun cooled down. As compensation for their native moistened sunshine, grow garden gentians in part shade. Gardens in the North or at elevations are especially suited to gentians — the farther north or the higher on the mountain (up to the snow line), the better. However, at the hands of skilled shade gardeners, gentians can be managed in the hottest, driest climate: Our consultant Margaret Williams, who gardens in the Nevada desert, flowers gentians in the shade of a lath canopy. And the shade gardener anywhere on the continent lucky enough to have a stream or spring or weepy slope in the garden, with plantable soil saturated by fresh, percolating water (yet safe from flood), may well be in possession of ground perfect for the robust growth and flowering of gentians and of a great variety of rare primulas, terrestrial orchids, saxifrages, and other hard-to-please shade flowers. There the gentians and the others will want only light shade.

Gentiana acaulis (Stemless Gentian) is an easy-to-grow plant, but not always an easy one to flower. It hugs the ground, a close aggregation of little dark green glossy leaves in rosettes. The deep blue urn-form flower, stemless or nearly so, stands several inches tall and is huge for the plant. Best chance for flowers: superrich soil, constantly moist; sun, with just enough shade to keep the plant from scorching. NE, GN, NW, C.

Gentiana Andrewsii. NE, GN, NW, NC. The Closed Gentian of eastern North America. Grows 1–2 ft. tall, with dark blue flowers that are the shape and size of Christmas tree lights. A plant proffered by dealers in native species; a relatively easy grower and a sure flowerer, in July and August.

Gentiana asclepiadea. NE, GN, NW, NC. European. Strong, leafy plant, to 2 ft. tall if grown to a lushness (as it should be). Summer flowers in numbers at the branch ends, bell-form, *Lycaena*-blue with purple dots inside.

Gentiana septemfida (Crested Gentian). NE, GN, NW, NC. Fully tested by rock gardeners, New York to San Francisco; a success across the land. In high summer, a well-grown, several-year-old septemfida sends up dozens of flower stems about a foot high, each holding a cluster of lapis lazuli bells with rims that break and recurve in five starpoint lobes.

Gentiana sino-ornata (NE, GN, NW, NC) heads a group of Himalayan species with narrow grasslike leaves in tufts (easily divisible) and trumpet-shaped autumn flowers with conspicuous stripes of green and darker blue on a blue ground. Not difficult to grow in a moist garden.

Related species, such as *G. Farreri* and *G. Veitchiorum*, are challenging plants for gardeners located in the foggy dews of the Maine coast and the Pacific Northwest, or in Alaska.

Geranium. Not the window box and bedding annual "geranium" (which is technically pelargonium), but the true geraniums, a group of perennials of mounded or straying habit. Although these plants are relatively new and unknown to North American gardeners, they are, to the British, pieces of Edwardiana prized since the day of Gertrude Jekyll, doyenne of the perennial border — and are, by the British, still featured in community with such summer flowers as Foxglove, *Lunaria*, *Campanula lactiflora*, *Hosta*, and *Cimicifuga;* in part shade.

True geraniums have maplelike leaves, several inches across in the species described below. They produce five-petal flowers, rounded into a cup, in quantity during high summer and then a sprinkling until fall. An old English name for the plants is Cranesbill, after the long-beaked seed head. This singular structure, green at first, ripens dry-brown and firm to its purpose, that of seed catapult: The "bill" of the device serves as a support post for five slings, each carrying a single seed. The ripened slings burst from the central post and fling the seeds several feet or yards.

Geraniums are hardy in all climates, with the exception of certain species, noted below.

Geranium ibericum. Russian Georgia. A foot tall with blue flowers over downy maple leaves. Closely allied is *G. platypetalum*, from the same region; 2 ft. tall, flowers violet. Both are clump-forming plants.

Geranium **'Johnson's Blue'.** Large bright blue cups; a glorious plant in flower.

Geranium madieriense. c, sw, t. Madeira. A rounded, tap-rooted plant, 3 ft. tall, with glossy green leaves; hot magenta flowers, scores together in panicles. Has a fascinating habit of growth: The big leafy hemisphere props itself firmly on many elbows — leaf stems that point down to meet the ground, then angle up to fit the leaves into the green dome. A biennial, it sows its own seedlings to carry on.

Geranium palmatum (*G. anemonifolium*). c, sw, t. A Madeiran wildflower deservedly popular with plant collectors in California. To 2 ft. tall, flower warm magenta; short-lived, freely seeding — a weed most welcome in the casual garden.

Geranium phaeum. European. British folk name is Mourning Widow. Small bird's-bill flowers (petals reflexed, pistil exserted) are black-magenta, magenta-rose, or mauve — seedlings are highly variable. Flowers over a long season; accepts full shade. Foliage clump 12 in. tall; flower stems 20 in.

Geranium sanguineum. Europe. The typical, magenta-flowered form should be planted only in the garden of one's enemy, by secretly shooting the seeds forth with a slingshot or blowpipe. These will come up and flower ingratiatingly and will be accepted as one of those mysterious floral strangers that show up; but having flowered, the seedlings will fling their own seeds everywhere. Very soon the garden will be filled with this deeply rooted, ineradicable pest.

Two forms of *G. sanguineum* don't have the weedy proclivity, however, and are among the best of shade flowers. One of them is *G. sanguineum* 'Album', an open, wiry-stemmed clump, 18 in. tall, with small leaves that have a bird-foot cleft, and white flowers, May to September. The other is *G. sanguineum lancastriense* (from coastal cliffs in Lancashire, England), a dense, flattened bush, a foot tall (or less), 2 ft. across, flowering all season; the corolla cup is crepe-textured, white with rose veins (one's eyes blend the colors and make a pink flower of this). Lancastriense can be used as a ground cover.

Geranium Wallichianum 'Buxton's variety'. NW, C, SW, T. Himalayan, at temperate mid elevation. Flowers, violet-blue with a white eye, open all summer. The plant stands somewhat more than a foot tall and is modestly stoloniferous, spreading to a couple of feet across in several summers. A possible ground cover.

Two other geraniums are definitely ground covers, and of the finest; They are listed in chapter 11.

Gunnera chilensis, G. manicata. NW, C, SW, T. Two mammoth perennials for shallow water or boggy ground in part shade (with strong, sunbather's sun for several hours). The rounded, wavy leaves are lobed, as large as open umbrellas (or even twice that big — beach umbrella–size), and as high as umbrellas held overhead. The two species are closely similar. In *G. chilensis* (Chilean), the leaf lobes are deeply and finely toothed; in *G. manicata* (Brazilian), the teeth of the lobes are coarser. Hardy down to 15°F, if the crown of the plant is protected by being covered with its own huge leaves (once they've turned brown in autumn), the leaves weighted with stones. In the Southwest, gunneras require total shade in the afternoon and shelter from drying winds.

Heliconia (false bird-of-paradise). T. One of my dreams (not to be requited by reality) is to be a tropical shade gardener specializing in heliconias, to plant them beside a path winding through a lignum vitae grove, and to muse upon the Mayan extravagance of their flowers. Never mind. The heliconias are several dozen tropical American forest plants, 18 in. to 18 ft. tall. They are clump makers, with leaves large and firm, shaped like a canoe paddle (typically), and arranged in two ranks. They are relatives of bird-of-paradise *(Strelitzia)*, with an even more ugly beauty. The inflorescence of *Heliconia* is a bract structure flattened and segmented into a semblance of a rattlesnake rattle. In scale with the plant, the various species have "flowers" the size of a playing card, of a book, of a Mosaic tablet; many are blood-red, or red with green tips on the bract segments. These plants grow naturally in tree shade, but flower best when warmed by several hours' sun. Use ideal shade garden soil or a loam that would also grow good corn or tomatoes.

Helleborus (hellebore). Cup-form flowers in winter and early spring; handsome evergreen leaves. Plants for ideal shade garden soil and the shade of deciduous trees or north walls.

Helleborus foetidus. European. For all climates. Grows 18 in. tall, the green leaves divided into slender leaflets. February to April, the plant holds in abundance clustered flower cups, green rimmed with rose. Lives three years or so and leaves a flock of seedlings close about the parent plant.

Helleborus lividus subsp. *corsicus.* s, NW, C, SW, T. Corsica and Sardinia. Set this one out as a seedling or potling and let it be; the deep, sparse roots of the grown plant won't allow transplanting. Above ground, a cluster of several stout stems to a yard tall; at their tops, saw-edged leaves in threes, forming a palm about a foot wide, which is leathery and waxen to the touch. In various lights, tints of yellow, gray, or blue come forth from the basic green of the leaf. March to May, the plant carries yellow-green flower cups in clusters. Bees dote on them, and the honey they make may be imbued with helleborine, a drug that courses in the veins of hellebores. Corsicus lives three to five years and leaves a few seedlings.

Helleborus niger (Christmas Rose). All climates. A low clump of dark green leaves. The flowers open in January and February, 2-in.-wide white cups that age over a period of six weeks to a platelike flatness, while their color transforms from white to rose to green. Selected forms have flowers 4 in. across, unpleasantly outsize on the plant. Christmas Rose sometimes becomes shy about flowering. To re-enthuse the plant, pour on liquid fertilizer in the growing season and again in winter, before the flower buds begin to arise.

Helleborus orientalis (Lenten Rose). All climates. More than a species — a "hybrid swarm," as they say in field botany; involved are several species found in Europe and Asia Minor. Plants of the Orientalis group grow 1½ ft. tall and have divided dark green leaves that turn bronze by flowering time if winter sun reaches them. Flowers greenish white, pink, rose-purple, or maroon, nodding at first, later attentive; February to April.

Hemerocallis (daylily). For all climates. Half shade in the northern U.S. and Canada, dappled shade in the South, where notable use has been made of daylilies as a ground cover beneath high-shading pines.

Hepatica triloba. NE, S, GN, NW, NC. Hepatica grows as a wildflower around the northern world; in North America it ranges through Canada south to the eastern U.S. Spring flowers violet, rose, or white, in a small tuft. The tri-scallop leaves last through winter, and one of the memorable small pleasures of spring gardening after a snowy winter is saying hello to the plant (pressed flat as an herbarium specimen, but soon perking up into flower) when it reappears at the ragged edge of melting snow. There are

Christmas Rose (*Helleborus niger*) in early February. (DON NORMARK)

a couple of other hepaticas closely related to this, and of equal values. Grow any or all in moist ideal shade garden soil in dappled shade.

Heuchera (alumroot; coralbells). For all climates, with one exception, noted below. North American saxifrages native to cliffs and rocky slopes in part shade. Eastern America's *H. americana* (Rock Geranium), with mottled evergreen leaves, and *H. pubescens*, whose leaves are marbled, are attractive tufted plants for choice, moist soil in high shade or north-wall shade. Flowers greenish in the first-named, reddish in the second-named plant, not showy but nice when you stop to look. The western American *H. micrantha* has glossy dark leaves and little dipteran white flowers, many together in a flight above the foliage; likes woodsy conditions. *H. sanguinea* (Coralbells), native to the Southwest, is one of the several most famous American wildflowers and now has many garden forms that are used as edging plants or in ground-covering masses. In shade gardening, coralbells performs well in shade all afternoon or with no less than three hours' direct sun. California's *H. maxima* (c, sw, t), the giant of the genus, arises to 3 ft. tall, with cloud masses of little white flowers. Half shade.

Hosta (plantain lily). Some of shade gardening's most rewarding plants are grouped (chaotically) within this genus. Mainly Japanese in origin, hostas are growable everywhere — with one exception, pointed out below. Leafy clumps, so good-natured and, as a rule, so generous about allowing themselves to be divided that many of us who grow hostas end up using

Hosta 'Frances Williams' (heart leaves) beneath a Flowering Cherry (Prunus subhirtella). Ajuga as a ground cover. (GEORGE TALOUMIS)

them as ground covers. There is nothing handsomer or sturdier for shade gardening, so the ground might as well be given to these. Though hosta clumps really don't need dividing (in good soil they wouldn't mind being left alone for twenty-five years), they don't object to being lifted and made into many, even as often as every three years. Apply a knife to the corpulent rootstock in spring, just when the plants begin to lengthen and open their crown buds of leaves.

The few species and several hundred hybrids in cultivation carry leaves that are generally heart-shaped; these vary in length and width from the size of a newspaper page folded once, to the size of a postage stamp (miniatures for the miniaturist). Hosta foliages, decoratively deep-veined, are richly green all over, or white- or yellow-variegated, or, in a few cases, entirely aureate. The leaves are deciduous, turning soft yellow before going down and holding the color long enough to become a feature in the fall garden. Summer flowers lavender, violet, or white; in general form and carriage like small nodding lilies, but aligned on slender stems.

The plants have deep roots and are at their best in rich ground, moist or wet with percolating water. The biggest hostas of boldest foliage are effective in composition with the clear trunks of high-shading trees or with picturesque tree stumps; with Japanese Irises and *Iris orientalis (I. ochroleuca);* with equisetum, Joe-Pye Weed, or bamboo; or at the base of Black Alders, Vine Maples, birches, or Bald Cypresses in wet soil. Lesser hostas

Primroses at the edge of a bed of hostas. In flower, *Primula × polyantha.* The lustrous leaves belong to a hybrid of *Hosta lancifolia.* (DON NORMARK)

— with leaf blades approximately the measure of this book, or smaller — go well with practically everything else in the shade garden.

Largest in leaf of all the hostas are *H. plantaginea* (Fragrant Plantain Lily) and certain of its hybrids. The Plantagineas flower white and delicately scented. Hardy not much below 0°F, growable NE (shelter) and in all other climates except GN. Other large-leaved hostas are the hybrids of *H. Sieboldiana* — and the species itself with blue-green leaves as glaucous as a geisha's rice-floured cheeks; flowers lavender-white, close above the leaves. The popular hosta Frances Williams, with pearly flowers over whopping yellow-variegated leaves, seems related to sieboldiana. Unlike most hostas, the foregoing plants are slow to increase.

Among medium-size hostas, the hybrid 'Honey Bells' — bright green leaf blades 9 in. long — is distinctive for the light, pleasant fragrance of its pale lavender flowers, held on tall scapes well above the foliage. A large group of medium hosta hybrids, known as *H. Fortunei*, offers green or variegated foliages and lilac flowers. The white-variegated hosta 'Thomas Hogg' is perhaps the best known of the Fortunei complex (or perplex). *H. ventricosa* (Blue Plantain Lily), another hybrid swarm that has medium-sized leaves, contains plants with dark violet flowers.

H. lancifolia (Narrow-leaved Plantain Lily), as grown in gardens, is usually one or another of hybrids that bear some resemblance to the pure, narrow-leaved species. Of these, *H. lancifolia tardiflora* is readily recognizable for the lateness of the lavender flowers, which open full in October, over small leaves broader than lance form. A slow grower.

I won't name any more hostas, for their names are in a royal mess. Horticulture in Japan, Europe, and North America has made a busyness of the few hosta species — plants fervent about meeting and hybridizing — to a point where the Latin binomial system hardly makes sense when applied to the garden genus. There is a hosta society devoted to putting order in the house, but also bent on introducing new, minutely different hybrids each year. We plain gardeners may, with fair safety, rely on nursery catalog description, since almost any hosta is a worthy plant.

Iberis sempervirens (Evergreen Candytuft). All climates. Good performance in shade up to three-fourths of the day. A big flattish loaf of dark needle leaves, somewhat too dark for shade gardening, but milk-white flowers liven the plant for two months, beginning in mid-spring.

Impatiens Oliveri (Poor Man's Rhododendron). C, SW, T. A shrublike perennial, an invaluable quick filler and swift background plant for any soil, wet or dry, good or clay-bad; in all shades except dark, and a sun plant as well. A cluster of succulent cane stems, pale green, 4–6 ft. tall in shade. Attractive foliage, giving the general impression of rhododendron, with its leaves in the spoke arrangement characteristic of that plant. Closely viewed, the leaf of Poor Man's Rhododendron (I love that common name — so apropos) is seen to be about 6 in. long, as spatulate as a Dandelion leaf and with Dandelion's bright-dark leaf color and glabrous cool clamminess, but without its toothed edge. In flower all summer, with blooms that are pink or rose, 2 in. across, and shaped like a Pansy face turned upside down, but with a long upturned queue in back, as on a peruke (the flower's nectar chamber, fully two inches long). To propagate and plant, chop from an established specimen canes that have a bit of attached root and plant these directly into the ground where they are to grow — perhaps along a humdrum fence or wall, which they will conceal in a couple of seasons, while you wait the requisite seven years or so for real rhododendrons and other choice shade shrubs to grow up enough to take over the job that Poor Man's Rhododendron does so well and so quickly.

Iris. The bearded irises prefer full sun, yet are gracious about accepting shade up to half the day.

The Crested irises, *I. japonica, I. Wattii, I. gracilipes, I. cristata,* and several others, open spring flowers that sport a bit of a cockscomb at the base of the falls (the down-curving petals, as opposed to the upswinging ones, which are the standards). Native to moist woods, Crested Irises grow readily in a dapple-shaded garden, or in part shade with as little as three hours' direct sun; the most shade-tolerant of the group, *I. Wattii,* will flower in a north-wall bed. Their soil must be moist in all seasons. *I. cristata* is hardy everywhere except GN; the others are growable S, NW, C, SW, T.

Of the Crested group, *I. japonica* is vigorously stoloniferous and often used as a ground cover. Curving ensiform leaves arranged in rich-evergreen fans; above the foliage, on 2-ft. stems, small fringed flowers of palest violet with mustard- and blackberry-colored streaks and spots. The Himalayan *I. Wattii,* an enlargement of *I. japonica,* has 4-in.-wide flowers with familiar markings on yard-high stems, early spring to mid-spring; big, curved fan leaves — a landscaper's foliage that fits in especially well with ferns. *I. gracilipes,* a Japanese woodlander, is an enormously fetching little plant, paused over and spoken to by all my garden visitors who see it in flower — on the wing, let me say. The flowers are small mauvine moths, many at once, just above the foot-high tuft of curved grassy leaves. An albino as desirable as the typical mauve is sometimes cataloged, and also a double form, but the heavier flowers of this one are beside the point of the plant, which is buoyancy. *I. cristata,* eastern American, makes a low, slowly spreading mat of deciduous dirk-blade leaves and fresh, light violet flowers. Protect from snails and slugs.

Native West Coast irises (NW, C, SW, T) flower best in light shade, or half shade at most. Plant in moist, well-drained soil. There are two species that are generally reliable in gardens (whereas some others are not). One is *I. Douglasiana,* of many colors, including clear blue-violet, white, and yellow, the flowers held 1–2 ft. tall over a tough, yard-wide clump of sword leaves. The second is *I. innominata,* smaller by half, with leaves that are broadish grass-blades and flowers in a great hybrid range of colors (but to many wildflower enthusiasts, the classic innominata is a rich yellow with darker penciling on the falls). The whole group of western irises is poles apart from the bearded border iris — the German iris, as some of us still call them — with their good round burgermeister flowers. Western irises are

Iris cristata, light violet and pleasantly ambitious (notice the way the leafage is moving along). (DON NORMARK)

Iris Douglasiana on a streambank. (DON NORMARK)

particularly light and feisty, with falls that don't fall, but instead spread wide, like the wings of sunbathing swallowtails. Aerodynamic flowers. To anchor my accolade in practicality, pick the spent flowers from these plants, green basal pod and all, to prevent seed formation, for they would overdo it in the garden.

Iris foetidissima (Gladwyn). For all garden climates, in half or total shade. A dark upright tuft with little faded lilac flowers, it makes a saturnine addition to the shade garden — until fall and early winter, when its seed capsule opens wide as a flower and displays bright orange seeds.

Iris orientalis (I. ochroleuca), growable in all climates, stands 4–5 ft. tall, a handsome cattail tuft of a plant, in place at the back of the shady border or in the high shade of trees. Flowers large, yet slim in their segmentation; standards white, falls white with an inner blotch of turmeric yellow.

Iris Pseudacorus (Yellow Flag) loves moist soil or shallow water, makes a rushy clump of leaves effective in a shaded garden pool, where a submerged, 12-in.-wide pot of soil will sustain it for years. The water-loving Japanese Irises, *I. ensata* and *I. Kaempferi,* accept light shade or half shade. All these aquarians are fully hardy and growable everywhere.

Iris siberica (Siberian Iris). Any climate. Probably the sturdiest of all irises, it forms a broadening clump of narrow blades and lightly built flowers, violet, plum, or white, on clean shafty stems to 3 ft. tall. It grows as ebulliently in soils that are on the dry side as in those that are moist or waterside-wet; in three-quarters shade to full sun. And longevous: A clump undivided for twenty years remains leafy almost to its center and flowers undiminishingly.

Ligularia tussilaginea 'Aureo-maculata' (Leopard Plant). s, nw, c, sw, t. Can be taken out of the house and planted in a rich north-wall bed.

Lunaria annua (Money Plant). For all climates. A tall biennial, self-perpetuating from seed, usually permanent once you scatter the original packet in open, half-shady ground. The common magenta form is a satisfying flower for those rare souls who appreciate the color, but Money Plant also comes in clear white, violet, and purple, the various colors true from seed. *Lunaria* and *Vinca minor* together make an easy marriage: Sow seed of the biennial over the patch of ground cover, and presto, Money Plant rises through, to flower above the Periwinkle branches. Money Plant? Probably you've seen the branches in dry arrangements, with seed capsule septums like silver dollars.

Lysichiton americanum (Skunk Cabbage). For all climates. Found in marshes and stream margins in Pacific North America, in the shade of deciduous trees or conifers. A bold plant for a wet place in the garden. Arum flowers a foot long, shaped like a candle flame, bright yellow, rising from mud in earliest spring; in summer, a tropical clump of elephant-ear leaves, lustrous green, a yard long. A Japanese relative sends up white flowers; in all other features it is much like the American plant. Another Skunk Cabbage, *Symplocarpus foetidus,* of Atlantic North America and northern Asia, also takes to shady mud in any climate; the early-arising hood comes up tortive, streaked and spotted in moray eel colors — reddish purple and yellowish green, sinisterly attractive; large leaves unfurl as the flower ages.

The Skunk Cabbages are slandered in the name; their flowers and leaves are not in the least skunky. But they *are* redolent of fermenting cabbage, though it is a faint aroma in the garden, even entirely unnoticeable unless you get down on hands and (muddy) knees to investigate. In the house, however, their perfume is encouraged forth like that of brandy in a warm snifter. Well I remember. When we were small boys, we sneaked into the basement one day with bunches of the spectacular yellow flowers of our local Skunk Cabbage — the upstairs, we knew for certain, was taboo

Candle flames of *Lysichiton* rising from shallow water in March. Clustered globes are those of *Andromeda Polifolia* 'Minima'. (DON NORMARK)

to the flower; we'd been lectured the first time we'd tried to bring them in, sternly warned the second. So we attempted a basement breach with our nosegays (by now devilishly attractive because of all the fuss attached to them). We placed our trophies in Mason jars from the basement pantry and stood by adoring. But in no time their special odor arose and seeped through the basement ceiling, and down through the seams in those boards came words of wroth.

Marantha. See *Calathea* and *Marantha*, above.

Meconopsis betonicifolia (Blue Poppy). All climates. Tibet. A biennial or short-lived perennial, nowhere easy, but possible in any climate. Must have moisture, drainage, high humidity, and fresh air — but never a drying wind. Requisite conditions are most often to be found in Pacific Northwestern, far northern, or mountainous gardens. Here the blue bowl of a flower may be persuaded that it is at home in the Himalayas, inspired enough to present that ultimate tribute given by exacting wildflowers to gardeners for outstanding performance: seedlings self-sown. *M. cambrica* (Welch Poppy) is as easy as *M. betonicifolia* is recalcitrant. Yellow poppies, like sari silk in color and texture; in another phase, flowers of orange sherbet color. Will naturalize, in part shade, into a hundred, a thousand, a glorious pest the gardener will never want to banish.

Mertensia virginica (Virginia Bluebells). All gardens, except T; but not long-lived in a summer-dry garden. Give it moist, woodsy conditions. Soft-blue trumpet flowers in spring over arising, expanding, and coarsening gray-green leaves. Attractive planted behind pale yellow primroses. A western American relative, *M. ciliata,* succeeds in dryish shade gardens unacceptable to Virginia Bluebells; the westerner is a long-lived plant, flowering a hot blue in summer.

Monarda didyma (Bee Balm). All climates. Summer flowers in tousled heads, scarlet, lavender, pink, and white. Needs a damp spot in no more than half shade.

Monstera deliciosa (Split-leaf Philodendron). SC, SW (low deserts), T. Mexican. One of my least favorite houseplants (confined to a little post of tree fern wood, like an elephant chained to a stake), and my most favorite plant for tropical effects in outdoor shade gardening. Planted as a free-standing specimen at the back of a fernery, it gives the composition weight that nicely balances the effervescence of fern fronds. Propagate monstera by chopping 4–5-ft.-long rooted branches from an older plant, any month of the year. Planted directly where they are to grow, the branches carry on, lengthening about a foot a year. The plant is an arum, with the familial floral candle within a banana-yellow hood — a spadix in a spathe or a *santo* in a shrine; the candle ripens over a period of a year into an edible fruit the size and shape of a billy club, with the flavor of pineapple and mangosteen.

Peltiphyllum peltatum (Umbrella Plant). All climates. Saxifrage relative from the Siskiyous. Rosy cups in a corymb, in early spring. Round leaves about 8 in. across in ordinary soil, twice that in wet ground. Likes water and dappled shade.

Petasites japonicus giganteus (Fuki). From Hokkaido; growable in all climates, in half shade or dappled shade, and a lot of fun if you have the space. Cultivating this plant is a little like feeding and watering a sumo wrestler. The growth is gigantic — leaves 3 ft. wide on leaf stems rising 6 ft. tall from wet ground, where it has the strength to throw horsetail, or for that matter, horses. The plant is at its best — a 15-ft.-wide patch after a few years — in bottom-land mud, but will thrive in upland woods with ordinary moisture. Foliage collapses with fall frost; then in late winter, the plant erupts from the ground in heads of chartreuse flowers, quickly followed by arising, expanding leaves. Flower heads and young leafstalks are edible — the Japanese simmer them with sugar and soy. I've tried the recipe and will liken the product to sugar- and soy-laced mothballs: the fragrance of paradichlorobenzene suffuses the flavor of this plant.

Three-foot-wide umbrella leaves of *Petasites japonicus* 'Gigantea' and, in flower, *Iris Pseudacorus*, in a planting in boggy ground beneath alders. Garden of Roy Davidson.

Petasites speciosus (Coltsfoot). For all climates. American, native to wet ground at woods' margins. White flowers in early spring; large palmy leaves held about 20 in. high. Half shade or dappled shade.

Philodendron. Important brutes in tropical shade gardening. For the best leaf color, give them a rich tree shade or lath shade.

Phormium tenax (New Zealand Flax). NW (warm shade), C, SW, T. Sword leaves of various colors and many sizes, 1–9 ft. tall, in a tough, drought-tolerant clump. Arresting talonlike flowers on gaunt branching stems high above the foliage (but usually absent in the more dwarf varieties). Tall forms are old-time popular plants in our warmer states: As outsize and out of place as moas, they fill thousands of front yards. New Zealand horticulture has lately developed a range of smaller flaxes more suited to the average small garden, in such leaf colors as purple, bronze-rose, green with white or yellow stripes, and tricolored green-white-red. American nurseries have already snapped up many of these. In shade gardening, the swords of phormium contrast artistically with finer, divided foliages and blend with other blade leaves; or use flax by itself as a clean, strong leaf sculpture. Shade up to four-fifths of the day or full sun.

Polemonium caeruleum (Jacob's-Ladder). All climates except T; half shade or dappled shade. Soft, richly green pinnate leaves, in an upright tuft to 30 in. tall in some varieties, in condensed forms, a third that height: a greatly variable plant of wide natural range in the northern world. Soft, blue-violet cup-form flowers, in a cluster, last a long summer season. A plant of melding gentleness, easy company for ferns and any forest flowers. The taller (30 in.) forms of Jacob's-Ladder are free seeders and apt to be a nuisance if you grow choice miniatures within the plant's broadcasting range.

Polemonium reptans (acclimatability and shade as for *P. caeruleum*) is an eastern American wildflower hardly distinguishable from Jacob's-Ladder in leaf and cup; it is, however, an outward instead of an upward grower, and will form a small mat. *P. reptans* 'Blue Pearl', a selection commonly offered by nurseries, has flowers 6 in. tall in spring, 10 in. in summer; needs frequent dividing and replanting in freshly turned soil, every year or two in early spring.

Polygonatum multiflorum (Solomon's Seal). European; growable everywhere except T. A spreading network of fleshy rootstocks, giving rise in spring to 4-ft.-tall arching stems with lily leaves and pendant long bells, white with melon-green rims. Easy in moist soil, nearly full shade; spreads into a wide patch at the rate of about a foot a year. It will harmlessly intergrow with clumps of hardy Maidenhair Fern, and will flower there almost as if in a bouquet — with the fern serving as florist's filler foliage. Related eastern American wildflowers *P. biflorum* and *P. commutatum* are big, easy-to-grow woodlanders with greenish bells. These easterners prefer moist conditions, but once they've become established, they don't mind woods that dry out in summer.

Primula (primrose). The genus numbers half a thousand species, mainly Himalayan, but the few European and Japanese representatives are of foremost importance. North America's several wild primroses (with the exception of willing little *P. mistassinica* — Bird's-Eye Primrose — of Alaska, eastern Canada, and a few stations across the U.S. border) have rarely been grown successfully in gardens. They are used to the high life, a mile or more up in the mountain air or well up toward the North Pole, with an abundantly moist brief summer and a nine-month sleep beneath a protective snow blanket.

Most of the world's other primroses crave these same conditions of short, moist summer and long absolute winter. On the whole, the genus *Primula* grows more easily in Canada and in the parts of the U.S. that have cold or chill winters: NE, S, GN, NW, NC; less easily SC, SW, and T. However, the primrose species and garden hybrids that follow will grow and flower in the entire range of garden climates (there is an exception in *P. mala-*

coides, a half-hardy species). Primulas especially adaptable to warm-winter climates will be noted. sc, sw, and т gardeners: The montane species of primrose may not be easy in your region, but skilled growers do succeed with the plants. A garden location in a moist, cool canyon is a big help; otherwise, try container gardening in a spot protected from drying wind and burning sun. (But the natural mineral soils of sc and sw are the wrong stuff.)

In all climates, grow primroses as if they were floral beeves: fast and fat in a rich, airy soil, with a spring and summer boost of fertilizer — and be not mingy with water.

Professional growers sow primrose seed in spring, grow the plants fast for a summer, and sell them in flower the following spring. Prize plants — double Polyanthuses and slow-growing species that have attracted a waiting list of customers — are propagated by division. Professionals divide their plants in summer (late July and August, usually) and afterward water the plants daily until fall rains come. Summer division produces the strongest, most floriferous plants the following spring. Many home gardeners, however, prefer dividing in spring, the season of frequent rains that assist the less than professional waterer of plants.

Primula Auricula (Auricula). A conglomerate: in the wild, a number of related European mountaineers, saxatile plants with roots and stems in shady rock crevices and hard little grayish leaves in the sun; in gardens, a spate of hybrids. Grow auriculas in light shade, in moist yet fast-draining soil. A raised bed or pot culture helps assure drainage: In sc and sw, potting is practically mandatory as a means of supplying enough, but not too much, water in every season. Fancy forms — the "show" and "alpine" auriculas — require pot-and-cold-frame (or cool-greenhouse) gardening in all climates.

Primula Beesiana (rosy purple), *P. Bulleyana* (deep orange), and *P. burmanica* and *P. japonica* (both of them magenta) are characteristic "candelabra primroses": flowers in several circlets, spaced one above the other on a slim 2-foot pole of a stem; foliage a clump of massive thirsty leaves shaped like long tongues. Plants for streamside soil or damp ground in a half-shady woods. The pure, Asian species are difficult to obtain; hybrids are the usual provision, in the near-rainbow range of the modern primroses. The Candelabras particularly abound in orange-red, salmon, and apricot. They die down in autumn to a large conical crown bud, sitting there tempting every slug and snail — beware.

Primula Juliae and the Julianas. A brisk stir in horticulture — not quite a storm — followed the relatively recent discovery (1901) of the dwarf primrose *P. juliae* in the Caucasus Mountains. This species is the parent of the popular Juliana primroses. It stands 2 in. tall, is made up of dense, dark little earlike leaves and small, nearly stemless magenta flowers. *P. juliae* spreads by stolons into no more than a flowery doily — never a big grower. Developed from this plant, the Julianas are now

Candleabra primroses (*Primula japonica*) in a damp hollow with tufts of Japanese Iris. Mollis azaleas in flower on higher ground. Background foliage, upper right: *Rhododendron quinquefolium*. Garden of Izetta Renton. (DON NORMARK)

available in nearly all primrose colors. *P. Juliae* 'Wanda', with a warm magenta flower, was one of the earliest Julianas and remains one of the most popular. *P. juliae* and the Julianas are as easy (or as difficult) to grow as the Polyanthuses. Part shade; moist soil.

Primula malacoides (Fairy Primrose). C, SW, T. Short-lived perennial that is profligate in flower — how often those plants that have not long to live throw caution (and plenty of seeds) to the wind. Flowers purple, rose, lavender, pink, or white; late winter to mid-spring. Will self-sow and naturalize in open soil that is semishaded.

Primula ×polyantha (Polyanthus). The universal garden primrose, a clump of elongate and netted dark green leaves, and on each 9-in. stem a clutch of flowers colored — almost any color. Growable in all climates and capable of giving a great show anywhere, including SC and SW gardens (with provisos already mentioned). An old citizen in gardens, it is an English plant created by the hybridizing of two wildflowers of British and Continental range.

The ancestral wildflowers that gave us the Polyanthuses are *P. vulgaris* (English Primrose) and *P. veris,* plants that can be fancied entirely for themselves. *P. vulgaris* is the original holder of the name Primrose (or "prime rose," in an earlier spelling). Flowers — in the native British variety — are light "primrose-yellow" with a saffron-yellow eye, held singly on short stems. *P. veris* received its folk name of Cowslip for its noted habit of following cattle in pastures. Unlavish flowers have small petals and a puffed and baglike calyx collar and are held clustered on upright 6–8-in. stems.

The rodlike stems and clustered flowers of Polyanthuses have been inherited from the cowslip. Fullness of petal and variety of color have come from the prime rose, which, in the Near Eastern end of its range as a wildflower, runs to pinks, purples, white, and violet. Grow the Polyanthuses and the parent species in dappled, afternoon, or bright full shade. The moister the soil and the more humid the garden, the less shade these plants will need. In an especially primulaceous garden, full sun is not too much.

Primula rosea. A tuft 1 ft. high; bright rosy pink flowers in early spring. A bog plant in its native state, it requires wet or constantly moist soil and half shade. One of the easier primroses for SC gardens.

Primula Sieboldii. Japanese; in moist open woods and mountain meadows spongy with snow water. As a garden primrose, one of the most accommodating: growable everywhere in moist soil and dappled shade, with lettucy humidity. But the leaves die down in fall, and the dormant flat root plate of a young plant is usually no bigger around than a penny — if not marked, it's easily lost in weeding (I've found that pencil-size sticks, poked into the ground on either side of the plant, are a saving reminder). Up early in spring, with its leaves and flowers arising together; foliage large and crinkly, of a soft grayish green, and flowers clustered on staffs a foot tall — flat, upward-facing flowers very like phlox in their form and colors (rose, pink, white). Named selections imported from Japan prove to be every bit as splendid as the flowers yielded by the sowing of a packet of seeds from any local seed rack or a mail-order seed house.

A number of other primula species are available as seed or as pot plants from specialty nurseries: *P. denticulata,* with its violet flowers in cornball-shaped heads; *P. Vialii,* violet, in muscari heads; *P. alpicola,* reedy-tall and graceful, flowers trumpet-shaped, lunar yellow, violet, or white; *P. frondosa, P. farinosa,* and *P. mistassinica,* little tufted plants with grayish-farinose leaves and lilac flowers. All these are usually of short garden duration; but once grown and flowered, always a delight to think back on.

Rehmannia elata (*R. angulata*). C, SW, T. Big showy flowers, spring to fall; 2–3 ft. high, with nettlelike leafage, bristly and saw-toothed. Flowers are tubular, as long as 4 in., with a broad, deep, red-dotted yellow throat one cannot help peering into, past the wide-spreading purple petal-jaws of the flower. It looks like a hippo's head in an open-maw salute to food, glorious food. This plant is somewhat lacking in finesse but gives a passel of color over a long season. Spreads a foot a year by root-branches. Needs good, moist soil; any shade except dark.

Reineckia carnea. NE (shelter), S, NW, C, SW, T. Of the Liliaceae, and a charmer. A plant that seems to average the features of several other members of the same family: Lily of the Valley, liriope, ophiopogon, and *Hosta lancifolia*. It is as if color transparencies of all these were superimposed and somehow projected as one sharp image. Reineckia is a Chinese and Japanese forest plant: fresh green strap leaves 6 in. or more long, and in late summer, small coblike inflorescences, studded with starry little mauve-pink flowers, the anthers pronounced and of a chalky white-yellow, like a peeled banana. The plant creeps along on slow stolons; in time, a broad colony. Full, part, or light shade.

Rodgersia. S, NW, C, SW, T. Grand saxifrages of China and Japan. To 3 ft. tall or more, in damp soil; leaves like those of Horse-Chestnuts in *R. aesculifolia* or like elderberries in *R. sambucifolia,* or round, like May-apple leaves, in *R. tabularis* — but larger in every case; big panicle display of small white flowers. Half shade or dappled shade.

Rohdea japonica. (Why is it that so many great plants come from a rather small place like Japan?) A liliad for garden climates S, NW, C, SW, T. Dark evergreen strap leaves in a tuft narrow at the base, broadening to 3 ft. at the top. Suggestive of its relative Aspidistra; like that plant, growable in dark shade, in a container or in open ground. Slow-growing, with variegated forms slower still.

Sanguinaria canadensis (Bloodroot). NE, S, GN, NW, NC. Deciduous plant, native to eastern North America. A thoroughly bewitching filler of woods, where it is happiest. Grow it in moist soil in the dappled or half shade of

Primula elatior in flower. This primrose is considered by many botanists and gardeners to be the original Polyanthus — a natural hybrid of two British wildflowers, *P. vulgaris* and *P. veris.* (DON NORMARK)

deciduous trees, or near a north wall that receives a bit of sun, or as a companion for not too heavy wild grass in a shady-sunny glade — it will naturalize there. Less than a foot tall, with bluish-gray leaves as big as the palm of one's hand, roundish, lobed, and scalloped; flower a simple white star composed of eight or more petals, or a fully double flower of slow growth, a collector's acquisition. But the great sport in growing Bloodroot is to pry up a section of the fleshy rootstock and break it in two for the benefit of some visitor. It bleeds an almost blood-colored, orange-red sap. To the Indians this plant was a source of body paint.

Sansevieria trifasciata (Mother-in-Law's Tongue). c, sw, t; lightest frost only. The narrow, upright habit of the plant lends itself to line planting in several situations: as masking in front of ugly building foundations, as greenery along a fence or wall (particularly where there is no more than a skimpy ribbon of plantable ground), or as a narrow hedge. Best in bright full shade or afternoon shade.

Schizostylis coccinea. s, nw, c, sw, t. South African iris relative. Blade leaves in the family tradition and businesslike stolons that will bring on a sweep of flowers a few years after you plant a single potling from the nursery; late-fall flowers, six-petal wonders colored burnt carmine or shell-pink. Moist soil; semishade.

Sedum Morganianum (Burro's-Tail). sc, t. A gray-green clump of drooping, shaggy rope branches a yard long — a live macramé mop. Plant in a shady rock-wall pocket or in a hanging container in filmy tree shade.

Sedum Sieboldii (October Plant). All climates. Choice late summer–early autumn flower for a moist, half-shady rock garden. A low cushion, about 16 in. wide, with deciduous leaves that are like rounded disks of sea-tumbled shells, blue-green with a pink rim; rose-pink flowers in umbels. Closely similar — but smaller by half — is *S. cauticola;* both plants are Japanese. *Sedum* 'Ruby Glow', a hybrid of *S. cauticola* (with *S. Telephium* the other parent), has won an Award of Merit in England and a prominent place in the North American trade; grows 8 in. tall, a foot wide. Has the leaves and late bloom of Sieboldii-cauticola, but a larger flower display; the plant is a strong grower and is moderately drought-tolerant (whereas cauticola grows daintily and Sieboldii thoughtfully slow, and both require unfailing moisture).

Sedum spathulifolium. For all climates. A patch plant. Sometimes planted as a ground cover, but soon runs out at the middle — and then weeds pop up in the open space. But a small patch (1–2 ft. wide) composed of the powdery gray rosetted form of the plant is entirely manageable, and there is no more soothingly freshening plant in shade gardening: a flat, refined mat of leaf-roses, the rosettes 2 in. wide (an inch wide in the form *S. Spathulifolium* 'Cape Blanco'); starry yellow flowers in summer. Half shade or dappled shade.

Clockwise: *Sedum Morganianum* in a hanging container, *Schlumbergera* (cactus foliage), *Dicksonia* (fern), *Ajúga reptans* 'Atropurpurea' as a ground cover, young rosettes of *Agave attenuata*. Garden of John W. Pitman. (DON NORMARK)

Senecio cruentus (Cineraria), in its garden forms. C, SW (in primula conditions), T. Glorious daisies that come in mixed colors from seed — purple, violet, rose, and white — in late winter and spring. A bed of these is a chromatic big bang. The tumultuous flowers are especially effective with tall, cool, poised ferns. Cinerarias are usually considered annuals (and, indeed, they can be planted as such), but in moist, half-shady gardens they behave like biennials, self-sowing in early summer: the seeds, with their thistledown parachutes, drift everywhere. By late summer, the seedling Cineraria develops as a large, handsome rosette of big, roundish cordate leaves with a lacy edge.

Garden Cinerarias are of two main types: low plants with bigger daisies that seed themselves modestly, and 2–3-ft.-tall plants with smaller flowers that seed violently. The tall Cinerarias are known popularly as *C. stellata*. In my own garden, with great reluctance, I must pull out hundreds of the attractive young summer plants of stellata that have germinated in beds of low-growing shade perennials. It is a matter of saving the smaller competitors from being overgrown and shaded out. Stellata seems best suited to a wildish garden. I keep it (or try to keep it) confined to a semishaded wooded area in which the ground is covered with Indian Strawberry *(Duchesnea indica)*. Here the daisy's seeds drift down into the interior of the ground cover and later come up as rosettes whose strength of growth exactly equals that of the strawberry. They are livelocked, neither of them gaining over the other. Artistically and practically, the foliage association of these plants is so good I'm envious of Nature, in not having planned it myself.

Shortia galacifolia (Oconee-Bells). NE, S, GN, NW, C. Woodlander from North Carolina's mountains, one of the choicest American wildflowers. Round leathery leaves, bronze-green and polished, low to the ground in a mat; flowers fringy pink bells on short stems. Very slow-growing. Ideal shade garden soil, moist in all seasons; shade, with a little sun.

Sisyrinchium angustifolium, S. bellum, S. bermudiana (Blue-eyed Grass). All climates. Small iris family members, much alike: little grassy tufts, 5–9 in tall; flowers are bright blue-violet saucers, $1/2$–$3/4$ in. wide, that last through a long spring season. For moist or spongy-wet soil; half shade or sun. *S. macounii* 'Alba' is lower — 4–6 in. high — an iris mimic in its little broadish gray-green fan leaves; 1-in.-wide white flowers.

Smilacina racemosa; S.r. amplexicaulis; (False Solomon's Seal). All climates. These nearly alike North American woods' edge plants rank among the most rewarding of our wildflowers for shady gardening. It is puzzling that they have never become popular and that they remain rare in gardens. A creeping rootstock; large Solomon Seal leaves walking (left-right, left-right) up yard-high stems; cream-white flowerets in big torch heads in spring; beadlike red berries in fall. Tough plants that will come up a little stronger and more widespread every spring for twenty years without being divided or fussed with in any way. Moderate growth in good soil, slow growth in terrible soil — but sure growth. Drought-tolerant.

Shortia galacifolia in spring, with pristine flowers above last year's eroding leaves.
(DON NORMARK)

Thalictrum (meadow rue). All climates. A muddle in nurseries, but under whatever name, you'll receive the herbaceous counterpart of a fling of confetti: a fine, airy woodland flower for dappled or part shade. *T. aquilegifolium* (when true to name) stands 3 ft. tall and bolt upright in its slender firm stems of compound leaves, a narrow clump topped with little white or purple flowers in fluffy bunches; the easiest of thalictrums, it is tolerant of dryish soil and will self-sow. *T. dipterocarpum* grows its limber, spare stems to about 5 ft. long, but usually not that tall: in shade the plant bows toward the light. Small flowers in open sprays, powder-violet with a fluff of cream-colored stamens; tender-green leaves divided into ferny leaflets, in a construction very like a maidenhair frond.

Foamflowers (*Tiarella cordifolia* 'Albiflora') beside rhododendrons; Pacific Dogwood (*Cornus Nuttallii*) in flower at the back. Garden of Betty Miller. (DON NORMARK)

Tiarella. North American woodland flowers of the saxifrage family. Foot-high plants, more or less; leaves mapleish in outline, soft to touch, several inches wide; little star flowers in sparkler heads. Tiarellas crave moisture.

Tiarella cordifolia (Foamflower). All climates. This eastern species is determinedly stoloniferous, romping over low logs and mossy ground at the rate of a foot a year. (Perhaps I should have included this plant with the ground covers, but then again, maybe it's better here with its relatives, where you can compare them all at a glance.) *T. cordifolia* is a twofold flower, with a green-leaved, white-flowered form (*T. cordifolia* 'Albiflora') and a bronzy purple–leaved, rose-flowered form (*T. cordifolia* 'Purpurea').

Tiarella laciniata and **T. trifoliata,** growable in all climates and both of the Pacific Northwest, are leaf tufts no bigger than a tussy mussy, with delicately thin ensembles of white stars over their foliage.

Tiarella unifoliata (Sugar Scoop), growable in all climates, is native from California to Alaska, grows as a hearty mat of dark leaves and clustered white sparks. Fairly drought-tolerant (the others are not at all). *T. Wherryi*, of southern mountains, has the amplest and showiest flowers of any, salmon-pink or white, over a widening tuft of leaves. Divide the plant in late summer every two years — helps keep it young.

Tolmiea Menziesii (Piggyback Plant). All climates. Wherever I encounter this plant ensconced on the windowsills of the world, I greet my fellow native son with the pride one takes in someone from down home who has gone out into the world and become a household name . . . little old Piggyback Plant that I've collected in the bogs not two miles from my West Coast home. Internationally famous as a houseplant, Piggyback grows as a woodland wildflower in wet soils, California to Alaska. In shade gardening the foliage looks the same as indoors, a soft-green mound of heart leaves with serrated edges. But outdoors the plant carries small, softly reddish-brown flowers in abundance. Moist soil will do for it if you haven't a gumboots spot in the garden. (Incidentally, I quickly accede to the opinion that Piggyback is a native daughter rather than son.)

Tovara virginica. All climates. Thin, kinky canes in a narrowly upright tuft, to 30 in. tall. Eastern American woodlander that seems a fancy greenhouse plant, with its attractive alderlike leaves maculated with broad maroon chevrons; tiny red flowers aligned on wand-slim stems. Full or part shade.

Tradescantia virginiana (Flower-of-a-Day). For all climates. An eastern North America wildflower, now of many garden forms in the violet-red-white color range, with all the in-between hues. Three-petal flowers riding on a leaf clump built, like a day lily, of flexible strap-form leaves, but black-green. Flowers short-lived, arriving daily for a long summer season. Grow t in soils wet or well-drained; in any shade down to nearly full, or in sun.

For company: ferns; broad leaves such as hosta, tolmiea, alocasia, and caltha; and blending foliages such as iris and carex. You'll have quite a garden there.

Trillium (wake-robin). All regions except T; not easy in SC and in low SW deserts, but entirely possible in favored gardens, sheltered and moist as well as shady.

Trillium erectum (Purple Trillium) and ***T. cernuum*** (Nodding Trillium) — two easterners — are the easiest plants in the genus, tough survivors in soils that go dry, and relatively fast growers. This is a worthy pair, though the earthy brown-red petals of erectum are far from the bright cartoon-red blossoms promised from the plant in magazine ads. But the under-the-leaves flowers of cernuum are a surprise, concealed until you get down and poke around.

Trillium grandiflorum, white, of eastern North America is, to many gardeners who know the genus, the supreme species. *T. ovatum* (Coast Trillium), western, is closely related and a close second, with flowers as large as those of the easterner, but narrower of petal. Both are shade plants that settle in to stay: Each spring for many years the root clump will send up an ever more generous number of stems — one, two, or even three more annually — each topped with the three-leaf collar and three-petal flower celebrated in their name. Such moderate annual gain is top speed among trilliums.

Trillium sessile (burgundy-colored, grape-scented) of the East, together with greenish-white *T. sessile californicum (T. chloropetalum)* and the maroon-flowered *T. sessile californicum rubrum (T. sessile giganteum)*, both of the West Coast, are robust plants native to soil muddy in spring, moist in summer. Their green leaves are darkly marbled; flowers are sessile, with upright, elongate petals that form a kind of three-column cloister on a leafy plaza — not a flowery arrangement, but a striking one.

T. undulatum (wine-striped white), ***Trillium Catesbaei*** (*T. stylosum;* rose-pink), *T. viride* var. (*T. luteum;* light yellow, with lightly scented lemon blossoms), and *T. recurvatum* (claret), are all slow-growing easterners. These are choice plants: After about four years, they yield two flowers for every one you plant.

The miniature white *T. nivale* of the East and the equally little (4–5 in.) purply-speckled-white *T. rivale* of the Siskiyous need a carefully watched position just off the edge of the walkway, for they are easy to lose to larger plants that would overwhelm them. Protect from mollusks, as well.

Trollius (globeflower). All climates. Summer flower, gold or orange, cup or bowl form, over a clump of raggy-edged ranunculus leaves. Requires moist ground or fresh boggy conditions; part shade.

Trillium grandiflorum, a species variable in flower form, as these seedling plants reveal. (DON NORMARK)

Zantedeschia aethiopica (Calla). S, NW, C, SW, T. Tropical in character and out of keeping in most of the places where planted. But as a new gardener in the subtropics, I've come to appreciate this plant, which I still can't accept in my life as a plantsman in the northern U.S. The huge white arums are held 3 ft. high and the arrowhead leaves extend 2 ft. when it is grown in muck soil, in which the plant delights; it will also grow in moist well-drained ground.

In a warm climate Calla flowers throughout an exceptionally long season — spring and summer — and the leaves remain fresh nearly the whole year. For a bog extravaganza, plant Calla in half-shaded mud with other talls and toughs — *Woodwardia,* Yellow Flag, *Cyperus, Equisetum.*

Is this really the end of the line? Is *Zantedeschia* the last stop? I dare not think how many worthy perennials I've had to bypass for want of space. Shade gardening, now that I've investigated the field, turns out to contain a practically inexhaustible supply of plants suited to our medium, and each of these species is a culmination in natural design, in its separate way the perfect thing.

14

Annuals

Seasonal touches. Certain annuals tolerate shade well enough to provide the shade garden its best source of color in the months following the explosive spring flowering of its perennials and woody plants. In the summer and early fall, the green quietude of ferns, overhead leaves, and shadow pattern is the most refreshing aspect of the shady garden. And some of the most inviting shade gardens I visit belong to naturalistic gardeners who consider annuals inadmissible, who prefer their shade gardens Spartan-green during summer. I'm greatly attracted to their philosophy. In fact, I seem to have a Spartan-green garden without even trying, along about July every year. Then I weaken and stipple in a few annuals here and there for a color lift. (July is about a month too late for best results.)

The annual that flowers best in shade is, above all others, *Impatiens*. In my own experience, it makes a great splash of color in full sun, daily carrying about twenty-eight flowers on each square foot of plant surface while it is in full production. *Impatiens* in the dappled shade of mature trees in my garden, where the ground probably receives two or three hours of sun a day (totaling all the transitory spots of sunlight), flowers less than when in full sun, but still gives a good show: about seventeen flowers on each square foot of plant surface all season long. And in the full shade of my north wall, *Impatiens* grows well but flowers lightly: about eight flowers on each square foot. Roughly, then, *Impatiens* carries its full potential of flowers in full sun, two-thirds in part shade, and one-third in full shade. This same 3-2-1 formula applies to the several other most shade-tolerant annuals, as well as to nearly all shade garden plants that also accept full sun. It applies even to our native shade-loving wildflowers, whenever these plants prove adaptable to a sunny location (an acid test to be tried only when one has plants to spare).

In my garden conditions, at least, three other "annuals" — *Browallia*, Wax Begonia, and *Coleus* — approach *Impatiens* in shade tolerance. Botanically, none of these plants is an annual. They are all tender perennials of tropical origin (as is *Impatiens*). Horticulturally, though, these are annual plants to gardeners outside warm-winter areas. This chapter includes many such de facto "annuals" (tender perennials, tuberous plants, and one biennial) along with the true annuals, all of which are plants most gardeners buy or sow in the spring and let frost claim in the fall.

In any cool-summer climate (one in which tomatoes are an unsure crop), growing annuals from seed sown out of doors usually brings poor results. The problem of a cool growing season is solved in the greenhouse, where crops of annuals are best sown in flats or pots during late winter, in any potting mix that holds air and drains water rapidly.

For seed sowing I use ideal shade garden soil (*see* p. 28) that has been baked to kill weed seeds and other malefactors. I cook the soil in an old galvanized iron bucket, in the kitchen oven. The bucket has a reliably strong handle — an important feature, since a bucketful of soil weighs as much as a brace of large turkeys. I wait, though, to carry out the job until I'm alone in the house for a night or so. Experience has taught me that even the most serene and sensible of souls with whom one may share a house will quite possibly exhibit starbursts of high dudgeon over the harmless baking of soil in the household oven.

The bucket of soil should cook overnight — twelve hours or more, in a 250°F oven. Keep the kitchen blow fan going, because the smell of baking soil is oddly pungent. After it has cooked, take it outside to cool to air temperature before sowing the seed, a delay of some hours. Meanwhile, if you are a cigar smoker, light up a fat corona in the house to mask the earth smell. One's rare and apparently aberrant indulgence in the verboten indoor cigar is, I have discovered, more understandable and forgivable than one's true purpose. But do clean soil crumbs from the oven, or else "the jig is up."

Many professional growers sow annuals in a one-to-one mix of sphagnum and perlite; both materials are lightweight and essentially sterile. (An average-size flat filled with ideal shade garden soil weighs about 47 pounds fully wet, compared to about 24 pounds for a flat of sphagnum and perlite.) The sphagnum-perlite mix has one drawback. After a few weeks of frequent watering and resultant settling, the mix can become a miniature sphagnum bog, sopping wet and draining sluggishly. Water with finesse if you're working with this mix: While you are waiting for the seeds to germinate, apply water sparingly over the entire surface of the mix, but frequently enough to keep the surface moist. You may have to cover the container with a cotton cloth while you're watering, to break the force of the water and keep the seed from washing out. After germination takes place, water generously but let the container drain and half-dry between waterings.

Guard against damping-off, a fungus condition that knocks down an entire stand of seedlings as quickly as coccidiosis ravages a flock of chicks.

There are specific fungicides, but prevention is better. Crowding and excessive moisture encourage damping-off. Be ready to separate the seedlings when they attain the first pair, or pairs, of true, vein-bearing leaves (spreading above the bean halves known as cotyledons). Professionals separate seedlings into 2-in. plastic pots — inesthetic, compared to terra-cotta, but lighter, cheaper, and incapable of drawing life moisture away from the plant (a bad habit of small clay pots). Apply liquid fertilizer lightly and frequently — about once a week — when you water.

Set out annuals neither too early nor too late — "after the danger of late spring frost has passed" in your area, and "after the ground has warmed up," (famous slogans) but not until your own gardener's instincts tell you it is time; for the seedling set out too early sits there cold and motionless except for the battering it takes from the weather. I suggest going out and sniffing the air and measuring the enthusiasm of spring. I take spring readings by simply looking at the soil. If it is still sodden and morbid-looking, I go back inside to reread the season's crop of nursery catalogs, wherein it is always paradise in full dazzle. But when the soil is breathing deeply and weeds are coming up alarmingly, when robins are pulling up earthworms and not eating them, but stacking them crosswise in their bills like rubbery cordwood, then it is nestling time and seedling time. "In nestling time seedlings will climb" should be added to the repertoire that includes "Knee-high by the Fourth of July."

Early May is approximately the best time to set out annuals in warm southerly gardens. Early June is usually best in New England and westward across the Great Lakes states and the prairie states to the Pacific Northwest. Annuals set out early in the month proper to your area will often attain twice the size of annuals set out five or six weeks later and provide twice the number of flowers.

Fork or spade work should precede sowing. Deeply dug and aerated soil that is rich and moisture-retentive, and not congested with tree roots, is essential. Where the soil is forbidding — perhaps so filled with roots that digging would be well-nigh impossible — plant annuals in containers. When you plant in pots or boxes, you control, of course, the plant's root run, nutriment, and water (in rainless weather).

Annuals flower best when they are watered and fertilized plentifully. I prefer liquid fertilizers, because the dosage is easier to control than with dry fertilizers. Fertilize every two weeks from the time you set out the plants until the end of the growing season.

Most of the rest is reward. There are some fine perfumes among the annuals, and cornucopias of flowers. Only one or two small but menacing clouds remain.

A few annuals — particularly Tuberous Begonias, and *Coleus* — are so attractive to snails and slugs during approximately the first two weeks after you set out the plants that you might have to scatter a few grains of poison bait around each plant every evening; otherwise you may wake up next morning and find only stubs of stems remaining. I speak from cussed experience. Luckily, Nature places a time limit on the superallure of these particular annuals, a progressive lessening of attractiveness. After about two weeks, the plants become only moderately attractive. A scattering of bait every few days will then be adequate. And after a month, an application once a week or every ten days protects the plants. Garden mollusks are drawn by leaf aromas too subtle for human noses, but apparently equal in olfactory seduction to sizzling steaks or bread just out of the oven. Newly set-out plants probably exhale a larger volume of these leaf volatiles as a kind of distress signal at finding themselves in a strange environment less cozy than a greenhouse. Mollusks respond to distress aroma as swiftly as the distress vibration of fish brings sharks.

The annuals described below will thrive in all of North America's garden climates.

Begonia semperflorens (Fibrous Begonia; Wax Begonia). Small and neat, a rather glassy dome of brittle, translucent stems, glossy leaves and flowers. Beloved around the world as the stuff of floral clocks, the soldiers of flower battalions ordered to spell out city mottoes on civic lawns or to stand in curliques in front of clubhouses. For all this worldwide regimentation, the plant remains remarkably itself; there is left to it some wildflower character that comes forth when Fibrous Begonias are planted informally for summer color at the edge of the fernery or in the wildflower garden. A well-grown Fibrous Begonia stands only about 8 in. tall, by 7 in. wide. Because of its small size, it is perhaps the most expensive annual for planting en masse — if you buy the plants. They're economical when grown from cuttings in a home greenhouse; or, in a warm climate, merely break the plant to pieces and plant the fragments in the open ground.

Fibrous Begonias are one of the great producers of color in shade. For a solid mass of flowers by high summer, set plants 6 or 7 in. apart in finely worked, humus-enriched soil. White or white-and-pink bicolored forms with green leaves show up better in shade than red-flowered, bronzy-leaved forms: Red, a light absorbative color, appears rather black in shade.

Fibrous Begonias make an accommodating pot plant, indoors or out. Prepare an open garden plant for windowsill gardening by cutting it back to 4 or 5 in. tall in late summer. Bring the plant indoors before the first frost (32°F will finish fibrous begonias). Fertilize it every two weeks throughout winter.

Browallia (Amethyst Flower — but I have never heard the common name used). Several species of similar appearance. All browallias are shade plants of first value and will follow nearly as far as *Impatiens* into the deeps of shade. Browallias grow about a foot tall, with upright branches. The 1¾-in.-wide blue-violet or white flowers are asymmetrical. Face on, the flowers of the white phase resemble snowmen with fat limbs spread-eagled. *Browallia* is also a valuable houseplant, flowering the winter through.

Coleus. A tropical perennial and worldwide garden favorite, grown as an annual outside the tropics. The leaves are the main attraction. Nettlelike in size and shape, the foliage of *Coleus* is fantastically maculated. Seedling plants come up in endless variety. Many commercial growers select superior seedlings for propagation by cuttings. (Easy work for the home gardener, too; merely place stem cuttings in a glass of water.) In a well-stocked greenhouse nursery you might find *Coleus* available in pale spring greens and in shades of wine, maroon, and russet — autumnal colors rich as Sugar Maple leaves.

I never used to be able to resist planting the whole assortment of *Coleus*, but I have learned to specialize in the more light-reflective leaf patterns and colors. If my garden collection of *Coleus* verges on being too much of a muchness, my enjoyment of it raises me above self-criticism and the carpings of others. Big ferns and Aspidistra go well with *Coleus* and help insulate the different colors.

If you're growing a *Coleus* that you consider too special to let die with the first fall frost, you can save the plant by potting it up in the fall and placing it indoors in a well-lighted window. *Coleus* makes an easy-going houseplant. To prepare it for indoor gardening, cut it back halfway to the ground in late summer.

The *Coleus* saved over and grown as a perennial is potentially a large plant: Pot plants on window sills will probably attain a height of a couple of feet; plants in greenhouses or in tropical gardens grow (with pruning) a rounded 3 ft. tall by 3 ft. wide. Pruning *Coleus* grown indoors or out is a good practice; they are inclined to legginess. Many gardeners prune away the flower ensemble at an early stage to encourage fresh leaf growth. The flowers, in all charity, are not much — a paucity of violet petals carried on spikes — but the naturalist will find enjoyment in the wildflower quality of the small display. You may want to retain at least some of the flowers to collect the ripe seed that will follow.

Coleus is one of the easiest annuals to grow from seed; in a greenhouse or under growth lights, germination takes place in about a week, or even in several days. When seedlings are 3 or 4 in. tall, snip them back to 2 or 3 in. and wait for them to branch before setting them out.

Geranium Robertianum (Herb Robert), a small European annual or biennial with scented maple-form leaves and light rose flowers. In scattered regions in North America, the plant — unplanted, a complete surprise — sometimes ventures into woodsy gardens and naturalizes. But it is neither common nor well known. Naturalized along with Forget-Me-Not, Herb Robert will sprinkle the blue equally with its rose: The two plants make matched competitors. Herb Robert is a neat plant in the spring; lax, like Forget-Me-Not, by midsummer, but never unsightly if the rest of the garden is fairly tall and fairly wild. Sow from seed available (rarely) from herb specialists.

It is one of those plants gardeners pull out but never really want to banish. I know a garden where Herb Robert grows, and a gardener who is apologetic for the plant (which she secretly loves, I haven't a doubt). "Just a weed," my friend said, belittlingly, not knowing its name; meanwhile, was steered toward what I was supposed to see. But the sanctioned weed is the touch that I remember.

Heliotropium arborescens (Heliotrope). A tall, tender, semiwoody perennial grown as an annual in most areas. Heliotrope is famous for its fragrance, which is most intense in the forms that have dark violet flowers. Pale violet and cloudy sky–colored Heliotropes are often disappointingly weak in scent and barely worth planting. The plant flowers well in half shade, poorly in dappled shade. Grown in a container, Heliotrope can be wintered indoors; or the roots alone will winter when given the same treatment by which so many gardeners keep over fuchsias — in barely moist dirt in a chilly garage. In a warm climate, where Heliotrope is perennial, cut the open-ground plant halfway to the ground each spring to induce thrifty growth.

Impatiens. The smaller-growing species (there are also large shrubby ones, rarely used as garden annuals) are several and similar, with tallish and dwarf forms within each species. Dwarf *I. Walleriana* (*I Holstii* and *I. Sultanii*) — 9–15 in. tall — along with their hybrids (altogether a wealth of versicolored and particolored flowers known collectively as Busy Lizzy) are the best providers of summer color in the deeper places, the most reliable ones for the summer edging of shady beds of shrubbery, of ferns, or of woodland perennials that are past season. One small shortcoming: the 1½-in. flower is a dummy — five blank, roundish petals with no visible center parts and nothing to say. Picky criticism of a plant that gives so much. You get back a bushel of greenery and flowers from every *Impatiens* you set out in fertile soil. A plant in a northern garden grows about 15 in. wide within two months; or in a warm climate, twice the northern size.

Lobelia Erinus (Edging Lobelia). Suitable for shade gardening only in hot, sunny climates, where the plant flowers well in shade up to half the day. In cool climates, *Lobelia* requires full or nearly full sun. There are several named seed strains of differing garden values: 'Sapphire', a favorite hanging basket plant, has deep violet, white-eyed flowers on trailing branches; 'Crystal Palace', a compact plant with violet flowers and bronzy leaves, is somber in garden shade; 'Cambridge Blue' has a light violet flower, a light green leaf, and the compact habit of 'Crystal Palace', but in the shade garden this is a more refreshing plant, as is 'White Lady'.

Myosotis sylvatica (Forget-Me-Not). Technically a biennial, but a spring seedling often completes its life by fall. Forget-Me-Not comes in blue, pink, or white forms, the last two not so much loved or planted; the blue one seems more the symbol of constancy. Judging from the frequency of its appearance in flowery antique valentines, the blue Forget-Me-Not has been a cupid collaborator for at least a hundred years.

This is one of two shade garden annuals (Herb Robert is the other) so easy to grow from seed that you can scatter it where you want flowers. However, you'll get a larger number of flowering plants the first season if you follow the seed-sowing routine outlined at the beginning of the chapter. Easily naturalized, Forget-Me-Not will almost surely reseed itself and become a permanent feature of your spring garden. A classic plant combination in shady spring gardens all over Europe and North America is a drift of Forget-Me-Nots beneath flowering cherries, particularly that grandam tree, *Prunus subhirtella* 'Autumnalis'; the combined clouds of blue and pink are a definition of spring.

You can fill open soil in a sizable woodland with Forget-Me-Nots by scattering a few packets of seed one spring, and then merely standing by, idle as Thoreau, while the plants increase over the years. Among the most memorable "wildflower" displays I've seen is just such a bread-on-the-water return of Forget-Me-Nots broadcast some years before: an acre of forest bottomland covered with millions of Forget-Me-Nots — a Renaissance-blue carpet spread over a blackening pad of the previous fall's maple and alder leaves. Forget-Me-Nots will flower year after year in mature, deciduous woods too shady during summer for the health of most perennials. The annual or biennial Forget-Me-Not accomplishes most of its flower and leaf production and begins coding life in its seeds before the trees leaf out and fully shade the ground.

In more meticulously kept home garden areas, the Forget-Me-Not going-to-seed appears coarse by midsummer. I pull out many during summer, but before I toss them on the compost pile, I strip off the seeds and scatter them.

The wildflower quality of Forget-Me-Not allows the plant to fill in harmoniously and harmlessly about the stems of nearly all sorts of shade plants, especially the larger ferns; only shade garden miniatures, easily overwhelmed, would be unsuitable company.

Nicotiana alata (Flowering Tobacco). A tall plant, up to 30 in., and narrow. Group *Nicotiana* plants to give them body. Half shade at most. The flowers are fragrant, giving their scent most pervasively during the evening, so *Nicotiana* has special value bordering a terrace or other entertainment area of the garden; or plant it outside a bedroom window. Flowers come in white, chartreuse, lavender, and a Victorian red–velvet color; white, as usual, is the most effective flower color in shade, and in the case of *Nicotiana*, the most fragrant. *Nicotiana* can overwinter in the open ground where the temperature does not fall below 20°F. The plant that comes through as a perennial grows twice as big and twice as floriferous the second summer.

Tuberous begonias. A skirt of petals as grand as an eighteenth-century gown, a flower that queens it over every other plant in the shady garden. A flower of many forms and many silky colors. The tuberous begonia is gorgeously out of place in naturalistic gardens, but it fits well against formal architecture. My favorite images of tuberous begonias I've known include those in flower-filled window boxes on a century-old carriage house, in hanging baskets within an Edwardian pavilion (Butchart Gardens), and in big unglazed Mexican pots at both ends of a flight of pink sandstone steps, shaded by a wistaria overhead. Dappled shade or half shade suits these flowers best.

Most gardeners start tuberous begonias from nursery pot plants or from dry tubers. Set out plants or tubers in late spring, after you are sure the last frost is behind you and when the soil has warmed enough to leave your fingers supple and eager for garden work when you plunge your hand experimentally into the ground. Soil for tuberous begonias must be loose enough — sandy-humusy and airy — that you *can* plunge your hand into it without the help of any tool.

Tubers started in pots indoors a month before your outdoor planting season begins will give earlier flowers. Barely cover the tops of the tubers with ideal shade garden soil (*see* p. 28) or with fluffy planting mix, place them in full light (but out of direct sunlight), and keep the mix moist — not saturated. Take the growing plants outside when night temperatures average at least 45°F, with no expectation of a reversal toward winter. Tuberous begonias demand fast drainage during all stages of their growth and flowering and on through their autumn time of dying down. To winter begonia tubers for flowers another year, cut off the sloughy flower stems in the fall and wash soil from the tubers. Place them on an airy shelf, or in some other airy location out of the sun, and let them dry and harden for a week or more. Then pack the tubers in dry sphagnum or in crumpled newspapers and store them in a cold but frost-free location until the following spring. (In this, we've gone beyond "annual" gardening.)

Then, when the shade garden is in the fullest rush of growth and spring flower, take the tubers outdoors . . . And take my hand in congratulations for having attained, in the successful wintering of tuberous begonias, one of the high levels in shade gardening. It is not the easiest of our tasks.

15

Edibles

The shade gardener stands at the seed rack in the garden store extracting packet after packet — corn, peas, beans, lettuce, beets — turning over each one to read the cultural notes on the back, hoping for an encouraging word about culture in shade. Nope. Full sun, as in "plant in an open, sunny location," is the canonical advice given vegetable gardeners by seed packets — by virtually all garden literature, for that matter. But the fact is that many kinds of vegetables tolerate shade up to half the day, and plants that are somewhat shade-tolerant have the potential for being more so. Yet, for all their constant proliferation of new vegetable varieties for particular climates, seed merchants have left shade the last unexplored environment for vegetables: No seeds selected for shade are to be found in seed racks.

Gardeners who have tried vegetables and other crop plants in shade know that, in moderate amounts, it is by no means an abomination. I've grown a number of edibles in half-shaded or dapple-shaded beds with rather good results overall. Certainly the harvest has been worth the effort.

Vegetable seed is slower to germinate in shady soil than in sun, so instead of planting your seeds early and having cold, pelting rains wash them away, plant late, when warming ground encourages germination. Or start seeds early in peat pots or other biodegradable containers and then plant seedlings in the shady bed when the soil warms.

For partly shaded ground I especially recommend beets, sweet cicely, cucumbers, turnips, leaf lettuce, Chinese peapods, comfrey, kale, radishes, scallions, shallots, chives, leeks, broccoli, cress, watercress, carrots, sweet potatoes, spinach, zucchini, cabbage, mustard, and French sorrel. As a rule, leafy vegetables accept more shade than do seed vegetables such as corn, pole beans, and peas, which will tolerate only about three hours of

Half-shaded vegetable garden in a woodland clearing.

shade daily without noticeable impairment. (The vigorous corn plants in the photograph don't seem to believe me.) Other vegetables not often successful in shade include okra, eggplant, squash, peppers, and tomatoes — but better news about tomatoes is soon to come in this narrative.

Shade tolerance in plants is relative to total sun and warmth; the brighter and warmer the summer in one's garden climate, the more shade one's plants absorb without weakening. I happen to garden in the darkest, coolest summer climate in the U.S., a climate sometimes cavelike: During one particularly summer-forsaken August, little gray toadstools sprouted in the damp carpeting in the back of my car. So if you garden almost anywhere else on this continent, your chances of getting a shade crop of any of the above plants are even better than mine.

As it happens, I also garden in New Zealand's North Island,* in a sunny climate much like that of the warmest Mediterranean coast of Europe or that of southern California. In my Auckland garden, a grapefruit tree fruits satisfactorily and a lemon bears heavily in half shade. Tomatoes (in the Pacific Northwest, an uncertain crop even in the fullest sun) ripen in my Auckland neighbor's garden on four hours' sunshine in the afternoon — great big beefsteaks, in a mural planting; the wall behind them reflects heat and light, which is helpful to their ripening.

Herbs as a shade crop in the Pacific Northwest are amazingly successful — amazing in that nearly all the common kitchen herbs are native to hot sun in Mediterranea. Parsley, sage, rosemary, thyme, savory, borage, lovage, fennel, oregano (both the plain green and the golden-leaved kinds), lemon balm, and costmary — all southern European — grow strongly in half shade or even three-fifths shade in my garden; the last three perform even better in shady ground than in full sun. A single plant of any of these herbs (except for parsley: plant several) will almost certainly provide all the aromatic foliage a family of herb enthusiasts can use, plus a bumper crop to give away.

In abandoned farmyards many years overgrown by tall native trees that have come on their own from seed, one sometimes finds an old apple tree, shaded but carrying on the apple business. There, at the right time, I have found ripe apples handy on old bent-down branches, apples of less than store size, and usually with scruffy skin, but fragrant, tart-sweet, and equal, in my memory of living off the land, to the crispest spring water.

Apples, pears, lemons, tamarillo, pie cherries, plums, elderberries, raspberries, strawberries, loquat, and rhubarb (technically a vegetable) are capable of bearing in half shade, probably not as heavily as they bear in full sun, but good fruit.

My own lists of shade garden edibles add up to merely the first word. Consultants located in several states report success with a wide variety of crops in shade: alpine strawberries and black raspberries in half shade (Pennsylvania); blueberries, brambles, muscadine grapes, and squash, in patterned shade and sun throughout the day (Georgia); asparagus, lettuce

* I've learned there is at least one other peregrinating New Zealand–American gardener. In a jet enroute from Auckland to Los Angeles in late April, during that level, mid-ocean time when passengers wander like the Ancient Mariner and stoppeth strangers, I heard a fellow American talking to other passengers about his double life as a vegetable gardener. He was on his way to Los Angeles to plant his "veggies" (he used the New Zealand word). Then in late October he would fly back to Auckland to grow veggies there. For years he had pursued this winterless life with vegetables (and with whom, he didn't say). I did not break into his glad monologue and never even introduced myself, which I now regret.

spinach, and turnip greens in half shade — the last three as fall crops (Alabama); *Ugni Molinae* — a shrubby relative of guava with huckleberry-size fruit — in full shade (California).

From Virginia: "My blueberry bushes ripen fruit with only four hours of morning sun. The alpine strawberry Baron Solemacher, a happy plant here, has seeded itself into all parts of my garden, even the shadiest. (It is at its best with three or four hours of sun.) Lettuce grows better here and lasts longer if shaded in the afternoon."

From vegetable gardener Jim Howard of Yuma County, Arizona, who grows two-thirds of his vegetables under lath panels:

We have learned by trial and error which plants benefit from the shade and which do not. Grapes do not. They bear plenty of fruit under lath, but they tend to get powdery mildew. All melons, squash, and corn do best in full sun; fruit trees, too. Root vegetables and greens grow better in the lath shade, holding longer in mature form under shade, not becoming old and tough before picking. Under lath we have carrots, beets, chard, spinach, celery, cauliflower, artichokes, and parsley. Tomatoes, lettuce, and onions are O.K. under the lattice work, but I've learned how to grow them in full sun, too (with more water). Beans and peas do not like this country under any conditions. Peas make weak growth; beans fold up quickly and expire.

From Ohio:
In my vegetable garden all the conventional vegetables receive at least four hours of shade daily. The only effects of consequence are a slower maturing — perhaps as much as two weeks later than the same vegetables in a fully sunny garden across the road — and a reduced crop of okra. An acquaintance in Hillsdale, Michigan, grows vegetables and fruits in shade morning and afternoon, with no more than a few hours of direct sun at midday: magnificent tomatoes, cabbages, leaf lettuce, root vegetables, strawberries, raspberries, currants, gooseberries. Plants are staked and trellised to expose the foliage to the maximum amount of light. The soil is crumbly to a one-foot depth with compost. In addition to compost, he uses fertilizers, intensive watering, and cultivation to offset the effects of shade to a major extent.

That's just the way to do it.

16

Getting Away at Home

Shade gardening is ultimately a kind of vanishing act, and to set it up, we shade gardeners go to work like magicians. For stage paraphernalia we assemble a selection of shade plants. Our vanish-all cabinet is a bower that we construct of shady foliages: We step inside — and disappear for a while. A little magic with leaves.

Thus the shade gardener begins as a grower of plants and becomes the cultivator of a certain phase of mind: that of retreat and solitude, of the need to drop out, to disappear — poof!, as all of us must, I think, hanker to do now and again. For some of us, surely, the serenity of shade gardening — as the counterpart of sun gardening, with its festive mood — is just what the inner doctor orders.

At a bargain price. The garden composed of livable outdoor rooms, entertaining in the detail of their leafy decor, probably pays for itself in the money one does not spend searching for entertainment in public places. Good times are there for the finding, of course, but they should also be here in the garden. We plan and plant and care for a garden, and it becomes the complete creative hobby, recreation, and body builder. Jogger, here are your shorts — what's your hurry? We gardeners have it all just outside the door.

I show in the drawings a shady-sunny garden whose emphasis is on privacy, a place where one can get away alone or in company. The garden surrounds a conventional bungalow, all within a typical small lot. The shape and size of the house and its grounds are not important; they could take any form. And the arrangement of the plantings isn't significant in itself, either. What you see could be revised to fit any property. This garden is a sampler, then, showing shade garden solutions to common landscape problems.

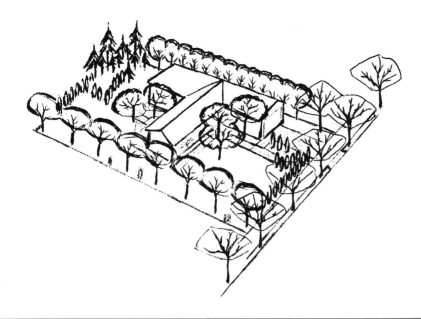

Getaway garden, aerial view.

The usual lonesome, open yard of suburbia has been banished from the site. In its place stands a garden made up of ten or so leafy rooms and hallways, in nearly all of which you could plod around in robe and slippers on a fine morning, in a life-style happily unconventional and unseen. The property is rich in that rarest luxury in modern life, privacy. You find it immediately on entering from the street.

At the public sidewalk end of the garden, columnar conifers such as junipers, yews, or thujas screen the house from public view (or one could use fencing here, or a hedge). I know from my dealings as a designer that there are architects and homeowners who will throw up their hands at the idea of obscuring the house ("What about security?"). With the exception of the enclosed entry garden of Southwestern Spanish architecture, we still generally obey the antique design dictum of presenting the manse to the street with a grand sweep of lawn — design etiquette in the nineteenth century, when there was plenty of space to indulge it, but these days an empty gesture. By now, with home lots in North America shrinking to European and even Asian dimensions (in Tokyo's nicer neighborhoods, twelve by twenty feet of walled garden is a park, nowadays), our traditional no-man's-land of the open front yard seems an insupportable waste of ground.

The unpalatability of yard life extends to every sector of the home lot. It comes not only from lack of privacy but from the plainness of grass lawn all around. Perhaps there is a remanent Puritanism in this reluctance of ours to plant for shade and delight. In any case, grass lawn takes up far too much of North America at the front, sides, and back of the house. The

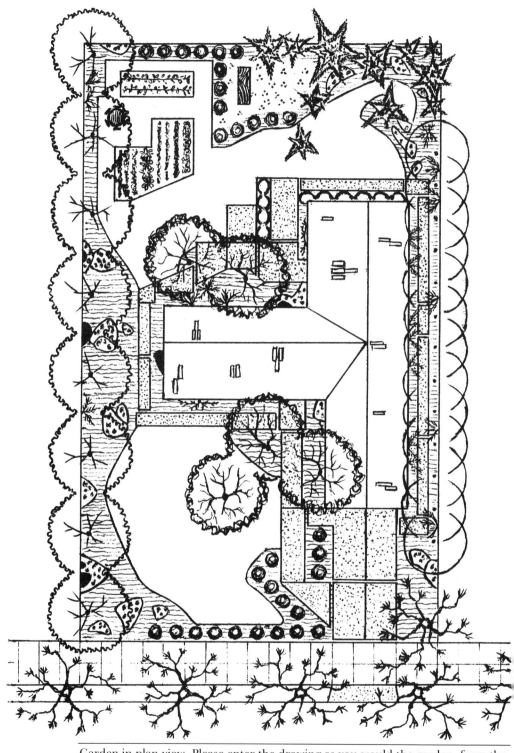

Garden in plan view. Please enter the drawing as you would the garden, from the lower right.

majority of us probably carry a general picture in our minds of hundreds of home properties we've peered into from the street or sidewalk (in our learning to be gardeners), a view of a yard that consists of a strip of planting along the property's edges. The grounds are merely an ornate picture frame, inside of which a bare canvas of lawn covers the ground.

Not so the lawn (shown blank white) in the garden plan at hand. Deep notches incise its edges, as if the greensward were a leaf that had met up with a caterpillar. In place of grass I've used ground covers (wavy lines). Gardeners not keenly interested in plants will probably want to limit the variety of cover plants to one or several of the least laborsome, most serviceable kinds listed in the ground cover chapter. The plant collector, on the other hand, will disdain my wavy lines, which represent uniform ground cover planting and simplification of garden care, and will plant five hundred or a thousand little rarities requiring inch-by-inch gardening, with all its satisfactions.

In the midst of the ground cover plantings, the plan view drawing includes shapes that look rather like pebbles, some of them spotted, some black. Each spot represents several low or middling shade plants, shrubby or perennial, all of one kind; each black shape stands for a single upright plant. There is nothing holy in the proportions. The spotted areas could be more extensive (at a reduction in the amount of ground cover) and the black areas more numerous.

The ground cover sea and its pebbles approximately equal the measure of lawn and pavement (speckled areas), creating a balance that is important, I believe, for the comfort of the human creature: on the one side, ample space for roaming, and on the other, plant variety to engage one's eyes and hands. Another of the garden's balances is the evenness of sun and shade effected by the trees. Shade and sun share the garden and fall equally on the house. But how easy it is to install this pat apportionment in my paper and ink garden, and how uneasily transient are garden shade and sun in real life, changing with every year's plant growth.

I suppose we all know intuitively that different people prefer different amounts of sun and shade on their properties. For a factual basis, I've consulted experienced gardeners around the country. A few gardeners reply that they want shade in only a small part of the garden; a majority would have sun and shade in equal measure and work to maintain that balance; and several deeply dyed-in-the-woods shade gardening specialists among my correspondents prefer a garden mostly shaded, with a small area of unmitigated sun. Only desert gardeners hanker for homes completely shaded by trees (but where one gardens on desert rocks, trees usually grow too slowly to shade the house satisfactorily).

At this point in the gardener's magic show, I would like to demonstrate the best trick of the designer's trade: Gardener, be repetitious. My garden plan is filled with architectonic repetitions of trees and shrubs, the largest example of it being the line of eight trees along the left edge of the property: Dogwoods, Pie Cherries (you'd have all the birds in town), birches, crabapples, magnolias, or any one of dozens of kinds of smallish trees named in chapter 9. But only one kind, please, for all eight. Mixing of varieties in this lineup would jumble and jungle the garden.

You gain not only structural strength and order by planting a single kind of tree in a long line, but also a certain grandeur that is as proud in its way, I'll have to confess, as that of the old open front lawn. However, planting the same kind of tree (or shrub) along two sides of the property risks the beginnings of a boxed-in feeling, and the same planting on three or four sides of the property will plunge many viewers into a claustrophobic funk.

My other long line of planting, in the sideyard at the right edge of the property, is composed of a narrowish kind of tree or shrub (such as stewartia or Lemonwood; fastigiate forms of birch, oak, or cherry; aucuba or nandina) or perhaps of a nonrunning bamboo. The side garden becomes a tunnel formed by branches overhead and to one side, and by the house on the other side. Along the walk, large ferns peacock their fronds up through a ground cover planting. In all, this place is an adventuresome go-through, instead of the usual storage area for scraps of waste lumber, oddments of brick, and a hopelessly leaky hose. Such treasures have been relegated to the garage; more obtrusive there than if limboed in the sideyard, they'll be taken to the dump years sooner. Sideyards are generally the most abused and long-suffering strips of ground in civilization. Many backyards have it bad enough, but the average sideyard is a material Bedlam. Pity, because this space can become a journey of delight to the child mind in all of us.

Near the front door (located slightly below and to the right of dead center in the garden plan) stand three spreading trees, perhaps small maples, flowering cherries, palos verdes, or hawthorns. My case for including them is to gain overhead foliage and the atmosphere of an anteroom in the dooryard. But after drawing them in, I've become uncertain as to whether they are really needed. Of course, anything superfluous to a garden is wrong, and very wrong if it is a thing as large as a tree. Can't decide. The trees may very well be exactly and boldly right for the spot. But perhaps it's less a matter of artistry than of psyche. When I sketched the trees, I was no doubt thinking as a shade gardener, which is to think of sequestered places; my second thoughts have been those of a sun gardener.

The two trees that shade the rear terrace need not be the same kind as the trees in front; if different, the change will contribute a little more spice

---

Narrow side yard — but not anymore. Now something of a leafy tunnel of many foliages. To create a tall, dense, informal grovelike planting in a narrow space, use such trees as birch, Lacebark, Amur Maple, Vine Maple, Sourwood, or Quaking Aspen, or such shrubs as boxwood, *Enkianthus campanulatus*, *Ilex crenata* 'Convexa', *Mahonia Aquifolium*, or *Nandina*. If you decide to use trees, a single kind for the entire planting will probably give a better effect than a mixture. With shrubs, uniformity seems unimportant — and perhaps less joyful than a welter of different foliages. Garden of Mo Yee.

of life. Yet, neither the front planting nor the one in the rear should comprise a mixture of trees, I would say. But that, of course, is only one opinion. More important, what do you say, reader — old compadre of these many pages? I would not be in the least surprised to hear a rationale for a mixed bag of trees that is quite as sound as, or sounder than, my idea of planting them in nice uniformity. There's no one way of going about it.

As a mere idiosyncracy — indulge me here — I've divided the pavement of the terrace with a short hedge, loosely pruned (four connected bead shapes): Japanese Holly, boxwood, camellias, or any of the other more trimmable shrubs presented in this book, or compact rhododendrons.

The lawn leads from the terrace to three garden rooms at the back of the property. The first of these, upper left on the plan, is a place for cooking out and picnicking — as much the primordial heart of a home garden as Frank Lloyd Wright's fireplaces are to his houses. I show a table with chairs on the half-shaded lawn, beds of edible plants and flowers, and space for a party celebrating the crops in their midst. (The table and chairs will need to be shifted frequently to keep the grass beneath them in health.)

At upper center is a garden room screened with columnar conifers, surfaced with sand or sawdust (depicted on the plan by trios of dots.) Here is a potting table that can also be used to display plants. The open ground nearby might be employed for making compost.

And, at last, there is a hideaway, located at upper right, a glade of lawn within a grove of conifers — perhaps Hinokis, Dawn Redwoods, or Douglas Firs, or the grove could be of deciduous trees. You could stretch a hammock here. Or two of you could carry the picnic table over for lunch in the "redwood room." Only millionaires and shade gardeners live in such luxury.

17

Recent Findings

Here are some shade plants new to me since I wrote the first edition of this book, and also some plants I knew about all along but omitted from the original opus. Nothing so nags a writer on gardening — this writer on gardening — as the important or especially interesting plants he has left out for lack of space or memory.

When the book came out in 1984, a friend who read one of the first copies challenged me: Where are the uvularias? I exactly recall my reply, "Oh my gosh, I forgot 'em!" A certain species of the genus *Uvularia* is one of eastern North America's handsomest wildflowers for shade gardening, and I had forgotten it. Now is my chance to instate the plant, together with all the others of the omitted I can think of. Climate codes (NE, S, NW, and so on) are explained on p. 87.

Achillea ptarmica (The Pearl). All climates. This well-known white button flower will grow and flower in up to two-thirds shade. It is a mighty traveler at the root, plunging through the underground parts of any perennials in its path, sending up stray stems in their midst. These neighbors had better be as tough as or tougher than The Pearl. In the border where I grow the plant, shaded by a Marmalade Bush, its 2-ft. stems topped with flowers interweave harmlessly with Shasta Daisies and *Phygelius aequalis*.

Actaea (Baneberry). All climates. American woodland plants, available from a few nurseries. While hardly memorable for their small white flowers, the actaeas are among the showiest berry-bearing perennials for the shade garden. *A. alba* and *A. pachypoda* are 2–3-ft.-tall clumps of graceful, compound leaves, surmounted by stems of rounded, dead-white berries, like tribal beads made of bone. *A. rubra* is a similar grower, shiny lacquer-red of fruit. Slow to increase, actaeas need moisture and a half-shady or mostly shady location. Shiny bright though they are, red actaea berries lack specialty in a garden world filled with the red berries of holly, firethorn, and cotoneaster. White actaea, though, is extraordinary, unmatched by anything in the garden.

Caution: the berries of these plants are poisonous.

Adlumia fungosa (Allegheny Vine). Hardy everywhere. Mauve or white lockets like those of bleeding hearts on delicate stems that delight in scrambling a yard or so up on shrub branches, say, those of *Abeliophyllum* or *Rhododendron mucronulatum*, or any others more filmy than bushy; in a moist, half-shady setting. This eastern American wildflower, a biennial, flowering in spring and summer, is well established as a harmless weed in many parts of the world. It comes up mysteriously in the garden, and if the gardener does not know its name and biography, the gardener will try to find out, for the plant looks well mannered and no one would take it for a weed. In my twenties I asked a gardener in her eighties about this plant, which I had but had never planted — and quick as a wizard, she gave me the name. Indeed, she seemed a wizard to me at the time, and still does. There is evidence in her magnificent shade garden planting shown at the top of p. 213.

Allium. The wild onions add up to a large genus, native all around the northern hemisphere. Many of the species thrive in shade: two of these appear on pp. 207–8. Below are two more, spring-flowering.

Allium neopolitanum. All climates except GN and T. Heads of white on 2-ft. reedy stems, nodding in a breeze. A graceful flower and a harmless self-sower amongst large rhododendrons and other shade shrubbery.

Allium ursinum (Ramson). Hardy everywhere. A British wildflower and a wild self-sower, turning many a woodland floor into a sweep of white flowers in Maytime. Showy bulb, useful in wild gardening. But the plant seems to evoke little sentiment or poetry. We hear only of Britain's bluebell woods, not of its ramson woods.

Artemisia. All climates. Many of these sun plants will take to shade, up to nearly the day long, with surprising ease. Their silvery leaves impart an astringent freshness to neighboring shadowy greenery. The upright-growing perennials and subshrubs in the genus are the ones most usually amenable to shade. However, one of the mat-forming artemisias happens to be among the best for our purposes: *A. stellariana*, a ground cover that spreads to a yard wide in about 2 years, with gray-white leaves divided into many irregular toes, held mostly flat and close to the ground. This plant makes a dapper team with bronzy-purplish forms of *Ajuga*, not intermingled, but planted as near neighbors.

Shrubby *A. absinthium*, the absinthe of mind suicide and the wormwood of Shakespearean verse, offers gray, dissected foliage and gray flowers, effective in shade (or in sun) with puce-leaved forms of *Canna* or *Phormium*.

Artemisia stellariana, silvery gray, as a ground cover in a bed framed by railroad ties silvered with age.

Astrantia maxima, mauve florets backed by a rosy collar.

Such appositions of silver and bronze have perhaps become conventionally artistic by now. Yet who can resist?

Astrantia major. NE, S, NW. A clump-forming perennial, summer-flowering, now showy but most elegant and entertaining: a yard-tall cluster of thin, mostly upright stems terminating in inch-wide flowers, each a floral arrangement in itself: a nosegay of tiny, greenish white florets backed by a serrated collar of chartreuse. This dramatic arranger's flower needs rich, moist soil and half shade, or the dappled shade of tree branches. *A. maxima* is a similar grower, with similar needs. The flower has mauve-pink florets and a rosy collar.

Blechnum brasiliense (C, SW, T) and **Blechnum chilense** (S and NW with shelter from the worst of winter; C, SW, T), are 3-ft.-tall South American forest ferns with big, dark green fronds, coarsely segmented and leather-thick in their fabric. The fronds of *B. brasiliense* are rose-bronze in new growth. Add these species to those listed in chapter 12 as the best of home landscape ferns. *B. brasiliense* tends to stay put and form short trunks; *B. chilense* wanders. The two blechnums require nearly full shade; moist, cleanly draining soil.

Canna. s, nw (with deep mulch on the rhizomes in winter), c, sw, t. For a marshy waterside, for average moisture, or even for a summer-dry hillside. Their adaptability to wet soil is perhaps confined to the tropics, where cannas are often grown in marshes or as aquatics in shallow water, rhizomes clutching the mud.

Ginger-cane plants, 4 to 6 ft. tall, with somewhat orchidlike flowers at top. The two kinds I've tried successfully in shade (about two-thirds in measure) are *C. indica* 'Purpurea', tall, with coppery purple leaves and canes, topped with a small show of glowing orange-scarlet flowers in late summer, and *C. lutea,* less tall, with fresh, peapod-green leaves and red-spotted yellow flowers in summer.

The taller of the two I grow mainly for its foliage, which I have found to be a highly effective toner of the landscape in several places in the garden. Adding bold form and magnetic color to undecided groupings of perennials and shrubs, the canna pulls together any timid or wispy plants, like a storyteller gathering a cluster of children.

In certain compositions, the macaw-red flowers scrawk at others in the violet and rosy range. In that case, I lop off the canna heads when they first bud out. Sounds callous, and it's got to be. Gardening calls for both an understanding hand with plants and high-handedness. The ruthless but creative throwaway is the second most important event in gardening, after planting. I often think of it as editing the garden.

Carex (Sedge). Add the following species to those enumerated on page 211.

Carex flagelliformis. s, nw, c, sw, t. A New Zealander, a 2-ft.-tall, yard-wide clump of almost hair-fine leaf strands that arch outward and then downward, until many of the tips touch the ground. Shiny dark green or, in the more commonly cultivated form, shiny copper red. Flower and seed show is minor. Serviceable as a ground cover when planted as a group. Half or more shade, or sun. The metallic color form yearns, with the usual passionate affinity of bronzy or coppery plants, for gray foliages close by.

Carex pendula. For all climates, in upland soil or marsh. Best in half or three-quarters shade; growable in light shade. A great grassy fountain, 4 ft. tall, upward- and then outward-arching, with green blades about as broad as a rapier. Stems of grasslike green flowers surmount the foliage and then bend gracefully downward: *pendula.* Hardly anybody uses the supposed common (say, rather, comic) name of the plant, Great Drooping Sedge, which almost demands to be followed by an exclamation point, as in Great Balls of Fire!

This species has become secretly stylish in recent years with a few

North American landscape architects who are, as well as builders, connoisseurs of garden plants (a rare combination). The tall carex is particularly effective as professionals generally use it, in small groups or in swales. Homeowners with less space at their command will find that a single sedge clump makes the perfect counterpoint to shade plants with big leaves: rhubarb, hosta, calla, *Lysichiton,* and others — not all of them together, but one or another of the elephant-ears.

Carex trifida. Growable everywhere except GN. A coastal plant, native to sub-Antarctic islands and other southern hemisphere shores. Two feet tall, with broad, sickle-curved strap leaves. Of a greenish gray, it has the look of Lyme Grass; spreads modestly, though, not at all like that invader. Light yellow flowers in early summer ripen into big club-clusters of brown seeds. A sun plant in nature, it needs semishade and steady moisture in the garden, which conditions keep the foliage fresh.

Chrysanthemum parthenium (Feverfew). A Victorian antique, a quaint old party in the shade garden. The single-flowered forms of Feverfew grow readily in shade; short-lived, the plants perpetuate themselves by seed. One form is green, 2 ft. tall, with little yellow-centered white daisies all summer. The other form is *C. parthenium* 'Aureum,' shorter of stem, with glowing greeny yellow leaves and the same flowers. Either variety seeds true. These pesky-pleasant plants come up everywhere and should be left to flower wherever they fit in, weeded out where they interfere.

Clintonia Andrewsiana. S, NW, C. Elegant in leaf, flower, and fruit, a 2-ft. liliad native to the redwood forests of the West Coast. Leaves, broad and glossy, spread close above the leaf mold. The height is in the slender flower stem, topped with rosy bells in late spring. Berries follow, round and shiny, violet and jewellike. A slow grower for a cool shady position in moist, humusy soil.

Green-yellow-flowering *Clintonia borealis* of our northeast is faster and has blue jewel berries.

The white-flowered *C. uniflora,* so abundant in western mountains, so tempting to the transplanter, refuses life in a lowland garden.

Cornus alba (Tatarian). For all climates. Deciduous shrub, especially valuable in its color varieties of leaf or twig. Accepts much shade or full sun. In shade gardening, Tatarian is ideally placed in the shadows of deciduous trees, whose leaflessness in winter will allow sun to reach the shrub. Sun induces bright red coloring in twigs formed the previous summer. Brightest of all in winter twig is the green-leaved variety, *C. alba sibirica.* Variegated leaf forms of *C. alba* are among the most freshening of splashy leaves for the shade garden. Of these, *C. alba* 'Argenteomarginata' (often sold as *C. alba* 'Elegantissima') has green leaves irregularly marked with white toward their margins. The young bark is purplish brown in summer, reddening in winter.

C. alba and its varieties flower in spring, an effective display of small white flowers clustered in cyme heads. As for power of growth, these

Garden niche in nearly full shade. At left, *Cornus alba* 'Argenteomarginata' as a pot plant. Lower right, the crinkly leaves of *Hosta sieboldiana elegans.*

shrubs have the copsy strength of willow and will grow tall and loose if unpruned. Cut back to the desired height after their flowering each spring; if back to 4 ft., new growth will present the bright winter bark at about eye level. Plant *C. alba* singly, or in a line to make an informal hedge.

Codonopsis clematidea. NW, NC. A twining perennial that would admire an *Abeliophyllum* or *Vaccinium* or some other airy small shrub as a host for its climb. The late summer flowers are pendant bells of a ghostly pale violet with hidden interior decorations in orange and oxblood. Needs a cool, moist, woodsy place.

Crinum Moorei. S, NW (with shelter), C, SW, T. From a bulb the size of a large rutabaga, flower stems arise to 3½ ft. and crest in nodding, lily-form flowers, pale pink, flared at the rim to 6 in. Below the flowers, broad, almost spatulate strap leaves curve out to catch the rationed sun of the woodland. The foliage, as handsome as the flowers are Junoesque, remains fresh and glossy a couple of months after the late-spring, early-summer flowers melt away. In all, a substantial summer landscape plant, combining well with ferns.

My garden experience with *C. Moorei* is in subtropical New Zealand, where I grow the plant in a rich, moist woodland soil of leaf mold and silt, shaded almost fully by trees. In more northerly countries, the conventional place for *C. Moorei* is in the sun. So grown, it flowers well but always appears mangy of leaf. Shade is essential to keep the foliage from flagging and eroding prematurely.

When you plant the bulb, its long neck and part of its shoulders must show above ground. Flowering improves when the bulb is left undisturbed for years or even decades. Neither slug nor snail nor possum nor anything else will attack this bulb, which must be very nasty tasting.

Cyananthus. NE, NW. I used to stock these miniatures in my mail-order nursery, and they were usually sellouts, popular with rock-gardening connoisseurs in both the northeast and the northwest. These people weren't gambling on hardiness (for once), but knew the plants to be successes in their regions.

Cyananthus is a small group of Himalayan relatives of bellflowers. Taprooted; leaves in a low tuft; blue-violet, tubular flowers with spreading petals. The plants live only a few years but are easy to renew from seed. Grow them in a peat wall or a woodsy alpine garden. They require cool semishade and abhor drought.

Danae racemosa. S, NW, C, SW. Related to *Ruscus* (described in this chapter), with that shrub's 2–3-ft. height of flattened branches, and red berries. *Danae* will grow in full shade, but not in the darkish places its *Ruscus* relative will tolerate. *Danae*'s branches are useful in floral arrangements.

Disporum (Fairy Bells). Gentle woodland plants, minor relatives of Solomon's Seal. If you know that plant, you know the habit of these: creeping rootstocks, arching stems of winglike leaves, pendant bells; afterward, pendant berries; then retreat beneath the leaf mold during winter. The fully

Disporum hookeri in a shady rock garden. This display of half-inch, grape-red berries lasts through the summer and early autumn.

hardy western American species, *D. hookeri* (greenish yellow of flower), *D. oreganum,* and *D. smithii* (both ivory-white), stand about 18 to 30 in., the better the living conditions, the taller the plant. Abundant moisture, fertile soil, and cool, dewy, part shade, are to the liking of disporum. The various species display sizable berries: apricot-colored in *D. oreganum* and *D. smithii,* grape-red in *D. hookeri.* The American Indians used the berries as food, and those of us non-Indians bent on enriching our acquaintance with our plants are sure to sample this fruit (a bland, sweetish goo).

The only commonly cultivated disporum is the Japanese *D. sessile* 'Variegatum' (NE, with shelter; S, NW, C, SW), a moderately fast spreader; flowers, green-and-white, lost against the eye-walloping green-and-white variegated foliage. Unlike this species, the American disporums are slow growers in gardens.

Two other smallish relatives of Solomon's Seal, in appearance similar to *Disporum,* and both also gently effective in the shade garden, are listed at *Streptopus* and *Uvularia.*

Dodecatheon (Shooting Star). All climates except T. Spring wildflowers of North America, belonging to the primrose family but nothing like that plant in the appearance of the flower. The common name, Shooting Star, says it all: meteorite flowers in flight, pointed at the fore end, with a whoosh of reflexed petals aft; on thin, straight-up stems that connect with a basal tuft of pointed or rounded, auricular leaves. Tallest is *D. Maedia* of the east, lavender, flowering at 2 ft. Of the several westerners, *D. pulchellum* 'Red Wings' is the most colorful, rose-red, on a foot-high stem. Dodecatheons grow best in moist, cool, humusy soil, with the sun well broken by boughs, lathing, or netting overhead.

Doronicum pardalianches (Leopard's-Bane). Hardy everywhere. My notes on doronicums (p. 217) worry too much to suit this tough species. Since that writing, I've met the plant as a naturalized escapee (probably from somebody who dug an excess of it from the garden and dumped it) into open woodland. There it stood 3 ft. tall, a host of yard-high daisies as gaily yellow as daffodils, though not quite 10,000 at a glance. This plant belongs to the list of nonnative flowers capable of entirely maintaining themselves in the midst of woodland rabbits, snails, caterpillars — and seasonal drought. What list? Under the heading *Lactuca muralis* in this chapter.

Equisetum variegatum (Northern Scouring Rush). For all climates. A plant of marshes and moist soil, found around the world in sub-Arctic and more northerly temperate latitudes, descending in North America to the northern United States. Adapts readily to well-drained garden soil or pot culture in sun or shade. A patch of vertical cylinder-stems, leafless, branchless, evergreen, with blackish bands, and most strange. The stems attract and hold the eye, primevally, like a snake. They are narrower than chopsticks, broader than spaghetti; some are topped with spore-bearing cones; all stand about 16 in. high.

This plant fascinates people, I've discovered, having planted it in a bowl-shaped pot and taken it to a public garden where we have a permanent display of foliage plants and miniature landscapes, together with a seasonal display of annual flowers, all in containers. The *Equisetum* is one of the most attention-getting plants in the display. People ask where it can be purchased. I have to tell them — and you, as well — that I've never seen or heard of it being for sale (I collected it in the wild, a small piece whose removal did not threaten the broad colony). This would make a see-it, buy-it item in garden centers, especially if planted in an attractive pot. The plant is easy to maintain. It likes moisture but is drought tolerant even as a pot plant. More on *Equisetum*, p. 217.

Eucomis comosa (Pineapple Lily). s, c, sw, t; nw with shelter from winter sun and wind. It is easier to caricature the oddity of this plant than to describe the quiddity that makes it fascinating. A bulb plant of boozy appearance, as if somebody had poured a pitcher of piña colada over it. Leaves and flowers sprawl disreputably and have a pudgy flaccidness. The strap-form leaves are 2½ ft. long, soft green with darker, froggy spots. Flowers develop in summer, pale greenish and small, but several hundred together in a corn-ear cylinder about the length of this book at first, stretching longer by autumn with the ripening of the flowers into purplish seeds. Too weighty to stand upright, the floral cylinder leans, but turns upward toward its tip and terminates in a curious tuft of pineapplelike "leaves" (actually bracts).

Slowly I've learned to appreciate this plant, a surprise gift from a friend I could hardly offend by refusing. I gave it a killer location, but it didn't die; it grew, unabashed. Its floppiness, increasing with the bulbs, peeved me for years. My accord with the Pineapple Lily began with my construction of a dry stone wall that needed to be gentled with plants that would partly conceal it. Since the wall planting would receive little watering or attention, I turned to the *Eucomis,* having discovered it to be a survivor. I separated the bulbs early in autumn, pressed their roots into spaces in the stonework, and draped the lolling leaves and flowers down over the wall. The result was immediately good and has bettered with the renewed growth of the plant. Its sprawliness is advantageous here, and the greening of the wall is just enough. *Eucomis* needs only an hour or two of sun but can be grown in a fully sunny place. A similar species, *E. bicolor,* is not to be despised either, if some kind friend offers it.

Eupatorium. Two very different eastern American perennial wildflowers join under this name. Both plants can be purchased from nurseries listed in this book; both are hardy everywhere, easy and permanent in moist soil and part shade. The one, *E. ageratoides* (White Snakeroot), forms a clump of strong, upright stems to 3 ft., dressed with nettlelike but nonstinging leaves and topped with flattened cotton-boll heads of white flowers in autumn. Its stance and size suit the plant to the shady flower garden. The other, *E. purpureum* (Joe-Pye Weed), stands 8 or more ft. tall in a rich place, one of the more august and dignified perennials in the garden repertory. Attractive from foot to head, a neat, narrow canebrake of bolt-upright stalks, so sturdy it knows no ill wind. Across the summit of the canebrake, late summer–autumn flowers spread as floral cushions of fuzzy texture and rosy color. Harmonious with Japanese maples in autumn leaf. But who was Joe Pye and what did he have to do with this plant? These questions comprised a gardening mystery fully as long-running in my life as Agatha Christie's *Mousetrap* on the London stage. At last I have the answers, from the 1893 classic, *How to Know the Wild Flowers,* by Mrs. William Starr Dana, recently republished by Houghton Mifflin. Joe Pye was a Native American who used this plant to cure typhus fever in New England.

Euphorbia (Spurge). Among the many species is the Poinsettia *(E. pulcherrima),* which amounts to more than a Christmas victim in a pot; in tropical gardening, Poinsettia, grown to 10 or 15 ft., massed with flowers, forms a spectacular background shrub in shade or sun. The Poinsettia plant — stem, leaf, bracts, and florets — presents a pattern for all the other, far less showy euphorbias. They all bleed a gummy and poisonous white latex if you pull off a leaf or cut a stem; they all blossom with bract collars, yellow or green in most species, the collar holding at center a cluster of functional little flowers.

Euphorbia cyparissias, hardy in all climates, grows as a 6–10-in.-tall, furry or firlike carpet of grayish green needles, soft to the eyes and touch; a goldish carpet in spring flower. The plant is a known weed, hectically stoloniferous and inadmissible to a fine garden community, but valuable as a ground cover in dry, tree-robbed shade. Margery Fish, of cherished memory in gardening, wrote that this plant worked well for her as a cover beneath a large specimen of the desert mountain conifer *Cupressus arizonica.*

Euphorbia Griffithii 'Fireglow' (hardy except in GN) has become increasingly popular in Britain in recent decades and has lately been imported and cataloged by several North American mail-order nurseries. Green, a yard tall, with early-summer flowers of orange-red that manage to defy both those hot colors with a pastel subtleness of hue. 'Fireglow' is a long-lasting arranger's flower and is finding a place in the florist industry. The plant needs rich soil, moisture, and full sun, or shade up to two-thirds of the day.

Euphorbia Robbiae, native to the Near East and hardy even in the coldest regions, has been employed in Britain for at least half a century as a filler plant in shade or sun. It is especially valued for its almost matchlessly tough luxuriance of growth in dry shade beneath trees or in awkward scraps of soil at the base of a building. From 2 to 3 ft. tall, with somber black-green foliage and green bracts. It is one of those plants more popular with professionals than with home gardeners. In recent decades, British landscape architects have made increasing use of *E. Robbiae.* In North America, this nostrum for difficult ground is as yet nearly unknown. The first 5,000 pros in this continent who start using the plant instead of ivy as a shade ground cover will make their reputations as vanguard landscapers.

Euphorbia Sibthorpii and *Euphorbia characias Wulfenii,* s, NW, C, SW, T, are closely related, gray-green bushy plants, 3–4 ft. tall, flowering in early spring; every stem is topped with yellow bract heads, almost as big and insistently jolly as cheerleaders' pompoms.

There. I hope I've made amends; a nurseryman scolded me when this book first appeared for neglecting euphorbias except for one mention. He was quite justified in his criticism. This is a plant group of first value in our *sombra* world.

Grasses and grasslike plants. Members of the grass family (Gramineae) and other plants of grassy appearance have lately undergone one of those surges of popularity characteristic of gardening through the centuries. The grass-gardening trend took off in the 1960s, as a part of the turn toward nature and away from ostentation. Grass plants possess an agrestic simplicity that probably connects them, at some level of mind, with wholesome grain and the restorative country life. At its beginning, the grassy trend was a youth movement; as a nurseryman, I found very young gardeners were the buyers. But then the advance of horticulture always begins with the young. The proposition must of course include those of us up to age ninety-plus, youthfully adventurous in our gardening.

See *Carex, Luzula, Melica,* and *Melium.*

Hedera Helix (English Ivy), as shown on p. 163, has climbed a two-story masonry wall at a rate of a foot a year. This same plant will descend with more alacrity. Ivy in balcony planters, with ample water and fertilizer, vines its way downward at about three feet a year.

English Ivy in its small-leaved forms often grows much more slowly in the subtropics and tropics than in northern gardens. Such small-leaved ivies as 'Golddust,' 'Pittsburgh,' and many others, which ramp yards wide in the north, may spread across only a few feet of ground in a subtropical climate, and in the tropics remain for years as choice pot plants. It seems that winter chill stimulates English Ivy, as it does apple trees, and that warm or hot winters devitalize the plant. But ivy in the tropics still makes attractive dwarfed growth.

Heracleum mantegazzianum (Giant Hogweed, Cartwheel Plant). All climates except t. White, umbellate discs 3 ft. across, lofted like jugglers' plates on poles 10 ft. high over a clump of enormous, jaggy, maple-form leaves. A plant especially attractive to the young and unwary. In my gardening novitiate, I planted out a couple of first-year clumps of this giant biennial. I had dug them with heroic effort, for they were massively rooted, from a patch of the plant growing in a farm yard. Those plants flowered, seeded, and died the next summer, but their progeny have never left me. This species seeds about widely and cunningly. One never knows where it will next erupt; it's like *Rafflesia* for size and shock. This year it is bursting forth from a dignified bed of lavender 150 ft. from the original planting site. Still, everybody in my family of nongardeners or occasional gardeners looks forward to the spectacular flowering of this plant each summer. They've never done battle with its excess seedlings.

I called this suburban property The Wild Garden when I had a nursery here, but the place has never been wild enough to accommodate the plant. A country setting would be better, perhaps along a stream bank in shade or sun, or in an opening in the woods. The seed head of this colossus, when dried and divested by time of its powerful herbal scent, is grand material for dry arrangement.

Heucherella. Bigeneric hybrids between *Heuchera* and *Tiarella,* with much of the latter's sparky daintiness of flower. Hardy perennials, the heucherellas require part shade or a north slope; fertile soil, steadily moist. Drought will quickly ruin them. The best known is *Heucherella tiarelloides,* 18 in. tall, spring-flowering on upright stems that terminate in clusters of tiny, salmon-pink bells. The close basal foliage, intermediate in character between those of the parents, spreads slowly to 18 in. across in about four years. At age 4, or even younger, heucherellas should be divided in late summer. Keep the transplanted divisions watered until autumn rains take over.

Hyacinthus (Hyacinth). All climates except T. The common garden hyacinth is unsuited to the shade garden (or, as far as I am concerned, to any other garden, poisonously sweet-smelling Medusa coiffure that it is). But there are two perky, dwarf species of hyacinth, *H. amethystinus* and *H. ciliatus* (*H. azureus*), that belong squarely in our domain of shade. The names describe their colors. I recall flowering them in one year from seed (which I obtained from a rock-garden society). They prospered in a half-shady bed in my Pacific Northwest garden, increased by self-sowing, and carried on for a good two decades, until ferns and bleeding-hearts overwhelmed them. My fault for not stepping in and playing umpire in time.

Hydrangea petiolaris (Climbing Hydrangea). All climates except GN. A climbing vine that will, in decades' time, ascend four stories of wall or tree trunk, carrying showy plaques of creamy white flowers that measure about 8 in. across. Back in chapter 1 I wrote about a Climbing Hydrangea I'd planted at the base of a brick wall of my home. The vine was a slow starter and has always declined to fasten itself to the brick work. Wires help it upward. I can't account for this tepid performance, which I now know to be atypical of the vine (something distasteful about these particular bricks?). Another Climbing Hydrangea of my acquaintance has climbed a two-story wall in about a decade, securing its heavy wood firmly with its own hold-fasts. Throughout its long summer flowering, this vine is of enchanting aspect, especially when viewed from a distance. Then the thousand or so white flower clusters, dotted over the dark foliage, resemble a flock of migratory butterflies resting awhile on branches. The flowers open on stems held — as the vine wants them positioned — 30 to 36 in. out from the wall. Any closer pruning would reduce the display.

A related hardy vine, one of confusingly similar appearance, *Schizophragma hydrangeoides,* will in time scramble three stories high. In the Pacific Northwest, either of these climbers is often planted at the base of a Douglas fir whose trunk has been cleared nearly up to telephone-pole height (see p. 77 for an example). In the midmorning to midafternoon shade cast by the fir boughs, the vine cloaks the tree trunk with a dense shag of ovate leaves and an abundance of summer flowers.

Hydrangea Sargentiana. S, NW, C, SW. Himalayan. Equally attractive for its foliage and its summer flowers. The leaves are nearly a foot long, ovate, soft green and furry, held mostly flat. Flowers assembled in a structure about as flat as a domed pie, half a foot in diameter, of a smoky, pale violet, with white sterile flowers around the rim.

This large shrub fits perfectly against boles of trees limbed well up to provide high shade. The hydrangea tends toward a tall lankiness, but can be held down to 6 ft. by pruning in early spring, shortening the branches to round and compact shrub. A memorable plant; once seen, pleasantly reviewed in mind.

Ilex (Holly). S, NW, C. The English Holly (*Ilex aquifolium),* the American Holly *(Ilex opaca),* and others are generically tolerant of shade, producing good crop of berries in half (or more) shade, as in the lee of tall trees.

Leaning over a bubbling brook: *Ligularia dentata,* with 3-inch orange-yellow daisies and round dark leaves. Daylily leaf blades, above; the little round leaf coin of Creeping Jennie beneath.

However, as with the cultivation of practically all plants in shade, and most certainly plants such as holly that are natively sun-loving, there is an un-determined boundary between the amount of shade the plant will accept willingly and the amount that will prove ruinous. Don't overdo it.

Jeffersonia (Twin-Leaf). All climates except т. A two-part leaf, like two hands cupped together to drink water from a spring; a foot-tall clump of such leaves rising from an underground crown of yellow wood; and an intricate basket of tough, wiry, yellow roots, typical of the barberry family, to which *Jeffersonia* belongs. There are only two species in the genus, both perennial plants. *J. diphylla*, eastern North American, was the first named, after Thomas Jefferson. He was pleased enough at the honor to include a big bed of *Jeffersonia* in his sketches for the garden at Monticello (does history know if the plants were ever set out?) Better that he had planted one, or only a few together, for the plant is deciduous, leaving a winter barren in the space clothed by its summer leaves; its spring flower is a little white cup, very short term.

The other species, *J. dubia*, Manchurian, differs in being rounder in the divisions of its twin leaf and in flowering pale violet. Neither of the species is a show-stopper in flower. Even so, *Jeffersonia* are distinguished citizens in the shade garden. They catch and hold the eye — and memory. Propagate from seed; division of the woody crown is nearly impossible.

Kirengeshoma palmata. s, nw, c. Japanese, a cool-appearing woodland perennial. Three feet tall, and as wide. Soft green leaves, a rounded 4 in., serrate, and seeming to belong on some sort of tree, perhaps sycamore. Soft yellow flowers, bell-shaped and nodding, as in *Abutilon*. But such comparisons are forced. The plant is like nothing else. Grow it in a lush, woodsy situation, with unfailing moisture. Propagation by seed.

Lactuca muralis (Wall Lettuce). All climates except т. Hundreds of little cowslip-yellow stars in early summer, airily apart on nearly leafless, slim yet sturdy branching stems to 3 ft. tall. A biennial of stardust sparkiness in flower. It is also a weed, but a benign one, one of several plants of aplomb that arrived from Europe without documents long ago and that now add harmlessly to the color of woods and wild gardens. Others that I can think of are Lady's Mantle, Foxglove, Ground Ivy, Forget-Me-Not, Herb Robert, and Self-Heal; all but the last are described elsewhere in this book. These weeds provide easy pleasure in shade gardening, as long as the rest of the plant community is as tough, wildish, and tall (or taller). By the way, Self-Heal *(Prunella vulgaris)* is a plant so abundant and widespread that I won-der if you're not old friends/adversaries with it? — yanking it from some places, letting it alone to give color in others. I've known many gardeners who keep up such a relationship with Self-Heal, as indeed I do myself. The plant, if you're wondering, resembles *Ajuga* in leaf and flower — a violet-purple pagoda spike in spring and summer.

Ligularia. Daisies of bold, rounded, colorful leafage. Those described here are growable in all climates except gn. One receives scant mention on page 230. Others, tolerant of shade and demanding of moist or marsh soil, include the dark-green-leaved *L. dentata* and its purplish-leaved garden forms, *L. dentata* 'Desdemona' and 'Othello'. These stand 3 and 4 ft., respectively, and crown themselves with orange-yellow daisies in summer. The 6-ft. *L. Przewalskii* displays only small yellow summer daisies, but its dark foliage is deeply and ornamentally frilled within the round outline.

Lobelia syphilitica. All climates. Dark blue-violet flowers in summer, shaped like those of the ubiquitous annual lobelia of gardens. But this species is a 3-ft. perennial, an eastern American wildflower native to moist soils. Of the several eastern lobelia species, *L. syphilitica* is the most amenable to shade.

Luetkea pectinata (Alaska Spiraea). NE, S, GN, NW, C. Western alpine plant, a 4–5 in.-tall carpet, slowly extending to yards across where conditions are hospitable. Foliage finely divided, in a circular brush on each of many even-topped little branches, as in mossy saxifrages. This plant is even mossier, like a cap moss in aspect; shiny green, soft as chick feathers when you run a hand over it. White spiraea flowers in short spikes, early summer. A small-scale ground cover for shade up to three-fourths of the day. For solid cover, center the new plants at about 8 in.

Luzula. (Wood Rush). Hardy, probably even in GN, and growable in warm climates as well. Plants of upland woods, tufted, and like smallish grasses in leaf, but the leaves are broader than those of most grasses and held with the blade partly or completely flat to catch the light. Luzulas are good company for primroses and ferns.

Luzula campestris (often sold as *L. pilosa*) is one of the more engaging of the many species, a deep green starfish with its broad blade-rays flat on the ground; brown flowers in late spring on stems a foot or so high. *L. nivea* has broad blades seemingly margined with a thread-form frost. White flowers at the tips of 18-in. wands. *L. sylvatica* 'Marginata' is somewhat larger than the last-named plant, a tuft of green, with narrow white margins along the leaf blades. I've forgotten what the flowers are like, so they must be forgettable.

Meconopsis. Besides *M. betonicifolia* and *M. cambrica*, discussed on pp. 231–32, there are a couple dozen other species and varieties in cultivation, occasionally sold by nurseries specializing in rock-garden plants, more often available through the seed exchange lists of rock-garden and hardy-plant societies. These other kinds are biennials or short-lived perennials quite as challenging to grow as *M. betonicifolia*. Would that any of the other meconopsises were as happy-go-lucky as *M. cambrica*. Yet the others are all in the realm of reasonable dreams. The dreamer, exercising courage and skill, and blessed with luck, might see the materialization of *M. grandis*, with its nodding cloches, blue or purple, or of *M. sarsonsii*, with its ivory bowls, and go onward to additional blues and shades of lavender, lilac, yellow, and red.

The fastidious members of *Meconopsis* grow best in a northern climate that provides a cool, moist atmosphere; even so, I have seen *M. betonicifolia* flowering in a netting-shade house in a subtropical garden that also grows tangerines. The plants stood a mere 2 ft. tall (they will grow twice that high in a more accommodating region and favored garden), but were producing clear blue bowls, the purity of color indicating contentment in the plant.

Sow meconopsis seeds in flats filled with ideal shade garden soil (p. 28). Prick them out when they are tiny into pots about 4 to 5 in. in diameter. Or sow directly into pots, one precious seed in each, barely covered. Transplant to a sheltered position in fast-draining open ground, ideal of soil, as soon as the seedling stands 2 or 3 in., or by early autumn if it has not grown to size. If the seedlings make it through the winter (a percentage of them probably will not), flowers of some kinds will appear next spring or early summer; of others, a year or two later.

Meconopsis is endangered by soddening rains in winter and by droughty wind at any time. Some gardeners temper the weather by growing meconopsis, and many other delicate shade plants, in open soil or pots within cold frames, from which the lights (that is, the windows) are removed in spring and usually kept off until autumn.

Melianthus major. s, nw (with shelter), c, sw, t. A South African shrubby perennial, to 8 ft. tall. Leaves tropically huge and productive of tropical fantasies in gardens in more temperate climates. A British authority on perennials, Graham Stuart Thomas, rates this species as the provider of "probably the most beautiful large foliage of any plant that can be grown in these islands."

A serrated and deeply segmented gray-green leaf, a frond about 4 ft. long in its blade. *Melianthus* needs only a few of these giant chlorophyll-factory complexes for its livelihood; these few leaves, radiating from the plant's tough canes, build a perennial about as wide as tall in its first years. It grows wider with age as the plant advances stoloniferously. In late summer the cane tops erupt in large sprays of green-stamened flowers with red-brown bracts.

Melianthus grows and flowers well for me in two-thirds shade, in clay saturated in the winter and spring but so dry and hard by late summer that a spade rings like an anvil when I attempt to dig there. In this harsh setting, I grow *Bambusa multiplex* as a hedge at the back; the tall, coppery purple *Phormium tenax* 'Burgundy' at one side; the coppery red-brown sedge *Carex flagellifera* beneath the spreading *Melianthus* "tree." These four form a mutual admiration society of foliages. I've also grown *Melianthus* as a container plant in shade.

The plant does have a couple of serious drawbacks. One is a brutish smell, bothersome to a person who walks close by. Its other not-so-good quality is that *Melianthus* is mecca to white flies. If they ever get started, as they have on my plant, there's no stopping them. Spraying only teases them. My control method is somewhat the Pyrrhic victory: saw the plant down to soil level, every stem and scrap, in early autumn and bury it beneath compost. With winter and spring rains, *Melianthus* sprouts from the ground, renewing itself with leaves that are clean enough until midsummer.

Melica, a genus of true grasses, growable in all climates, is at its garden best in shady places, where the fine blades of the grass tuft are presented more airily than in sun, negating the prairie bunch-grass quality of the plant.

Melica altissima is a 4-footer with brownish flowers in early summer; *M. altissima* 'Atropurpurea' flowers bronze-purple.

Melica nutans grows as a concise clump, about 15 in. tall and 9 in. across, of especially fine green leaves. Seed heads, green in early summer, are reminiscent of the flowers of certain scillas. Once I made a garden feature of *M. nutans* as a path plant, perking up here and there along the outer eddies of a shady pathway topped with sand. Gray sand cozied closely around each rich green tuft of grass and extended outward to pathside ferns. I kept the planting for about ten years and then, having more garden notions than space, dug it up and planted something different in its place. I do that a lot.

Melittis melissophyllum. Hardy everywhere. A member of the Mint Family, Labiatae, with whorls of flowers ascending on 18-in. stems. The flowers appear in June, tubular and pouty-lipped, as is typical of the family, 2 in. long, white with a pink stripe. There is a pure white form, as well. Either one is effective in a shady border.

Milium effusum 'Aureum' (Bowles' Golden Grass). For all climates. A famous shade-garden plant. Two ft. tall and of open growth, this grass comes up in random tufts, spreading slowly to 2 ft. wide after several years. But some of the newer tufts are seedlings, which come true, and sparingly. The entire visible structure of the plant — leaves, stems, and flowers — is a peculiar and attractive pastel yellow, somewhere between wax-bean yellow and split-pea yellow in hue. Slow to establish, uneasy to divide and transplant. Best grown from seed and planted out from pots about 4 in. in diameter. Bowles' Golden Grass chimes mellowly with other goldish shade plants, such as *Chrysanthemum parthenium* 'Aureum' and *Lysimachia nummularia* 'Aurea', perhaps with ferns in the vicinity to substantiate those paler flowering plants.

Myrrhis odorata (Sweet Cicely). A relative of parsley, another culinary herb of European origin, to be added to those listed on p. 258. Any of these will grow readily in the blocky sun-and-shade of trees or in a mostly shady place at the base of a fence or wall in all climates. Sweet Cicely is a freely seeding perennial, 18 in. to 3 ft. tall, depending on richness and moistness of soil; a structure of sweetly scented leaves, cut rather like those of Italian parsley, and of umbellate white flowers, late spring. Grow from seed, sown into 4-in. pots filled with ideal soil (see p. 28). Thin the seed lings, retaining one or two or three of the lustiest in each pot. Plant out into the garden, pot soil intact, when their leafage stands 2 to 3 in. tall. This same seed technique applies to any of the other shade-tolerant herbs.

Nomocharis. s, nw, c. Bulb flowers, sometimes called Butterfly Lilies, for their wingy flowers aligned along 3-ft. arching stems in late summer. *N. pardanthina,* native to Yunnan, is the strongest in gardens, not difficult to establish in the cool, dappled shade of a moist woodland. Mauve flowers with many purple freckles and with fringes on the petals. The bulb — to be planted four times deeper than it is tall — slowly and safely multiples. This is not one of those bulbs that disappear into the maws of mice, at least not in my experience. And yet, for all its surety, the plant is an exasperation to me in the subtropical garden where I grow it. Here it flowers well every year but obviously does not altogether enjoy the hot, dry summer climate, displaying discontent like a Japanese maple in a Los Angeles suburb, by a browning of the leaf edges in summer. The nomocharis does this just as the flowers begin to appear, with detracting effect, since leaves and flowers occur alternately along the stems. I fight unsightliness by picking off the worst of the leaves. The extraordinary flowers are worth any effort.

But then I may lose most of the year's production to the flower arrangers with whom I share the garden. Nomocharis has the distinction or misfortune to be long lasting in a vase and is irresistible to those with ikebana eyes.

Omphalodes cappadocica. ne, nw, nc. Leaves of distinction, 4 to 5 in. long, furrowed, ovate, grayish green, tidily close together and close to the ground, in a plant less than a foot tall. Close above the leaves, flowers of Forget-Me-Not form, bright pure blue with a white eye, produced winkingly over a period of weeks in spring and summer. One plant will eventually make a ground cover, with help from the gardener. In late summer, divide the broad, well-grown clump to gain starts for more extensive planting; space out divisions at 6–8-in. intervals; keep them watered. This is a long-lived perennial, easy in moist soil and part shade.

Omphalodes verna (Blue-eyed Mary, Creeping Forget-Me-Not). Any climate. Said to have been the favorite flower of Marie Antoinette, yet it seems totally out of keeping with such an orchidaceous lady. A low, rapidly carpeting perennial, with dark green, heart-shaped leaves about 4 in. long and, in the spring, tiny, intensely blue Forget-Me-Nots in clusters. Not a great flower show, but an easy cover beneath trees. Will take full shade. Dies down in fall, comes back forever (40 years in one spot in my Pacific Northwest garden).

Origanum vulgare. This hardy culinary herb, mentioned with others on p. 258, is also useful as a small-leaved, small-scale ground cover in semi-shade. It is available in plain green or in the especially attractive *O. vulgare* 'Aureum', of Lodi apple color.

Paeonia Species (Peony). In many a book, the classic garden writers of his century chat enthusiastically about wild peonies, with their distinguished foliages and single flowers, rich with character. Yet the plants have remained almost exclusively in the province of fine gardening by such career gardeners. The popular mail-order nurseries and garden centers have hardly ever bothered to offer any of the dozens of peony species and natural varieties, probably because they *are* a bit of a bother. Grown from seed (available from plant societies), they take several years to reach flowering size. Division of mature plants (in autumn) would be too slow a means of propagation to supply a mass market.

In the shade garden, wild peonies enjoy the afternoon shade of an east wall or the semishade of open woodland. They are all big eaters, reveling in a soil fat with organic material, plus the tasty minerals of fertilizer, and liking plenty of water (with fast drainage).

Easiest of the species I've grown is *P. tenuifolia*, from the Caucasus (which gives clue of hardiness in any climate), an 18 in. plant with leaves divided into slim fingers; flowers are 4–5-in. saucers of a glistening dark crimson, a hussy color difficult to blend in with the debutante pinks, mauves, and violets of the late spring wildflower garden. But ferns complement this peony.

Other peonies especially at home in the shade garden are *P. peregrina*, a fully hardy 3-footer with flowers of a lighter, brighter, yet no less lurid crimson than those of *P. tenuifolia; P. Veitchii* (hardy, except GN), 12–30 in. tall, pea-green of leaf, dark purplish red, clear pink, or white of flower; and *P. Emodi* (hardy, except GN), a 2–3-ft. species that offers white flowers, scented, gold-stamened, and sumptuous. These three are all May-flowering.

Parochetus communis. s, c, sw, t; marginally hardy in the north (where it is sometimes grown as a hanging basket plant and wintered in a greenhouse). Pea flowers, gentian-blue, scattered on a carpet of exactly cloverlike leaves, in late summer. Moist soil, half shade or more. About 10 years ago I set out a single pot plant of *Parochetus* on a winter-wet, summermoist hillside in my subtropical New Zealand garden. That plant has romped ahead, north, south, east, and west, and now extends to 30 ft. across, a neat and glorious sweep of mock-clover. It puts down many weeds, but not the taller ones. In my occasional weeding of the carpet, I'm forced to make cruel footprints, mashing down the lush, clovery leaves. But in a few days the wounds heal as new foliage fills in. The *Parochetus*, a shallow rooter, sweeps harmlessly around clumps of New Zealand Rock Lily, stands of *Nomocharis,* and stems of *Fuchsia magellanica.*

Perennials: wildflowers vs. hybrids. Throughout this book, I deal with species plants rather than garden hybrids. The species — the other name for them is wildflowers — add sharply sculpted individuality of flower and leaf to the garden. The species usually need no staking to keep them from flopping in the wind and rain (Nature doesn't often make top-heavy flowers). Hybrid perennials add to the garden brilliant colors and a party-going quality of dressiness and sophistication, but to the degree they are big headed, these flowers will probably need staking.

Wildflowers happy in shade, reasonably colorful, growable in a border (if you would have them there), and in many cases useful in flower arranging, are many — too many to put them all into a book or a garden. Hybrid perennials for shade are rather few. They are really sun plants shanghaied into service in shade, up to two-thirds of the day, which they often take with surprisingly good will.

The top performer in shade among hybrid perennials is, in my experience, a single-flowered Shasta Daisy, which has pretty much taken care of itself for about six years now beneath deciduous trees, with perhaps three hours of direct sunlight, in all, on a summer day. Mind that it is a single, rather than a double-flowered Shasta Daisy; the relative sturdiness of head on stem has a lot to do with the flower's success. The soil I have it in goes dry in summer, proving drought tolerance as well as shade tolerance in this old-fashioned type of Shasta Daisy.

Under the same trees, near the daisy, I've grown Border Phlox *(Phlox paniculata* hybrids); they flowered abundantly, but I gave up on them after several years and grubbed them out, for reason that mildew incessantly attacked the foliage in shade, and I got tired of keeping the vector at bay with fungicide.

The old-time "pinie" of American gardens, *Paeonia officinalis*, serves up its soup-bowl flowers nicely in shade, provided the soil is superb: deep, airy, fertile, and moist. Given that same superlative medium, the Physostegia hybrids will produce plenty of their stiff rod flowers in shade.

Hybrid asters, especially smaller-flowered forms of Michaelmas Daisies and other hybrid asters with tiny flowers in billowy sprays, are good bets — good risks — for the shade gardener. It is always a risk planting flowers natively sunny in a shady place. Win some, lose some.

Philadelphus (Mock Orange). Hardy shrubs, so well known for nearly disappearing behind masses of late spring flowers, white, scented of orange blossom. In shade gardening, Mock Orange performs well against a north wall or at the north edge of a woods, provided the shrubs are not double-shaded by overhanging eaves or tree limbs in addition to the shade of the northern exposure. Flowering depends on crucial direct sun in early morning and late afternoon.

Phygelius. NE, north to Philadelphia; S, NW, C, SW, T. Brilliant orangy red (or, in a cultivated variety, softly yellow) flowers, tubular and lipped, toward the tops of awkward shrubby branches about waist high: *P. capensis.* Flowers of the same shape, of a pastel coral pink, on the same unshapely branches, up to chest height: *P. aequalis.* Grow either plant in rich, moist soil for prodigious branch and flower production; or in a poor, dryish spot for slow growth, shortened branches, and yet adequate flowering. The first-named species in its typical form is a fiery summer flower for shade or sun. The other, coral *Phygelius,* is a cool one, easier to blend in with other flower colors (I grow it in shade of a mature Marmalade Bush, together with *Achillea* 'The Pearl'). In England, both *Phygelius* species are favorites for planting in shady rock walls. The main flowering is in midsummer, after which flower heads crop out now and again, well on into autumn. Cut the branches back nearly to the ground in winter.

Podophyllum peltatum (May-Apple). Fully hardy. Eastern North American perennial, inhabiting moist soil in woodlands. A tropically prosperous leaf a foot across, shaped like an umbrella, on a 2-ft. high fleshy stem. Sequestered beneath the leaf, a nodding, white flower cup, followed by a big squashy fruit resembling a persimmon in color and shape. Country people gather these to make pies. The hardy *P. emodi* 'Majus' (the form of the species most often met in gardens) comes from the Himalayas, has mottled, bronze green/clear green leaves, pink floral cups, and big red fruit.

I find a sort of nostalgic fun in ducking down to discover the fruit of the May-Apple under the umbrella leaf; it is the same as the thrill I lost when I outgrew searching for, and espying, Easter eggs.

Primula florindae. Acclimatization ability almost universal (as detailed on p. 234, last paragraph). Of all Nature's half a thousand primula species, *florindae* ranks toward the top in tall handsomeness and in the deliciousness of its flowers to the eyes and nose. The plant loves water and self-sows readily if the soil is moist or wet, making a self-perpetuating community of itself. The individual in the colony is a tuft of 8-in.-long leaves; the tuft sends up 2–4-ft. stems (moisture induces height), capped with fragrant, lemon-yellow primroses in summer.

Prunus laurocerasus (English Laurel), cultivated varieties. Most surely hardy s, nw, c, t. Between the 6-ft.-tall *P. laurocerasus* 'Zabeliana' and the foot-tall *P. laurocerasus* 'Mt. Vernon' (both described on p. 128) are several other named varieties, in gradient sizes. All these are indispensable as solidly evergreen ground covers in shade or sun. More verdantly enriching than exciting, their best place is some yards back from garden paths or walks, with cheerier foliage and flowers toward the front. *P. laurocerasus* varieties are mainstays to a great many professional designers, who most often use them abusively, filling the planting beds right up to the sidewalk and the oppressed pedestrian. But used circumspectly, few plants are as able in the covering of shady ground with sturdy, all-season greenery, even in poor soil (dig in dry fertilizer).

The variety *P. laurocerasus* 'Otto Luyken', a narrow-leaved 3–5-footer (depending on pruning), with spikes of small white flowers and black purple berries, has an additional, excellent use as a container plant. Beside the door, it is like a good doorman, steady on, always spruce, soothingly polite.

Rheum rhaponticum (Rhubarb). All climates. The rhubarb of pies and sauces make a noble addition to a garden of ferns and woodland plants, in semishade. I grow it with Lady Fern, Meadow Rue, and Sweet Woodruff. Rhubarb's bold leaves form a centralizing feature for the other, finer foliages. I find that as a crop plant, rhubarb bears well in shady conditions. We harvest three times: spring, early summer, and midsummer.

Other species of *Rheum*, native to the Himalayas, are grown in high shade in woodland gardens for their imposing clumps of huge leaves and tall staffs of panicle flowers in early summer. The flowers are cherry red in *R. palmatum*, the species best known in gardens. All climates. Any of the rhubarbs need rich, moist soil in order to prosper.

Rudbeckia fulgida 'Goldsturm' (Black-eyed Susan). For all climates. Garden form of an eastern and southern American wildflower. Black-centered, dark yellow daisies on 2-ft. stems all summer. A sun-or-shade plant; in fact, it is one of the most shade-tolerant of perennials suitable for border planting. Commonly available in the mail-order trade if not at the local garden center.

Ruscus aculeatus (Butcher's Broom). S, NW, C, SW, T. A strange evergreen shrub, 2 to 3 ft. tall, formed of apparently leafless, flattened, angularly jointed branches. A slow grower NW, yet valuable in any region for its tolerance of dark places few plants will endure.

Saxifraga Fortunei. S, C, NW. Perennial, a neat clump of rounded, jagged leaves, glossy green with a purplish underside. In autumn, a flight of wingy little white flowers rises above the foliage to a height of 2 ft. in the tallest forms. These are suitable for the foreground of the flower or shrub border. Alpine reductions of *S. Fortunei* flower only a few inches high, rock-garden size. All are easy to grow in moist soil, half to three-quarters shade. Attempts to divide and transplant plants directly into open ground can be, as I've discovered, murderous. Divisions should be coaxed along in a cold frame or cool greenhouse before planting them out. Better still, propagate from seed.

Streptopus (Twisted Stalk). Fully hardy. Little cousins of Solomon's Seal, perennials assigned to the great family, Liliaceae. *S. amplexifolius*, native to much of North America, brings to the garden 2 to 3 ft. leafy stems; nodding, greenish-whitish flowers in late spring; and red berries. *S. roseus* divides into three regional subspecies — *S. roseus curvipes*, of Alaska and the Northwest; *S. roseus prospectus* of eastern North America; and *S. roseus longipes* of the north central United States — which are given full specific entity in some books. In all three varieties, small ash-rose or purplish bell-form flowers are produced on leafy, twisted stems about 30 in. high; red berries follow. Twisted Stalks are easy-to-grow woodland plants, pleasant without being showy, spreading modestly at the root.

Stylophorum diphyllum (Celandine Poppy). All climates except T. An American wildflower, found in parts of New England and of the Great Lakes states, westward to Missouri. Eighteen-inch stalks bear leaves tenderly green, deeply serrate of edge, like a coastline of fiords. Above the leaves, big, shiny, dark yellow poppies; full blown, expanded of petal, the flowers appear to be the world's largest buttercups. Easily grown in fertile soil, part shade. Valuable for its flowers, produced from about May until August.

Symphytum. All climates. Perennials, numbered in the borage family. Tubular flowers in spring, making you glad you planted them; coarse, hairy, beasty-ear leaves in summer, making you wonder why you did. But then spring comes around again. *S. luteum* (of gardens) flowers light yellow; *S. caucasicum,* light blue; *S. rubrum,* dark crimson. Useful as filler plants in the midground of the bed; part shade.

Thuja plicata 'Excelsa'. s, NW, C. This horticultural variety of the Western Red Cedar, fragrant and plumy of foliage, turns out to be a first-rate evergreen hedging plant in sun or in nearly full north shade. Twelve-year-old plants that I've been pruning annually stand a rounded 5 ft. and remain fully foliate to the ground. (Unpruned, the shrubs would by now be tall and conical.) They grow close to a solid north fence and receive brief sun early and late in the day.

Uvularia grandiflora. All climates except T. Woodland wildflower, native to Canada, south to Georgia, westward to Kansas. Soft to the eyes, with its pale yellow bells in spring, on arching, 18-in. stems additionally lined with pea-green perfoliate leaves. A liliad, related to Solomon's Seal, but much slower; fey in aspect where its relative is stalwart. *U. grandiflora* is easy in semishade but has little tolerance of drought. Other eastern North American uvularias, lesser lights, are *U. perfoliata* and *U. sessiliflora,* attractive little yellow bells, well worth space in the woodsy garden.

Veratrum. NE, S, GN, NW, C. Masterworks of natural art, tall towers made up of a multitude of cupped little flowers, singularly themselves, never to be doubled and enlarged by the mad doctors of hybridization into something resembling stems of Brussels sprouts. Such is my hope, spoken like a chant to scare away the dark spirits. I do appreciate Nature's art, as is.

Each veratrum species is a perennial clump of large, scoop-shaped leaves pointed at the end, with ornamental pleats running from leaf base to point. Small but abundant panicle flowers in summer on vertical stalks rising above most of the leafage. The individual flower is a six-pointed star, not flattened, but cupped like a hand clutching a ball. Flower colors are milky green jade in the European *V. album;* greengage-yellow in our western American *V. californicum* and *V. speciosum;* definitely green in our eastern *V. viride;* and in the European *V. nigrum,* eggplant purple.

Slow growers, best in half shade, and insistent on rich soil, moist through the summer.

If you will be transplanting veratrum from the wild (having found them unavailable from nurseries), late August to early September is the best time, after having of course weighed the morality of removing the plant from the place it grows. Flowers from seed require several years' wait, but that is the most considerate plan of all.

Weigela florida. Hardy everywhere. An old-fashioned deciduous shrub, grown for its megaphone-shaped flowers, rose or white, in spring. Shade-tolerant. I've never had the least interest in this old horticultural dray horse. My excitement is in the variety *W. florida* 'Variegata' as a shade

Veratrum californicum, tall towers of greengage-yellow flowers above foot-long leaves.

plant. This is a shrub whose variegation is understated, green-on-green in young leaves — mid-green at mid-leaf, green-yellow along the margins. At a little distance, one's eyes melt these greens into a parsley-butter color. In mature leaves the margins pale to a green-tinged cream.

Your author has high resistance to variegated plants, most of which seem to me garish. This one, however, casts a spell. I took it home from a garden center and planted it against a north wall, an experiment in the plant's shade tolerance, for the wall receives only early-morning and late-afternoon sun. With the shrub I planted other yellow-greens: that ball-of-string conifer *Chamaecyparis pisifera filifera aurea,* at the left flank of the Weigela; and at the right, *Chrysanthemum partheneum* 'Aureum' and *Alchemilla vulgaris,* the latter yellow-green of flower. This ensemble has worked out perfectly for more than ten years now. The chrysanthemum and the alchemilla are both prolific self-sowers well matched in strength: neither has been able to muscle out the other, and both have increased from a few into dozens.

The Weigela requires summer pruning to keep it compactly vertical. I've let it grow nearly 3 ft. out from the wall and have encouraged it to attain all the height, short of scraggliness, that it can manage: 8 ft., so far. The discordantly mauve flowers of this Weigela variety are, fortunately, few and hardly noticeable. When I notice them, I clip them off.

This fool's rush of an experiment in shade gardening with two known sun lovers, the Weigela and the conifer, encourages my beginning thoughts that location against a north wall or fence will sustain nearly any kind of sun plant, as long as the structure receives early-morning and evening sun. However, in order for the north wall or fence to work at all well as a shade garden locus, there must be nothing overhanging the structure, neither eaves nor boughs. I believe I've said as much elsewhere; it's an important enough point to harp upon.

My listing of plants for shade must, I suppose, amount to a sufficiency, for the present at least. There are still more plants I haven't named, so deserving of a place in the shade garden. Or are they? Do any of them need to be added to one's life? A gardener can never answer that, and wavers between wanting more plants and wanting total freedom from being their caretaker.

Yesterday — a hot, dry day in late summer — we went on a picnic in a forested park. We sat on a log in the deep shade of hemlock trees, a carpet of needles at our feet. The hemlock grove was too shady and needly to allow undergrowth. But at the edge of the trees, in more shade than sun, grew huckleberry and serviceberry bushes, freshly green. Altogether, a complete, restful shade garden, asking no care. The place personified the alternative dream of the shade gardener, supposing one's first fantasy is a shade garden unendingly rich with foliages and flowers, a banquet for the creature of fine senses; and for the insatiable mind, a volume of verdant knowledge whose pages increase with each day's experience in the garden. One has a choice, the simple or the intricate — if one could ever decide.

18

Shade Plants for
Special Uses

Here is a list of plants with the rare ability to grow in shade even fuller than the full shade described on p. 78; their tolerance of dim light extends somewhat over the near edge of dense shade. The "somewhat" is somewhat unknown, to be determined only by optimistic experiment. The plants' chances for healthy life in marginally dense shade are improved by placing them in ideal soil (p. 28), deeply tilled and loosened, free from competing roots, perhaps topped with light-colored sand or gravel, and always moist. The plants:

Acanthus, Ajuga reptans (no flowers in this depth of shade, but a handsome carpet of glossy leaves), *Alocasia, Arthropodium, Arum maculatum, Asarum, Aspidistra, Aucuba,* Baby's Tears, *Campanula poscharskyana, Carex morrowii* 'Variegata Aurea', *Cocculus, Crassula lactea, Crassula multicava, Cymbalaria muralis, Danae, Daphne laureola,* Deer Fern, *Duchesnea, Euphorbia robbiae,* Fancy Fern, *Fatsia,* Fraser's Sedge, *Gaultheria shallon, Glechoma, Ilex crenata, Impatiens* (Busy Lizzie types), *Iris foetidissima,* Ivies, *Luzula, Mahonia nervosa,* Mondo, *Monstera,* Mosses, Oak Fern, *Oxalis oregana, Nephrolepis cordifolia, Pachysandra,* Periwinkle, *Plectranthus, Polypodium, Polystichum munitum, Prunus laurocerasus* 'Mt. Vernon', *Rohdea, Ruscus, Sarcococca, Skimmia,* Spider Plant, *Tovara, Tradescantia fluminensis* (invasive), *Vancouveria hexandra, Waldsteinia,* Yew.

The Most Shade Tolerant of All

Following these notes is a list of shade plants especially suited to container gardening, an uneasy classification. As contemporary nurseries demonstrate, nearly every kind of ornamental plant in the world can be grown in

In Containers

Lists of plants suited to arid land and marsh appear on pages 27 and 28.

a container. Nurseries hope to sell their containerized stock quickly to avoid having to winter it over and eventually repot. But we container gardeners carry out those chores of wintering and repotting as technical necessities underlying the pleasure of the hobby.

Container gardeners in cold-winter climates winter their supposedly hardy plants safely under glass, for all but a few granitically hardy species will likely be damaged in an exposed location. And any kind of pottery container, except certain stoneware made for outdoor gardening, is almost sure to break when frost expands the soil within. Lacking a greenhouse or cold frame (I have neither), one must tap plants out of their pots and plant them in a shady, sheltered place. But before planting, I remove one-third of each plant's root mass. I use the ground beneath evergreen conifers with low-sweeping branches and the ground at the north side of the house, covering the plants with evergreen boughs or straw for the winter. When I dig the plants up in the spring, I repot using ideal soil (p. 28). Actually, I mix up something close to the ideal by blending garden loam with the fluffy, peaty or sawdusty stuff that comes with plants from a nursery. I never use any of the fluffy, manufactured soil substitutes as straight provision for container plants grown outdoors; all too easily the "mixes" dry out fatally in hot, windy weather.

Above all, be a diligent waterer or an inspirational delegator of such work. And apply fertilizer (to the plant, I think I must say here) once in a while, at least twice a year, spring and summer.

Container gardening provides, for those cold-winter gardeners who have a greenhouse or a well-illuminated room in the home, an opportunity to grow nearly any of the tropical or subtropical plants described in this book. If you plan to grow plants indoors in winter and outdoors in summer, it is important to place in shady locations outdoors any plants that have been grown out of sunlight indoors. This, to prevent sunburn.

Now come the lists of names, weighty with plants that supply bold, landscapers' foliages the year around and light on deciduous foliages and mere seasonal flowers — although I do include some of these.

Shrubs. *Acer circinatum, Aucuba, Bamboo, Buxus, Camellia, Cocculus, Coprosma, Cornus alba, Cycas, Danae, Fatsia, Fuchsia, Gardenia, Gaultheria, Hebe, Helichrysum, Hydrangea, Ilex, Mahonia, Nandina, Pittosporum, Prunus laurocerasus* varieties, *Pseudopanax, Ruta, Ruscus, Taxus* × *media, Trochodendron, Viburnum Davidii, Weigela.*

Ground Covers and Vines. Any of these combine well in a container with taller plants. In such combination, I love to let the naturally trailing plant spill down over the sides of the pot, romantic gardening at its most maudlin. The weepers, then:

Asparagus Fern, Baby's Tears, *Cissus, Cymbalaria muralis, Duchesnia, Episcia, Euonymus, Ficus pumila, Glechoma, Hoya,* Ivies, *Juniperus, Lapageria* (also a climber), *Parochetus, Plectranthus, Saxifraga stolonifera, Selaginella, Tradescantia, Waldsteinia.*

Ferns. The most effective as landscape furnishing when grown in containers include:

Adiantum hispidulum, Adiantum pedatum, Asplenium bulbiferum, Blechnum brasiliense, Blechnum chilense, Athyrium filix-femina, Cyrtomium, Matteuccia, Nephrolepis, Onoclea, Osmunda, Polystichum, Tree ferns, *Woodwardia.*

Perennials. *Acanthus, Acorus, Agapanthus, Agave, Alocasia, Angelica pachycarpa, Anthurium, Artemisia, Arthropodium, Aspidistra, Astilbe, Begonia, Bergenia, Billbergia,* Cacti, *Caladium, Calathea* and *Maranta, Canna, Carex, Clivia, Crassula, Crinum, Cymbidium, Cyperus, Dianella, Echeveria, Equisetum, Heliconia, Heracleum, Liriope* and *Ophiopogon, Melianthus, Monstera, Petasites japonicus giganteus, Philodendron, Phormium, Phygelius, Sansevieria,* Spider Plant, *Tolmiea, Tovara.*

Annuals. Every one in the chapter on annuals will do as container plants, although Herb Robert and Forget-Me-Not would provide only a minor note of temporary color.

Edibles. Herbs, Sweet Potato (as a cascading vine), kale, citrus fruits, Loquat, and strawberry can be effective landscape plants in pots.

Shrubs. *Chamaecyparis obtusa* and *C. pisifera* (dwarf forms), *Daboecia, Daphne, Epigaea, Gardenia jasminoides* 'Radicans', *Gaultheria* (any of the small-growing species), *Helichrysum* 'Limelight', *Ilex crenata* 'Mariesii', *Kalmiopsis, Leucothoe Davisiae, Leucothoe Keiskei* 'Minor', *Mahonia aquifolium* 'Compacta', *Mahonia nervosa, Nandina domestica* (drawf forms), *Pentapterygium, Prunus laurocerasus* 'Mt. Vernon', *Rhododendron* (smaller species and hybrids), *Ruta, Sarcococca.*

Small Plants for Edging or Rock Gardens

Ground Covers. Any of the ground covers and smaller vines listed in chapter 11 will serve.

Ferns. Ditto, any of the smaller-growing ferns.

Perennials. *Acorus, Actaea, Agapanthus* (dwarf forms), *Alchemilla* (invasive), *Aquilegia, Arthropodium, Arum, Astilbe* (the smaller kinds), *Billbergia* and other bromeliads, *Bletilla,* Bulbs, Cacti, *Caladium, Calathea* and *Maranta, Calceolaria, Caltha, Campanula* (smaller kinds), *Carex, Ceratostigma, Chrysanthemum parthenium* (invasive), *Chrysogonum, Clintonia, Corydalis, Crassula, Cyclamen, Cymbidium, Cymophyllus, Cyperus albostriatus* 'Elegans', *Dianella nigra, Dicentra, Disporum, Dodecatheon, Echeveria, Epipactis, Equisetum variegatum, Eucomis, Francoa, Gentiana, Geranium, Helleborus, Hemerocallis, Hepatica, Heuchera, Heucherella, Hosta, Hyacinthus, Jeffersonia, Luetkea, Luzula, Meconopsis* (most are tall but are best displayed as foreground plants; *M. cambrica* is invasive), *Melica, Milium, Mertensia, Monarda, Omphalodes, Phormium* (dwarf varieties), *Polemonium reptans, Primula* (smaller growers), *Reineckia, Saxifraga, Schizostylis, Sedum, Shortia,* Spider Plant, *Streptopus, Tiarella, Tolmiea, Tradescantia, Trillium, Uvularia.*

Annuals. Any. But any of them will get the snoot from rock-garden purists. Let's not invite them.

Appendix

Specialty Nurseries

uestone Perennials
'11 Middle Ridge Road
adison, Ohio 44057
l0-428-7535 or 800-852-5243
ww.bluestoneperennials.com

mong their perennials are both garden
phisticates and species. Their mail-order
talog indicates, by symbols (a partly or fully
clipsed sun), the shade tolerance of each
lant.

ovees Nursery
737 SW Coronado Street
ortland, Oregon 97219
03-244-9341 or 800-435-9250
ww.bovees.com

hododendrons and a selection of distin-
uished trees, shrubs, and ground covers for
hade. Readable and helpful catalog.

usse Gardens
7160 245th Avenue
ig Lake, Minnesota 55309
'63-263-3403 or 800-544-3192
ww.bussegardens.com

A vast collection of hardy perennials. Among
hose for shade, described in their catalog, are

hostas, *Bergenia, Dicentra, Epimedium, Heuchera,
Ligularia, Pulmonaria,* double-flowered bloodroot, and many more.

Carman Nursery
16201 East Mozart Avenue
Los Gatos, California 95032
408-356-0119

Collector's bonanza of rare plants. No catalog;
cash and carry; occasional mail orders.

Carroll Gardens
444 East Main Street
Westminster, Maryland 21157
410-848-5422 or 800-638-6334
www.carrollgardens.com

In business more than half a century, they offer
extensive selections of pines and other trees,
rhododendrons and other shrubs, herbs, and
perennials. Mail-order catalog.

Collector's Nursery
16804 NE 102nd Avenue
Battle Ground, Washington 98604
360-574-3832
www.collectorsnursery.com

Mail-order catalog.

Color Farm
1604 West Richway Drive
Albert Lea, Minnesota 56007
www.colorfarm.com

Coleus, and only coleus, especially antique varieties that Vern Ogren, the nurseryman, considers better plants for open ground than most modern kinds. Mail-order catalog only.

Cricklewood Nursery
11907 Nevers Road
Snohomish, Washington 98290
360-568-2829

Unusual and hard-to-find perennials from around the world for shade or sun. Mail-order list of Latin names with brief descriptions.

Eastern Plant Specialties
P.O. Box 226W
Georgetown, Maine 04548
732-382-2508
www.easternplant.com

A great variety of Maine-hardy shrubbery and trees for collectors: rhododendrons, kalmias, pieris, hollies, dwarf conifers, shrublets, and ground covers. Mail-order catalog.

Fancy Fronds Nursery
P.O. Box 1090
Gold Bar, Washington 98251
360-793-1742
www.fancyfronds.com

Descriptive catalog lists ferns of native and international origin, including "English variations."

Fieldstone Gardens
620 Quaker Lane
Vassalboro, Maine 04989
207-923-3836
www.fieldstonegardens.com

Astilbes, campanulas, epimediums, peonies, and many other perennials, generously described in mail-order catalog.

Foliage Gardens
2003 128th Avenue SE
Bellevue, Washington 98005
425-747-2998
www.foliagegardens.com

Approximately 100 different ferns, mainly fu hardy varieties. Descriptive mail-order catalog. Also available, a videocassette, "Short Course on Ferns."

Forestfarm
990 Tetherow Road
Williams, Oregon 97544
541-846-7269
www.forestfarm.com

Mail-order catalog.

Gardens of the Blue Ridge
P.O. Box 10
Pineola, North Carolina 28662
828-733-2417
www.gardensoftheblueridge.com

The Robbins family nursery, since 1892. One the great sources for shade-loving wildflowers and ferns of the East. Mail-order catalog.

Gilson Gardens
P.O. Box 277
3059 North Ridge Road
Perry, Ohio 44081
440-259-4845

Ivies, lamiums, periwinkles, and many other ground covers. No mail order.

Gossler Farms Nursery
1200 Weaver Road
Springfield, Oregon 97478
541-746-3922

Magnolias (over 60 kinds), stewartias, hamamelises, and many other woody trees and shrubs. Descriptive mail-order catalog.